MAR '04

W9-DFS-355

LP
B
KENNEDY/SCHLOSSBERG
ANDERSEN, CHRISTOPHER
SWEET CAROLINE

27.99

ELLENVILLE PUBLIC LIBRARY
40 CENTER ST.
ELLENVILLE, N.Y 12428

A FINE OF 5 CENTS PER DAY
WILL BE CHARGED ON EACH
ITEM THAT IS NOT RETURNED
ON TIME.

SWEET CAROLINE

Also by Christopher Andersen
in Large Print:

Diana's Boys
The Day John Died
The Day Diana Died
Jack and Jackie
Jackie After Jack
Young Kate

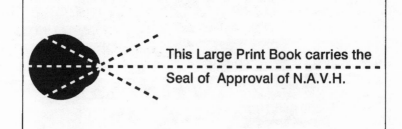

This Large Print Book carries the
Seal of Approval of N.A.V.H.

SWEET CAROLINE

Last Child of Camelot

CHRISTOPHER ANDERSEN

ELLENVILLE PUBLIC LIBRARY
40 CENTER ST.
ELLENVILLE, N.Y. 12428

WHEELER
PUBLISHING

Copyright © 2003 by Christopher Andersen.

Grateful acknowledgment is made to the following for permission to reprint the photographs in this book:
Stephen Allen, Globe Photos: 45
AP Wide World: 2, 4, 29, 37, 38, 40, 47, 52, 54, 55, 60, 61
Laura Cavanaugh, Globe Photos: 48, 50, 56
Jeff Christensen, Sipa Press: 59
Diane Cohen, Sipa Press: 58
CORBIS: 6, 7, 26, 28, 31, 46
Dalmas, Sipa Press: 1
Stephen Dunmore, Globe Photos: 44
Globe Photos: 30, 33, 34, 35, 36, 39
John F. Kennedy Library: 3, 5, 8, 9, 10, 11, 12, 13, 14, 15, 16, 17, 18, 19, 20, 21, 22, 23, 24, 25
Helaine Messer, Globe Photos: 42
David Ranns, Globe Photos: 41
Sipa Press: 32
Richard Sobol, Sipa Press: 43
Marcel Thomas, Sipa Press: 49, 53, 57
Stanley Tretick/CORBIS SYGMA: 27, 62
Robert Trippett/Sipa Press: 51

All rights reserved.

Published in 2004 by arrangement with William Morrow, an imprint of HarperCollins Publishers, Inc.

Wheeler Large Print Hardcover.

The text of this Large Print edition is unabridged.
Other aspects of the book may vary from the original edition.

Set in 16 pt. Plantin by Liana M. Walker.

Printed in the United States on permanent paper.

ISBN 1-58724-615-5 (lg. print : hc : alk. paper)

For Valerie, Kate, and Kelly

National Association for Visually Handicapped
------------------------ *serving the partially seeing*

As the Founder/CEO of NAVH, the only national health agency solely devoted to those who, although not totally blind, have an eye disease which could lead to serious visual impairment, I am pleased to recognize Thorndike Press* as one of the leading publishers in the large print field.

Founded in 1954 in San Francisco to prepare large print textbooks for partially seeing children, NAVH became the pioneer and standard setting agency in the preparation of large type.

Today, those publishers who meet our standards carry the prestigious "Seal of Approval" indicating high quality large print. We are delighted that Thorndike Press is one of the publishers whose titles meet these standards. We are also pleased to recognize the significant contribution Thorndike Press is making in this important and growing field.

Lorraine H. Marchi, L.H.D.
Founder/CEO
NAVH

* Thorndike Press encompasses the following imprints: Thorndike, Wheeler, Walker and Large Pr int Press.

All our lives, it's just been
the three of us.

— *John F. Kennedy Jr.,*
at the wedding of his sister

PREFACE

She is the keeper of the flame — heiress to a legacy of power, wealth, unfulfilled dreams, and unspeakable tragedy. Her father was gunned down before a stunned world, forever changing the course of history. Her mother became the most celebrated American woman of the twentieth century — an icon of style, glamour, and personal courage. Her brother was the most promising Kennedy of his generation — a global heartthrob whose chiseled good looks, personal charisma, and underrated intelligence might well have taken him to high political office had he not been killed in a plane crash at age thirty-eight within sight of his mother's estate on Martha's Vineyard.

Caroline Kennedy is the sole survivor of an American First Family that seized the world's imagination and continues to hold it more than forty years later. It is little wonder why we were infatuated from the very beginning.

9

Whatever harsh political realities may have lurked beneath, on the surface Jack and Jackie seemed ideally suited to lead America out of the drab Eisenhower fifties and into an exciting new era of peace and prosperity.

They were impossibly attractive, outlandishly wealthy, elegant, witty, headstrong, *exciting*. Youth, sex, power, and money — not to mention the dreams and aspirations of a generation — were embodied in the forty-three-year-old president and his thirty-one-year-old wife. Their young children completed the perfect family picture: he the tousle-haired scamp peeking out from beneath Daddy's desk in the Oval Office, she the freckle-faced girl sitting confidently astride her pony, Macaroni.

Still, our enduring fascination with the Kennedy children has less to do with what they are than with what they represented. For those of us old enough to remember, Caroline is one of the few remaining links to a more innocent and hopeful period in American history, a time before race riots, Vietnam, Watergate, the drug epidemic, AIDS — and terrorism.

To be sure, the Kennedy years were not without their moments: the Bay of Pigs fiasco, the Berlin Wall, and the Cuban Missile Crisis — not to mention the ever-present specter of annihilation in a nuclear exchange with the Soviet Union. It is astonishing how these events that so dominated our lives then have faded with time, while memories of the vigorous young president, his spellbinding wife, and his high-spirited children endure. No single image would prove more unforgettable — or more moving — than John, who turned three on the day of his father's funeral, snapping off history's most famous salute as JFK's horse-drawn caisson passed before him on a chilly November morning in 1963. Just a few feet away stood his big sister, tightly grasping their grief-stricken mother's hand. Caroline would turn six just two days later.

In the end, John Kennedy Jr. was not sure if he really remembered any of it; he admitted that he could not distinguish between genuine memories and what he had seen in television news footage and photographs over the years. But Caroline *does* remember it all — from scampering across the White House lawn to greet her father's helicopter to the death of her infant brother Patrick to the awful day Mommy returned from Dallas wearing a pink wool suit splattered with Daddy's blood.

The assassination brought an abrupt and bloody end to an era, but it marked a beginning for the family the slain president left behind. Over the next four decades, Caroline would grow up in the eye of a media hurricane as her mother's celebrity seemed to grow exponentially. There would be scandal — Jackie's tumultuous marriage to Greek billionaire Aristotle Onassis, the drowning death at Chappaquiddick that spelled an end to Uncle Teddy's presidential aspirations, the allegations of drug abuse, marital infidelity, recklessness, rape, and even murder that swirled around the extended Kennedy clan. There was also the unraveling of the Camelot myth, as her martyred father's myriad affairs, his connections to the Mafia through a shared mistress, his hidden health problems, and the First Couple's dependence on amphetamines supplied by "Dr. Feelgood," Max Jacobson, all became grist for the gossip mill.

Even more significantly, Caroline would be haunted by additional tragedies of the sort that had plagued her family for generations. The gunning down of her beloved Uncle Bobby, the untimely deaths of her cousins David and Michael, her mother's early death from cancer, and of course her brother's fatal plane crash — these events that also touched the nation would shape Caroline's life, determining the kind of woman Jack and Jackie's little girl would become.

More than the other three members of their tight family unit, Caroline has remained a mystery. In the 1960s, she and John-John were the two most famous children in America. Yet even as the First Son stole the spotlight with his antics — exhibiting almost from birth an affinity for the camera — Caroline was by comparison quiet and polite, shy, reserved. In a life lived largely outside the glare of media scrutiny, she handled every triumph and heartache with a quiet dignity, content to dwell in the looming shadow of her iconic parents and her movie-star-handsome little brother.

Mystique. The word was practically invented to describe Jackie, much of whose life was spent carefully tending to her own image. Caroline's mystique would prove to be more organic, growing out of her own desire to live as normal a life as humanly possible. It was a dream devoutly shared by her mother, who from the outset did everything in her power to steer JFK's two children clear of the excesses that destroyed so many of their overindulged peers.

Despite all the wealth, all the notoriety, all the pressures and expectations and the soul-crushing losses, Caroline and her brother would emerge as the stars of the Kennedy clan. They grew up to become — in stark contrast to some of their famously reckless Kennedy cousins — remarkably stable, unspoiled, socially responsible adults. On yet another of those sorrowful occasions when he was called upon to deliver a eulogy, Ted Kennedy knew just whom to credit for this outcome. Caroline and John, Uncle Teddy said in a voice choked with emotion, were simply "Jackie's two miracles." That is why, when she died of lymphoma in May 1994, Jackie took comfort in the assumption that at least her two children had somehow cheated fate.

Lamentably, she was mistaken. The plane crash that killed John and his wife, Carolyn, just five years later was an American tragedy — one that was all the more heart-breaking in light of the unique bond Caroline shared with Jackie and John. No one had experienced what they'd experienced, or could even imagine what it was like to have endured what they endured. For all the strength and dignity she summoned in the wake of her husband's assassination, those who knew her doubt that even the resilient Jackie could have survived this cruelest twist of fate — the violent and senseless death of her cherished only son.

But Caroline *would* have to face the emotional hammer blow of John's death, and the cruel realization that she had lost her entire immediate family.

Sadly, this burden is one Caroline is uniquely qualified to bear. So many times her private loss was the loss of a nation; when Caroline grieved, America — and the world — grieved with her. "Caroline is incredibly intelligent and strong-willed," said her uncle, Jackie's half brother, Jamie

Auchincloss. "But she's only human — a lifetime of anguish and tragedy takes its toll."

It is precisely because she is "only human" that we have come to view Caroline the way we would a member of our family — a daughter, perhaps, or a favorite niece or cousin. What has touched her so deeply touches us, never more profoundly than now. In the end, Caroline's is the story of a remarkable American family — and the one they left behind.

I have come to believe, more strongly
than ever, that after people die,
they really do live on through those
who loved them.

— *Caroline*

I am in awe of her.
Caroline *is* a profile in courage.

— *John Perry Barlow,*
family friend

1

Saturday, July 17, 1999
5:30 a.m.

Nothing. Not a dial tone, not a busy signal, nothing. He called his cousin's housekeeper back to make sure the number she had given him was correct. It was, she assured him. So Tony Radziwill tried again — this time enlisting the help of an operator.

"Yes, I'm trying to get through to Mountain Village Resort in Stanley, Idaho, operator," he said, "but I can't get through."

The operator tried, but no luck. "They must be having some trouble with the line, sir," she said politely. "I'll go ahead and report it."

Tony had also tried Caroline's cell phone, with no better luck. He checked his watch and did the math. It was still early in Stanley — not yet 4:00 a.m. — and Radziwill wondered for a moment if he should disturb the children. No, this was too important — they had to know. "Operator, this is an emergency," Radziwill said. She hesitated for a

19

moment, surprised by the sudden urgency in his voice. "I am trying to get in touch with the Schlossbergs — they are staying at the Mountain Village Resort, and I'm afraid there may have been an accident. . . ."

"Stay on the line," she answered. "I'll see what I can do."

As he waited, phone in hand, Tony gazed out at the brilliant sunrise over the Atlantic. He was sitting next to the sixteen-burner Vulcan stove in the kitchen at Red Gate Farm, the sprawling estate his Aunt Jackie had built on Martha's Vineyard. All the rooms at Red Gate Farm, decorated in pastels and lined with books, looked out over the ocean through multipaned windows made the old-fashioned way — with wooden pegs instead of nails. "It was a dream place, a sunlit place," her friend George Plimpton once said. "It's hard to explain the effect it all had on you — all the variations in color, water sparkling like diamonds everywhere you looked."

That is precisely why John had insisted that his cousin Tony spend the summer at Red Gate Farm. Radziwill had been battling cancer for over a decade, but now it was getting the upper hand. The soothing atmosphere that enveloped Red Gate Farm — Aunt Jackie's own secluded Shangri-la — could only accelerate the healing process, John had told him.

"Tony Radziwill's cancer was really tearing John up," his friend John Perry Barlow would later recall. "He did everything he could for Tony, but he knew that he was dying, and they really loved each other."

But right now it was Tony who was worrying about John — and Radziwill was not alone. John, who often piloted his Piper Saratoga to Cape Cod on weekends, had planned that night to fly his wife, Carolyn, up to Hyannis Port for his cousin Rory's wedding. They were not missed at the wedding rehearsal dinner that night, since it was understood that first they were making a brief detour to nearby Martha's Vineyard to drop off Carolyn's sister, Lauren.

But by 10:00 p.m., Lauren Bessette's friends had become concerned that she was more than two hours overdue. A thick blanket of haze had settled over the region, forcing many pilots to either delay or cancel their flights. Perhaps John had made the same wise decision. It was possible that they'd never left at all.

When John's plane had not turned up an hour later, a call was made to Ted Kennedy in Washington. He immediately phoned John's New York apartment. Someone answered, and for a fleeting moment the senator breathed more easily — until he realized that the voice belonged to a friend whose air-conditioning had broken down. John and

Carolyn had given him access to their apartment so he could escape the city's sweltering summer heat.

It was shortly before midnight when Tony was startled awake by the phone — Ted Kennedy wanting to know if perhaps John had checked in with him. For the next few hours, Tony was one of more than a dozen people manning the phones in an increasingly frantic effort to find John. At 2:15, family friend Carol Ratowell called the Coast Guard operations center in Woods Hole, Massachusetts. They then contacted the FAA, which scoured airports in the region, hoping to discover that John had decided to put down at the nearest airport and wait for visibility to improve. An hour later, having failed to locate the missing plane, the FAA alerted both the Coast Guard and the Air Force Rescue Coordination Center at Virginia's Langley Air Force Base.

Back in Stanley, Idaho, Caroline Kennedy slept soundly alongside her husband, Ed, blissfully unaware of the events unfolding twenty-five hundred miles to the east. The couple had planned to celebrate their thirteenth wedding anniversary and Ed's fifty-fourth birthday on July 19 by white-water-rafting through the region known as the River of No Return. That afternoon John had made his daily call to his sister's cell phone from the offices of *George*, the irreverent political magazine he cofounded in 1995. John did not want his nieces, Rose and Tatiana, and his nephew, Jack, to miss this adventure, and had insisted that Caroline not worry about missing Rory Kennedy's wedding. John and his wife would represent JFK's branch of the family at Hyannis Port that weekend.

They had always been close, but since their mother's death five years earlier, Caroline and John seemed to lean on each other for counsel and support more than ever. "She's an older sister, you know?" John once explained. "We're obviously very close. And as a young brother, you look up to your sister."

Caroline had taken up, said a friend, "where Jackie left off" when it came to worrying about John's daredevil streak. She was well aware that his friends had dubbed him the "Master of Disaster" for putting himself in risky situations and somehow emerging unscathed at the last minute. It had been only six weeks since he'd crashed his Buckeye powered parachute on Martha's Vineyard, breaking his left ankle; the cast had come off only the day before, and he still used crutches to get around.

As the protective big sister, Caroline, in the words of a friend, would "tell him to watch himself, not take any chances. But Jackie was not the smothering type, and neither is Caroline."

Despite the fact that Jackie forbade John to

pilot his own plane — a promise he had kept to his mother during her lifetime — Caroline was resigned to the fact that she could do nothing to stop him. When he told her that he intended to fly his new Piper Saratoga up to Martha's Vineyard and then on to Hyannis Port, she did not object. She assumed that, following John's usual procedure, a flight instructor would be on board to take over in case of emergency.

This final phone conversation between Caroline and John lasted nearly thirty minutes. To Marta Sgubin, who had been hired by Jackie as the children's governess and now worked as a cook and housekeeper for Caroline, it was the same sort of banter brother and sister had engaged in virtually every day since they were teenagers. "There was lots of laughter," Sgubin recalled. "They always seemed to know exactly what the other was thinking."

Accordingly, John knew that his sister would be worried that he was flying up to Cape Cod, and he ended the conversation by reassuring her that he would leave in time to arrive at his destination before dark. It was a route he had already flown several times without incident, he reminded her.

But Caroline still had her doubts. What about his injured foot? Would it hamper John in his ability to control the plane? In the end, Caroline took solace in the presumption that an experienced flight instructor would be alongside her brother in the cockpit. What she did not know was that one of John's flight instructors *had* volunteered to accompany him, and that her brother had turned him down. He was determined to fly solo. "Had Caroline known that," said Jackie's stepbrother, Hugh D. "Yusha" Auchincloss, "she would have stopped John in his tracks. She is just like her mother. Jackie would never have let John take off under those circumstances, and neither would Caroline."

But Caroline, unaware that her brother would be alone at the controls, could do little more than urge him to exercise caution. "Well, be careful," she said in a voice tinged with resignation.

"Don't worry," he replied, trying to quell her fears. "I won't take any chances. I plan on living to a ripe old age. . . ."

These were the last words John would speak to his sister.

After a full day of traveling, Caroline and her family finally checked in to the Mountain Village Resort's Suite 231 and rested up for the next day's long-planned outdoor activities. Nestled at the foot of Idaho's spectacular Sawtooth Mountains, the resort offered such diversions as trout fishing, horseback riding, and bathing in natural hot springs.

Nothing appealed to Caroline and the kids more than shooting the rapids on the winding Salmon River, which they planned to do first thing the next morning.

Meantime, the accommodations were decidedly rustic: Their sparsely decorated two-bedroom suite offered little more than the bare essentials. But no matter. By 11:00 p.m., everyone had basically collapsed from sheer exhaustion.

Back on Martha's Vineyard, Tony Radziwill was unaware that the answer to John's whereabouts lay within sight of Red Gate Farm. Determined to contact Caroline, he called Stanley's police department and eventually tracked down Philip Enright — not only Stanley's police chief but the town's sole law-enforcement officer. Chief Enright drove out to the lodge, and at 4:30 a.m. local time (6:30 eastern) asked the manager to ring Caroline's room on the Mountain Village Resort's house phone. There was an urgent call from Massachusetts, he told her. Caroline's cousin had been trying to reach her for hours, but apparently something was wrong with the phones.

For the first few moments, there was only silence. Caroline, better than anyone, knew what calls like this meant. No Kennedy took the word "emergency" lightly. How, she asked, could she get in touch with Tony Radziwill?

As it turned out, it was still possible to make outgoing calls from the lodge. Caroline gave the switchboard the number of Red Gate Farm and asked to be put through. "Caroline, I've been trying to reach you," Tony said as soon as he heard her voice. "It's John. . . . His plane was supposed to arrive here hours ago, and he hasn't shown up. . . ."

Caroline had learned from an early age not to betray emotion at moments like these. Panic would accomplish nothing. She wanted details. Had a flight instructor accompanied him? Did he file a flight plan? Were there other airports where he might have landed until the fog lifted? Couldn't someone have just made a mistake?

Tony, exhausted now, did not have all the answers. Over the next hour, Caroline would make a series of phone calls to family and friends in an effort to put together the pieces of the puzzle herself. Once she managed to get through to Uncle Teddy, he tried to reassure her that John had landed at a small airfield somewhere and simply neglected to check in. "You know how John always manages to come out of these things," he told his niece.

But Caroline knew better. Like her mother, she had always worried about her brother's flying, and with good reason. For all his devotion to aviation and his extensive training,

John was notoriously forgetful. Had she known that one of his instructors had noted John's lack of concentration and his difficulties with "multitasking," Caroline would have been even more concerned.

Then there was the family's abysmal history in the skies. Caroline's uncle, Joseph P. Kennedy Jr., had been killed in 1944 during a World War II bombing mission. Four years later, Caroline's aunt, Kathleen "Kick" Kennedy Hartington, was flying from Paris to Cannes with her lover, Earl Fitzwilliam, when their plane crashed, taking the lives of all aboard. Aunt Ethel Kennedy's parents died in a plane crash in 1955, as did her brother, George Skakel Jr., eleven years later. During Jackie's marriage to Aristotle Onassis, John and Caroline lost their stepbrother, Alexander Onassis, when his plane crashed after takeoff. Even Uncle Teddy had narrowly escaped death in 1964 when the small plane in which he was flying crashed during a thunderstorm. His aide and the pilot were not so fortunate; both were killed.

Less than thirty minutes after Caroline was notified, White House Chief of Staff John Podesta notified President Clinton at Camp David that John's plane was missing. Clinton ordered that all necessary measures be taken to find young Kennedy — regardless of the cost. Even as Podesta was implementing the President's orders, First Lady Hillary

Clinton — a steadfast friend of Caroline's ever since Jackie first invited the Clintons to Martha's Vineyard — called with words of hope and encouragement.

On the President's orders, the government promptly deployed a small air and sea armada to pinpoint JFK Jr.'s whereabouts. By 7:45 a.m. eastern time, dozens of patrol boats, search-and-rescue vessels, and Coast Guard cutters plied the waters between the eastern tip of Long Island and Martha's Vineyard looking for the plane. At the same time, fifteen Civil Air Patrol planes, a C-130 Hercules cargo plane, an Air National Guard helicopter, two Coast Guard HH-60 Jayhawk choppers, and a UH-25 Falcon had taken to the skies looking for the downed plane.

Perched on the edge of her bed at the Mountain Village Resort, Caroline talked nonstop to family and friends, trying to stay on top of the ongoing search-and-rescue operation. In the background, a television tuned to CNN broadcast what amounted to round-the-clock coverage of what was already being billed as an American tragedy.

As the hope of ever finding her brother, his wife, and his sister-in-law alive slipped away, despair turned to anger. "When she heard of John's disappearance, I think her instincts kicked in," said writer George Plimpton, a longtime family friend who was particularly close to Caroline. "First, she felt the Hyannis Port Kennedys, with all their machismo, encouraged John's risk taking — that they were somehow to blame for his not abandoning the flight once he realized he'd be flying in darkness. She knows they would have called John a wimp if he had decided it had gotten too late to fly." Plimpton mused at the time that "it is just their way. When Michael Kennedy died playing ski football in 1997, it was his mother, Ethel, who had mocked him back onto the slopes when he said he was too tired to play anymore."

For the time being, at least, Caroline would suppress whatever feelings of anger or resentment she harbored against her Kennedy relatives. "I think she wanted to maintain the dignity her mother thought was so important," Plimpton later said. "She wanted to have a cool head so she could say good-bye to her brother in her own way."

Despite reassurances from friends that John would somehow turn up alive — that perhaps he had landed on some remote airstrip and had simply failed to check in — Caroline knew otherwise. "I should feel him," she told one friend, "but I don't."

The Schlossbergs waited until 7:00 p.m. Saturday before boarding a private plane bound for home. As soon as they arrived in New York, the Schlossbergs drove to their two-story, brown-shingled summer retreat on Long Island.

By then, pieces of wreckage — a seat cushion, Lauren Bessette's overnight bag, a twisted plane wheel — had already begun drifting onto Philbin Beach, not far from Red Gate Farm.

Even before Caroline left Idaho, Rory Kennedy announced that she was postponing her wedding indefinitely. Meanwhile, Aunt Ethel was rounding up Kennedys at the clan's Hyannis Port compound to go sailing — one of the physical activities the family traditionally engaged in to distract themselves from the grim reality of yet another untimely death in the family.

John had taken the same approach, Rollerblading up Park Avenue with his then-girlfriend Daryl Hannah on the day of his mother's funeral. Now, scarcely twenty-four hours after Caroline learned of her brother's disappearance, she and Ed hopped on bicycles and pedaled past the horde of photographers waiting outside her Sagaponack house. The press chose not to pursue Caroline and her husband, but that didn't stop locals from heckling the paparazzi. "Vultures!" several yelled. "Why don't you leave her alone?"

By late Sunday, Coast Guard Rear Admiral Richard Larrabee conceded that finding John and the Bessette sisters alive was no longer a possibility. Still, the next day — Caroline and Ed's thirteenth wedding anniversary — the American flag flying over the Schlossbergs' house flew at full staff. Two squad cars were now parked at the entrance to the driveway, a yellow police tape emblazoned with DO NOT CROSS stretched between them.

A steady stream of family members and friends arrived throughout the day to offer words of support to Caroline. Among them was Uncle Teddy, who pulled up to the Schlossberg house shortly after 11:00 a.m. in a black limousine with police escort. Later, while Caroline holed up inside, the senator doffed his shirt to shoot baskets at a free-standing hoop in the driveway with eleven-year-old Rose, nine-year-old Tatiana, and Jack, six. After a half hour in the sweltering heat, Senator Kennedy retreated indoors. As it happened, this day also marked the thirtieth anniversary of the fatal accident at Chappaquiddick.

Next to Uncle Ted, the Kennedy who stayed longest that day was William Kennedy Smith, who spent over two hours consoling Caroline. Of all the Kennedy cousins, Smith, whose rape trial once riveted the nation (he was acquitted), was closest to John and Caroline. Determined not to be held prisoner, Ed talked his wife into going for a drive. That afternoon, reporters watched as their car pulled out of the driveway, slowly turned left, then disappeared down a gravel road. Her eyes concealed by dark glasses, Caroline betrayed no trace of emotion; her face was, in the words of one reporter at the scene, "emotionless, a complete blank."

Behind closed doors, however, it was a very different scene. "We are all waiting here," Marta Sgubin whispered at the time. "I can't really talk. It is very difficult, very difficult. . . ." Sgubin, who had helped Jackie raise her two children, was devastated by John's disappearance — but also concerned that this final tragedy might prove Caroline's undoing.

As soon as they returned to the house, Caroline broke down, retreating to a back bedroom, where she cried alone for more than an hour before emerging. The scene would repeat itself in the coming days and weeks. "Both sides of her family thought it just wasn't dignified to show emotion in public," Marta Sgubin explained. "But Caroline was also determined not to upset the kids." The strain on Mom, however, was incalculable. Caroline, Sgubin added, "was crushed by his death — shattered."

So, too, was America. An emotional Bill Clinton, who at age sixteen had shaken hands with JFK in the White House Rose Garden, offered the nation's condolences to both grieving families. While the rest of the Kennedy clan watched Clinton's remarks from Hyannis Port, Caroline stared blankly at the TV set in her cluttered, toy-strewn living room. No one was surprised that she refused to join the rest of the family on Cape Cod; Jackie had always made a concerted effort, in the words of her friend David Halberstam, to keep her children from being "inhaled" by the Kennedys. While she inherited the toothy, fresh-scrubbed good looks that characterized all the Kennedy women — in contrast to her brother's Bouvier matinee-idol appearance — Caroline was even less a Kennedy than John. In recent years, she seldom spent time at Hyannis Port, preferring instead to concentrate on her own young family.

Caroline was also thinking of Rose, Tatiana, and Jack when she made the decision to stay in the more familiar surroundings of Sagaponack. All three of Caroline's children were close to their Uncle John, and in addition to handling her own grief, she wanted to shield them as much as possible from the prying eyes of the press. "Children are understandably confused and frightened when something like this happens," a friend said. "Caroline and Ed wanted to be there to answer their questions, to focus on them as much as possible. Caroline appreciated that her aunts, uncles, and cousins were grieving, too, but she didn't want to become part of the circus atmosphere on the Cape."

Monday evening, Ted phoned Caroline from Hyannis Port. It was the call he had dreaded making from the beginning. The Coast Guard had determined that, given the chilly sixty-seven-degree water temperature, there was virtually no hope that John, Carolyn, or Lauren could have survived. "If it's all right with you, Caroline," he said, "I think I should issue a statement on behalf of the family."

"Yes, Uncle Teddy," she said, sounding more exhausted than he had ever heard her. "Go ahead . . . it's time . . ."

Finding the right words to convey the family's shock and sorrow would come relatively easily to Ted Kennedy; it was a task he had been called upon to perform too many times before. "We are all filled with unspeakable grief and sadness," the senator's statement read. "John was a shining light in all our lives, and in the lives of the nation and the world that first came to know him as a little boy.

"He was a devoted husband to Carolyn," Uncle Teddy went on, "a loving brother to Caroline, an amazing uncle to her children, a close and dear friend to his cousins, and a beloved nephew to my sisters and me. He was the adored son of two proud parents whom he now joins with God. We loved him deeply . . ."

The hardest part for Caroline would not be confirming for the world that her brother was now irretrievably lost. "What," she asked Marta Sgubin, echoing the same heartbreaking question Jackie had asked thirty-six years before, "am I going to tell the children?"

I remember many of the same things
people remember about me:
hiding with my brother under
my father's desk, riding my pony,
watching the helicopters
take off and land. I also remember
other things that people don't know
about, like the bedtime stories
made up specially for me.

— *Caroline*

2

Chicago, August 1956

"Oh, come on, Jackie," the junior senator from Massachusetts pleaded with his wife over the phone. "All the other wives are here. It won't look good if you're not."

Even though she was eight months pregnant and drained both physically and emotionally, Jackie found it hard to tell her husband that she was not up to boarding a plane for Chicago and joining him at the Democratic National Convention. After all, he had already been given the last rites of the Roman Catholic Church three times, was still in excruciating pain from two back surgeries that had brought him to the brink of death, and was battling Addison's disease.

None of this had so much as slowed Jack down, and there was no way he was going to let her sit this one out — especially since he was now determined to become his party's nominee for vice president. At Jack's insistence, Jackie stayed with his sister Eunice and her husband, Sargent Shriver, who ran the Kennedy-owned Merchandise Mart. Jack, meanwhile, would operate out of a suite at the Conrad Hilton — and continue to be free to see several of the women he always kept on the side.

Jackie hated politics, especially the Kennedy brand of politics. She complained nonstop about the cigar-chomping pols — the "Murphia," Jackie called them — and the rubber-chicken dinners. But she also did not shrink from doing her part whenever it seemed that her absence might be felt. Jackie dutifully attended cocktail parties, breakfasts, and receptions — and was photographed at the convention waving a sign for the party's presidential nominee, Adlai Stevenson.

For all her efforts on his behalf, Jackie saw little of her husband, who was always on the convention floor or in the proverbial smoke-filled rooms trying to wrest the second spot on the Democratic ticket from Senator Estes Kefauver of Tennessee. Jackie did not speak to Jack during the entire convention, and she saw him only once, when he strolled past their mezzanine box the night he placed Stevenson's name in nomination for president. According to their friend Chuck Spalding, Jackie wanted desperately "to be included in Jack's world . . . but Jack was too busy doing what he felt he had to do."

Still, when an emotional Jack stood on the

bed in his hotel suite and thanked his campaign team, Jackie was clearly crushed by the defeat. "The whole time Jack was talking," said another friend, Florida Senator George Smathers, "Jackie was standing next to him, crying."

In fact, ever since their storybook wedding three years earlier, Jackie had struggled with the pressures of public life, rampant rumors of Jack's infidelity, his own precarious health, and their difficulty starting a family. When doctors told Jackie in September 1955 that she was pregnant, the couple celebrated by going house hunting. A month later, they paid the then-impressive sum of $125,000 for Hickory Hill, a historic residence in McLean, Virginia. But only a few days after moving, Jackie suffered a miscarriage.

Understandably, Jack and Jackie were "very upset," said Jackie's stepbrother, Hugh Auchincloss III. But in keeping with their passion for privacy, "they really didn't share their feelings with anyone. They both had entirely too much dignity for that. It wasn't their style at all." They would not have to do much explaining; only a few close family members were even aware that Jackie was expecting.

By January 1956, she was pregnant again. While her husband shot to national prominence as author of the Pulitzer Prize–winning *Profiles in Courage*, Jackie busied herself redecorating Hickory Hill. No room got as much attention as the nursery. "Jackie was very excited about the baby," Spalding said, "and worried, too, because of the miscarriage."

Now that the convention was over, Jack and Jackie returned to New York, where they maintained a suite at the Carlyle Hotel. From there, Jack flew off to cruise the Mediterranean with his brother Teddy and George Smathers. Tired and vulnerable, Jackie pleaded with Jack not to leave her so late in her pregnancy. After all, she had stood by him in Chicago, and now it was his turn to give her the emotional support she needed. Jack, unmoved, went ahead with his plans.

"I'm sure it was obvious to Jackie that he was going to have his share of female company on the trip," Smathers said. "She didn't want him to go, and she let him know it, but in the end there just wasn't anything she could do about it." Defeated, Jackie headed to Newport, Rhode Island, and Hammersmith Farm, the twenty-eight-room shingled "cottage" owned by her mother, Janet, and stepfather, Hugh D. Auchincloss. In these familiar surroundings, Jackie could spend the final month of her pregnancy recuperating from her punishing week working the convention in Chicago.

Jack was cruising the Mediterranean aboard a forty-foot sailing vessel when Jackie awoke the morning of August 23, 1956, and screamed for help. Responding to her daughter's cries, Janet Auchincloss ran into the room and found Jackie doubled over on the floor. Hemorrhaging badly, Jackie was rushed by ambulance to Newport Hospital, where doctors performed an emergency cesarean. But it was too late. The unnamed infant, a girl, was stillborn.

As tragic as the loss of the baby was, Jackie was now in danger of losing her own life. She had required several transfusions during the operation, and was listed in critical condition. When Jackie finally came to several hours later, it was Bobby Kennedy — not Jack — who held her hand reassuringly. It also fell to Bobby to tell his sister-in-law that she had lost the baby.

Jack, meanwhile, was still at sea with Teddy and several accommodating young women — unaware of the *Washington Post* headline that screamed SENATOR KENNEDY ON MEDITERRANEAN TRIP UNAWARE THAT HIS WIFE HAS LOST BABY. It would be fully seventy hours before Jack's yacht docked in Genoa and he called home to learn the news from Jackie. Incredibly, Jack told her that he saw no reason to cut short his trip and come home. Jackie, understandably, was furious, and deeply hurt.

"You better get your ass back there right away," Smathers told him, "if you plan on staying married — or on getting to the White House." With that, Smathers later recalled, they "drove like a bat out of hell to the airport."

Jackie, who until now had faced the devastating loss of her child without her husband — Bobby had quietly made arrangements to have the baby buried in Newport — refused to move back to Hickory Hill and its empty nursery. The loss was felt even more sharply because two other Kennedy women had given birth to healthy daughters during the same period. Pat Lawford's daughter Sydney was born just two days after Jackie's stillbirth, and two weeks after that, Ethel gave birth to Mary Courtney, her fifth child. Four months later, Jack and Jackie sold Hickory Hill to Bobby and Ethel, who would wind up giving birth to a total of eleven children over a seventeen-year period. Jackie later gave Ethel a drawing she did of Hickory Hill in which the stately home was virtually overrun with youngsters.

Jackie would never confront her in-laws directly, but she did blame her failed pregnancies on the Kennedys' frenzied lifestyle and, more specifically, on Jack's unbridled political ambition. She also knew that behind her back the tables were turned. The Kennedys were blaming *her*, speculating that the aristocratic Miss Bouvier was just too fragile to see a pregnancy through.

For at least the second time in their short marriage, Jackie was seriously contemplating divorce. But her father-in-law, Joe, the powerful Kennedy paterfamilias with whom Jackie shared a warm and joking relationship, would have none of it. When *Time* magazine claimed that the notoriously ambitious Joseph P. Kennedy had offered Jackie $1 million not to divorce Jack, Jackie phoned Joe and cracked, "Only one million? Why not ten million?"

Joe had, in fact, made the $1 million offer. And according to his friend Clare Boothe Luce, Jackie confidant Gore Vidal, and several others, she took it. "Happily," said Vidal, whose mother had been married to Jackie's stepfather.

Jackie was even happier in March 1957, when she learned that she was again pregnant. By this time, Jack had — with his father's blessing — decided to run for president in 1960. But Jackie made it clear that this time she would not subject herself to the strains of politics. Instead she would focus her energies on decorating the redbrick Federal house they purchased that spring at 3307 N Street NW in Georgetown. As she had at Hickory Hill, Jackie lavished special attention on one room in particular: the third-floor nursery.

By the time Jackie felt she was far enough along to go public with her pregnancy, everyone in the family had already phoned to congratulate her — with one major exception. Jackie's father, "Black Jack" Bouvier, only learned he was about to become a grandfather when he read it in the *New York Times*. Bouvier, who had divorced Jackie's mother when Jackie was eleven and her sister, Lee, eight, was deeply hurt. A recluse living on the interest from $200,000 in savings, the once-dashing Black Jack was now emaciated and sallow. No wonder: Bouvier spent weeks on end drinking alone in his four-room apartment on New York's Upper East Side.

Jackie was summering in Hyannis Port when she learned that her father was upset with her for not telling him about her pregnancy before it made the papers. She flew directly to New York, only to have her father lambaste her and her sister, who now lived in London, for deserting him to embrace the wealthy Auchinclosses and even wealthier Kennedys. "I suppose this baby is going to grow up knowing nothing about his Bouvier heritage," he sniped. "We may not have as much money, but what we do have is considerably more valuable: breeding."

Jackie had always been close to her father, but there was nothing she could do to convince him that the slight had been unintentional. She flew back to Hyannis. When

46

Black Jack checked into New York's Lenox Hill Hospital complaining of stomach pains on July 27, the eve of her twenty-eighth birthday, Jackie called to make sure that he was resting comfortably and that her presence wasn't needed.

Five days later, Jackie's father lapsed into a coma. For the first time, she was told he had been diagnosed with liver cancer. Jackie, now five months pregnant, rushed to Black Jack's side, but too late. He had slipped away forty-five minutes earlier; according to the nurse on duty, Jackie's name was the final word on his lips.

Jackie, guilt-ridden over not being able to say good-bye to her father, assumed the burden of making all the funeral arrangements — from picking out the coffin and the flowers to writing the obituary. For Jackie, any hope of avoiding stress during this pregnancy was gone.

Things only got worse when Jack checked back into the hospital with a virulent staphylococcus infection along one of the surgical scars in his back. Jack quickly recovered, but his wife was "a basket case," said one friend. "Of course the strain on her was enormous. Everyone, including Jack, was worried about the baby." To cope with the stress, Jackie chain-smoked Salems (she later switched to L&Ms) — a lifelong habit that she would diligently pursue away from the cameras.

Notwithstanding her mounting anxiety and the smoking, Jackie's latest pregnancy would prove uneventful. On November 27, 1957 — the day before Thanksgiving — she gave birth by cesarean section to a seven-pound, two-ounce girl at the Lying-In Hospital of New York Hospital–Cornell Medical Center. As was the custom for new fathers at the time, Jack bided his time in the waiting room during the delivery. Jackie's mother and a handful of other family members and friends kept him company.

While they waited, Janet Auchincloss asked her son-in-law if he was hoping for a boy or a girl. "Anything," he replied, "will be fine with me." Then the doctor came in with a progress report. "I'll always remember Jack's face," said Jackie's mother, "when the doctor came into the waiting room and told him that the baby was fine. I will always remember the sweet expression on his face and the way he smiled. And the doctor said, 'She's very pretty.' "

Blinking awake from the anesthesia, Jackie saw her husband walking toward her, their baby in his arms. Jack handed Caroline Bouvier Kennedy to her mother, who until now had lived in abject fear that she would never experience this moment. The child was named after Jackie's only sister, Lee, whose full name was actually Caroline Lee. Jackie later described November 27, 1957, as "the very happiest day of my life."

One of the first visitors to the hospital besides the immediate family was Jack's old friend Lem Billings. When Jack took Billings to the nursery to see his daughter, he clasped his hand to the man's shoulder. "Now, Lem," he said, "tell me — which of the babies in the window is the prettiest?" When Billings pointed to somebody else's baby, Jack scowled. "He didn't speak to me for two days," Billings said. "Jack was more emotional about Caroline's birth than he was about anything else."

Janet Auchincloss was especially impressed — particularly in light of the callousness he had exhibited over Jackie's stillbirth the year before. "He seemed perfectly at home with babies," Janet marveled, adding that she was struck by the "sheer, unadulterated delight he took in Caroline from that first day on. The look on his face, which I had never seen before, really, was . . . radiant."

Caroline was eleven days old and still in the hospital with her mother when the new British nanny, Maud Shaw, assumed her duties. Breast-feeding, not particularly in vogue in the 1950s, was something Jackie and her fellow society mommies scarcely considered. Nor was Jackie inclined to give the baby her bottle or change her diapers — tasks that she, like her mother before her, felt should be left to the professionals.

"Neither Jack nor Jackie ever changed a diaper in their life," said Chuck Spalding. "If one of them was holding the baby and that smell began wafting up, well, it was, 'Maud . . . oh, MAUD!' and they held that kid at arm's length until they could hand her over. But that was the way they'd been brought up — with servants always sort of appearing out of nowhere to clean things up. They weren't your average people, and they weren't your average parents either."

Still, even before they left the hospital, the forty-year-old first-time father wanted to give Caroline her bottle. "He asked me to stand quite near him," Shaw said, "in case he dropped her." But Jack, a bundle of nervous energy who always seemed to be in motion, spent less than five minutes before he became bored. "Miss Shaw, how have you got the patience to feed the child all this bottle?" he said, handing Caroline off to her. "I guess this is your department after all. I had better leave it to you."

"But he really loved her," said Shaw, who moved with the young family into their new home in Georgetown when Caroline was three weeks old. Like virtually everyone who knew Jack and Jackie well during this period, the nanny regarded Jack as a devoted father, utterly smitten with his little girl. "When he came into the house, he always came straight upstairs to the nursery. That child always smiled for him when she never did for anybody else. Right from the very beginning, he loved her and she adored him."

The impact this unique relationship had on Jack was so profound that, according to several friends, it enabled him to connect with others in a way he had not been able to before. "Caroline's birth was a magical thing for Jack," said Billings. "It changed him. I'm not sure he ever would have had what it takes — that extra spark — to make it all the way to the White House. And her arrival really changed the whole situation with Jackie — made it stronger, at least for a while. If Caroline hadn't come along, I really don't think Jack would ever have become president."

"That was a marvelous relationship," family friend Betty Spalding said of Jack's love for his daughter. JFK, she said, "was able to release some of his emotions to her, and it freed him from the fear of it, and he was able to exchange better with Jackie and she with him. Until he had Caroline, he never really learned how to deal with people. It was fascinating to watch him grow in this capacity."

On December 13, Richard Cardinal Cushing, Archbishop of Boston, traveled to New York for the christening of Joe Kennedy's newest grandchild at St. Patrick's Cathedral. Jackie had chosen her sister to be Caroline's godmother. While a mink-clad Lee cradled the infant in her arms, the raspy-voiced Cushing dabbed holy water on Caroline's head. The baby's godfather, Uncle Bobby Kennedy, looked on somberly while Papa stood nearby. Caroline wore the same lace baptismal gown her mother had worn when she was christened twenty-eight years before.

Caroline's arrival seemed to signal a marital rebirth as well — in part because it served to bolster Jackie's flagging self-esteem. To some extent, Jackie had lived her married life in the shadow of her domineering mother and her formidable mother-in-law, Rose Kennedy. Now she was wife, mother, and the very-much-in-charge mistress of the first home she could call entirely her own. Of course, given her background — and her husband's resources — she required plenty of help: her personal maid, Providencia "Provi" Paredes, two other upstairs maids, a cook, a laundress, a full-time chauffeur, a valet, and her own private secretary.

No staff member would have quite the status of Maud Shaw, however. In the days before Pampers and Huggies, it was Shaw who, several times a day, pinned a neatly folded fresh diaper onto Caroline's behind, then gingerly deposited its soiled predecessor in a hamper so that it would be picked up by the diaper service the next day. And if Caroline awoke crying at 2:00 a.m., Jackie and Jack slept while the nanny made her way downstairs to heat up a bottle of formula over the stove. Jack and Jackie, as devoted as they may have been, were to an extent utterly oblivious to the nuts and bolts of infant care.

"It all seems very nineteenth century now," said a family acquaintance. "But that's the way rich people behaved back then. Few mothers breast-fed. It's not that Jack and Jackie weren't close to their children — they loved them deeply, and their kids loved them back. But there's always that slight air of formality, that distance that's put between them in the very beginning."

Still, Caroline's nanny remembered that in the coming years, Jackie would "do a lot of little things for Caroline — dress her, and take her out, and play with her in the garden." In the summer months, an inflatable pool was filled in the backyard. "We spent a number of hours playing in the swimming pool and having these little afternoon teas and lunches together."

For now, as Jackie tried to define her role as wife and mother, days in the house on N Street were structured, formal, and above all else quiet. In sharp contrast to her boisterous in-laws, Jackie insisted that there be no extraneous noise. That meant no radios, no television, nor any whistling, humming, or singing on the part of the servants. Caroline was more or less kept out of sight until Daddy came home, and then Maud Shaw might bring her downstairs from the nursery so that he could hold her for a few minutes before retiring to the study for predinner cocktails.

As much as he adored his daughter, there is also no doubt that he appreciated what she could do for him politically. Until now Jack could claim to be a Harvard graduate, a war hero — the courageous captain of PT-109 — a Pulitzer Prize–winning author, not to mention dashing heir to one of America's great fortunes. These qualities, aided in no small way by his father's wealth, influence, and behind-the-scenes string pulling, were enough to get him elected first to Congress and then to the U.S. Senate.

To go any further, Joe told his son in no uncertain terms, he needed a wife and family. Under duress from his father, who worried that persistent rumors about Jack's frenetic love life could derail his presidential ambitions, Jack had married the refined Miss Bouvier. Yet to overcome his youth and his religious affiliation — no Roman Catholic before (or since) had ever been elected president — Jack needed to take that extra step into fatherhood.

As 1957 drew to a close, Jack enjoyed a comfortable lead in the polls over all the

1960 Democratic hopefuls. Nor was there ever the slightest doubt that he would handily win reelection to the Senate in 1958. But if he was going to maintain enough momentum to carry him through to the presidency, he would need to win — and big. Joe figured that a margin of a half million votes over his Republican opponent, Vincent J. Celeste, would make it virtually impossible for the party to deny young Senator Kennedy the nomination.

While Robert F. Kennedy would normally have run his brother's campaign, this time he was busy making headlines of his own — as chief counsel for Senator John L. McClellan's select committee on racketeering. In that capacity, Bobby took on Teamster boss Jimmy Hoffa before a television audience of millions. With twenty-six-year-old little brother Teddy taking the reins as campaign manager, Jack crisscrossed the country honoring speaking engagements designed to spread his message nationally.

Toward this end, he fully appreciated the newest weapon in his campaign arsenal: Caroline. Even some of his closest friends speculated that this was the chief reason — some said the only reason — he wanted children in the first place. "Jack's desire was," his longtime pal Charlie Bartlett put it, "to get the bountiful positive publicity only a child might yield."

Jack was not yet the nominee of his party, much less president. Still, the editors of *Look*, the *Saturday Evening Post*, *Life*, and other major national magazines vied for the first candid photos of the Kennedy baby. No sooner did Jack give the nod to a *Life* cover story than Jackie "hit the ceiling," their old friend Chuck Spalding recalled.

"No pictures of the baby, Jack," Jackie told him. "That's final. I'm not going to let our child be used like some campaign mascot. I don't care how many votes it costs you."

Jackie would ultimately relent, but only after Jack promised that he would take a break during the campaign that summer to spend time with his wife in Paris. *Life* photographer Ed Clark arrived at the N Street house that April and took a series of family shots. When the April 21, 1958, issue of *Life* hit the stands, the cover featured Jackie and Jack in the nursery, beaming at the camera with the baby's canopied crib visible in the background. Caroline, perched on Daddy's lap, looked off to the right at the stuffed toy the photographer had brought along to keep her amused. Inside, the most beguiling photo was of Caroline playing peekaboo with Daddy.

Jacques Lowe, a political refugee from Nazi Germany who had befriended Bobby Kennedy, was another lensman who played a huge part in constructing the Kennedy image frame by frame. For Papa Joe's birthday, Bobby had given the patriarch an album of photographs Lowe had taken of the organized mayhem that was Kennedy family life at Hyannis Port. It had been this way since 1929, when Joe bought a rambling, green-shuttered "summer cottage" on the beach at Hyannis Port and expanded it to include fourteen rooms, nine bathrooms, and New England's first home movie theater. Over the years, the patriarch gave his children the money to buy adjacent homes, gradually forming what by the end of the 1950s would be known as the "Kennedy Compound." When, at Joe Kennedy's insistence, Lowe arrived at the compound to photograph Jack, the photographer found his subject "grumpy, awkward, and preoccupied. He was very tired. But," Lowe added, "he perked up whenever I asked him to sit with Caroline."

Caroline would be the subject of countless Norman Rockwell images provided by Lowe, Clark, and other photographers — images that belied the fact that all was far from well in her parents' complicated marriage. Despite the pressures of the campaign, his fragile health, and the demands of family life, Caroline's father somehow found the time to cheat on her mother with dozens of women.

It was around this time, in fact, that JFK embarked on his two-and-a-half-year affair with Marilyn Monroe. A year after divorcing Joe DiMaggio, Marilyn married the playwright Arthur Miller. The couple settled in bucolic Roxbury, Connecticut, but within months Marilyn was meeting Jack secretly in his suite at New York's Carlyle Hotel.

Determined to keep a closer eye on her husband that summer of 1958, Jackie joined him on the campaign trail for the first time. She stared adoringly at the candidate whenever he gave a speech at the Lions Club, posed for pictures, marched alongside him in East Boston's Columbus Day parade, and answered phones with her sisters-in-law as part of a televised "Ask Senator Kennedy" program. Caroline's mother gave her first campaign speech not in English but in French, to the Worcester Cercle Français. When she spoke a few Italian phrases in Boston's North End, the crowd cheered.

But Caroline was, at Jackie's insistence, kept out of the fray. Photographs were one thing, but there was no way Mrs. Kennedy would allow her daughter to be stared at and jostled by complete strangers. "He wanted to cart out Caroline as often as he could," Lowe said, "but he wasn't about to defy Jackie when it came to their child. Besides, Jackie was turning out to be surprisingly effective as a campaigner."

Still, Jack fretted that he might not score the landslide he needed to carry him to the nomination. He needn't have. Jack received 73.6 percent of the vote — a victory margin of 874,608 — the largest number of votes ever cast for a single candidate in Massachusetts history. Moreover, Jack's victory margin was the largest of any Senate candidate's that year.

No sooner had he won reelection to the Senate than Caroline's dad began running in earnest for president — although the next day he went through the motions of emphatically denying it on NBC's *Meet the Press*. In truth, Joe Kennedy had already purchased a presidential campaign plane for his son: a ten-passenger DC-3 outfitted with reclining chairs, overstuffed sofas, a curtained-off sleeping area, a dining area, and a galley that would always be stocked with the one Kennedy staple, New England clam chowder. Jack had no trouble coming up with a name for the aircraft: the *Caroline*.

Caroline, left behind in the care of Maud Shaw, never saw her parents argue. Nor did anyone else. If there was visible tension between the two, it was more likely to be over Jackie's profligate spending habits than Jack's rampant infidelity. "So long as she was not held up to public ridicule," Gore Vidal said, "Jackie accepted Jack's womanizing as a fact of life. It's not that they didn't care about each other. I think she eventually grew quite fond of Jack, and he took a certain pride in her."

Over the next several months, Jackie would grudgingly allow photographers to snap candid shots of Caroline — in her sunbonnet, being carried by Mommy as the handsome young family strolled on a Hyannis Port pier, tickling Daddy's nose, sitting in Daddy's lap as he read her a favorite book, *I Can Fly.*

But as the campaign picked up speed, Caroline was left home with Maud Shaw for longer and longer stretches while her parents made the case for JFK's candidacy to the American people. Jackie, who seemed chilly and aloof at first, was now considered a valuable asset on the hustings. "It turned out that the voters loved her," said West Virginia campaign organizer Charles Peters. "She was perceived as the princess, and they basked in her glamour rather than being offended by it."

By the time Jack formally declared his presidential candidacy on January 20, 1960, he had already logged tens of thousands of miles aboard the *Caroline.* Jack's attitude toward risk taking in the skies would resurface in the next generation, with tragic consequences. But at the time, Jackie seemed no less fearless when it came to flying. According to Jacques Lowe, Caroline's parents "flew in any kind of weather. Blizzards, thunderstorms, terrible fog. Even when the pilots were reluctant to take the chance, Jack really pushed the envelope."

At one point, the couple was headed for the airport after a campaign stop in Ashland, Wisconsin, when Jackie spotted a crow. "I told Jack we must see another crow, and I told him the jingle I learned as a little girl: 'One crow sorrow, two crows joy, three crows a girl, four a boy.' And you should have seen Jack looking for crows until he found more. He would have liked to find four crows. I guess every man wants a boy. But that was a tender thing, I thought."

That spring of 1960, after racking up primary victories in New Hampshire, Wisconsin, and West Virginia, Jackie told Jack that she was again pregnant. The baby was due in early December, and she made it clear that she would be taking no chances. Fearing a repeat of the post–Chicago convention tragedy of 1956, she would not accompany her husband to the convention in Los Angeles.

This time, Jack made no attempt to talk her into going. "After they had Caroline, he understood what it was to be a parent," one friend observed. "He already saw this baby as a human being, and not a thing. I think he felt guilty for the way he acted in 1956 — wanting to stay in Europe even after he got word of the stillbirth. A lot of us felt that was unforgivable. But he was a changed man in 1960. If something like that had happened then, he would have been devastated."

Given her father's frequent absences, Caroline's first spoken word — "Good-bye" — seemed especially poignant. But the next words she uttered — "New Hampshire," "Wisconsin," and "West Virginia" — also made it clear that she had already been imprinted with the stamp of a political family. Jackie joked that she was "very sorry so few states have primaries, or we would have a daughter with the greatest vocabulary of any two-year-old in the country."

Caroline was, and would remain, remarkably unspoiled despite the circumstances of her early years. There would never be any question that, from the beginning, she adored her father. During one of his increasingly rare weekends home, the presidential candidate was taking a bath when Caroline rushed in shouting "Daddy!" and waving a copy of *Newsweek*. Daddy was on the cover, and with a laugh she gleefully tossed the magazine into the tub.

While Caroline stayed in Hyannis Port with her mother, who was now five months pregnant, Jack was in Los Angeles fending off a last-minute challenge to his candidacy from powerful Texas Senator Lyndon Johnson. Incredibly, JFK still managed to find the time for extracurricular activities — alternating between mobster Sam Giancana's raven-haired girlfriend, Judy Campbell, and Marilyn Monroe, whose affair with French movie star Yves Montand had just ended badly.

News of Jack's escapades (Marilyn was telling friends that she found her private times with the senator to be "very penetrating") filtered back to Massachusetts, where Jackie chain-smoked as she watched black-and-white convention coverage on a small rented television set. Jackie pretended to ignore the rumors, but in private she worried that the convention might have changed the nature of their relationship forever. With Caroline in the picture and another baby on the way, she may have allowed herself to hope, naively, that Jack might change his ways. "She hid it from the press, from the cameras, the public," said Larry Newman, the Kennedys' longtime Hyannis Port next-door neighbor. "But I saw her practically every day, and there were plenty of moments when there was this look in her eyes — something between sadness and panic."

As a child of divorce herself, there was no way that Jackie would subject Caroline or her new sibling to the kind of wrenching emotional pain she had endured. But rumors persisted that, in light of her husband's infidelity, Jackie planned to file for divorce the day after he was elected president. When one of the chief purveyors of that story turned out to be a New York socialite who had known the Kennedys for years, Jackie snapped, "That little bitch. And she always acts like such a dear friend."

Such remarks were never made in the presence of Caroline — and especially not when she and her mother were in residence at Hyannis Port. Grandmother Rose Kennedy was a strict disciplinarian with distinctly Old World notions about child rearing and deportment. As a mother, Rose Kennedy did not so much raise her children as manage them, insisting that their days be filled with calisthenics, math drills, pop quizzes (Rose called them "brain teasers"), and impromptu spelling bees — as well as golf, tennis, swimming, and sailing lessons. All the while, Rose kept an emotional distance from her offspring, and Jack never forgave her for that. "My mother never really held me and hugged me," he once complained. "Never! Never!"

Mellowing somewhat with age, Rose treated her grandchildren differently. While always a regal presence, she would show an active personal interest in the young crop of Kennedys who now swarmed over the lawns at Hyannis Port. Caroline was a particular favorite — and not only because she was the child of the future president. Caroline impressed her grandmother as a thoughtful child, and, due in large part to Jackie's civilizing influence, Caroline was noticeably more well behaved than most of her Kennedy cousins.

On July 13, Jackie and Caroline sat in the living room at Hyannis Port and watched as Daddy clinched the Democratic nomination on the first ballot. He would now square off against the Republican candidate and his old Senate friend, Vice President Richard Nixon. A half hour after Wyoming put Caroline's dad over the top, the phone rang at Hyannis Port. "Congratulations, Jack," Jackie said before he could utter a word. "I know, I saw it all on television. It's wonderful. . . ." Jackie knew all too well that she would not have been the first person he called; out of respect for the man whose wealth, power, and behind-the-scenes maneuvering had landed him this prize, the first call Jack placed was to his father. After chatting a few minutes, Jackie held the phone up to Caroline so she could say hello.

The next morning, while Jack offered Lyndon Johnson the number two spot on the ticket, a small army of reporters descended on Hyannis Port. With Caroline scampering about, Jackie struck an apologetic tone as she explained that she intended to stay home for the remainder of her pregnancy — in contrast to Republican candidate Richard Nixon's wife, Pat, who was already campaigning on her husband's behalf. "I suppose

I won't be able to play much part in the campaign," she said, "but I'll do what I can. I feel I should be with Jack when he's engaged in such a struggle, and if it weren't for the baby, I'd campaign even more vigorously than Mrs. Nixon."

When Jack arrived back in Hyannis Port, Jackie and Caroline handed him his homecoming present. It was a sketch of the newly anointed Democratic presidential nominee making his triumphal return to the Cape aboard his aptly named sailboat, *Victura*.

For the next two weeks, Jack spent some quality time with his wife and daughter at Hyannis Port before resuming his quest for the White House. It would be the first clear memory Caroline would have of an extended period with her parents together. To summon his daughter, all Jack had to do was clap his hands twice. "As soon as Caroline heard that first clap," said Presidential Press Secretary Pierre Salinger, "she took off like a rocket." Nor did JFK waste any time coming up with a pet name for Caroline. For the rest of her life, the President's adored only daughter would remember the sharp sound of Daddy's clapping hands, and his voice calling out the name he and only he used to summon her: "Buttons."

If you bungle raising your children,
I don't think whatever else
you do well matters very much.

— *Jackie*

3

Caroline stood on the porch at Hyannis Port in her sundress, watching Daddy and her uncles play touch football on the lawn. Next to her, Mommy and Grandpa Joe sat on wicker chairs, sipping lemonade and trading gossip about everything from New York's latest society scandal to the love lives of Jackie's female staff members — young women Joe referred to as "les girls." Sitting on the porch steps just a few feet away was a tired and sweaty Jacques Lowe, loading film into one of the three cameras that dangled from his neck.

Suddenly Grandpa jumped to his feet as Bobby plowed into Ted, knocking him to the ground. Lowe leaped to his feet and began snapping away. "That's right!" Joe Kennedy yelled to Bobby, who was considerably smaller and more ferocious than his younger brother. "And what's wrong with you, Teddy? Get up! Don't be a loser, boy!"

Bobby tossed the ball to Caroline's father, whose worsening back insured that — at least for today — he would not be tackled. "Yeah, Teddy boy," Jack teased, looking up at his daughter. "Why, I'll bet Caroline is tougher than you are!"

Presided over by Caroline's fiercely competitive win-at-any-cost Kennedy grandparents, life at the Hyannis Port compound was a frenzied blur of outdoor activity. There was tennis, sailing, snorkeling, badminton, and, of course, the obligatory rough-and-tumble "touch" football game for which the Kennedy clan was already famous. Always a speed demon, Jack ignored his bad back and took the wheel of a golf cart, zooming around the grounds of the compound as Caroline and her cousins hung on for dear life. (Most of the time, the Kennedy kids rode around the grounds aboard the "Toonerville Trolley," a stretch golf cart that could easily accommodate a half dozen passengers and their golf bags.)

Intent on capitalizing on his family-man image — after all, his old Senate friend Dick Nixon carted out his two daughters at every opportunity — Jack invited Jacques Lowe to take as many photos as he pleased. Just happy to have access to her husband for a couple of weeks, Jackie went along. One afternoon the not-quite-visibly pregnant Mrs. Kennedy put on a one-piece bathing suit and a bathing cap to frolick with her husband on the beach. At one point, she pretended to steady him in a dinghy before tipping it over, toppling Jack into the surf.

Mother and daughter remained largely out of sight for the next twelve weeks as Jack campaigned virtually nonstop — buoyed by the amphetamine injections he received from Dr. Max Jacobson, better known as the notorious "Dr. Feelgood." The turning point came on September 26, when CBS aired the first of four historic televised debates between Kennedy and Nixon. "Look! Daddy!" Caroline shouted, pointing to the screen as her father was introduced. She had seen her father so seldom over the previous two months that, Jackie later said, "Caroline was thrilled just to see him — even in black and white."

So, too, was the rest of the country. Although those who listened to the debate on the radio felt that Nixon had scored a decisive victory, the millions who watched on television were won over by Jack's appearance and cool demeanor. Tanned and relaxed after several days at his parents' winter residence in Palm Beach — an oceanfront mansion Joe Kennedy had purchased in the late 1920s — the Democratic candidate looked, in the words of debate producer Don Hewitt, "like a young Adonis." Nixon, by contrast, had declined the makeup that he sorely needed to conceal his five o'clock shadow and the sweat that beaded on his upper lip. For the subsequent three debates, Nixon, whose darting eyes continued to be a problem, used Pan-Cake makeup — but it was too late.

After watching the first three debates at home, a very pregnant Jackie and her sister, Lee, accompanied Jack to the ABC studios in New York for the final showdown. Jackie had little to say about the candidate's performance ("I think my husband did very well"), but her mere presence on the set added an undeniable touch of glamour. "Everybody was comparing Mrs. Nixon to Mrs. Kennedy," said *Washington Star* columnist Betty Beale. "Pat Nixon was a very warm woman, but let's face it — she was drab in comparison to Jackie."

The Kennedy campaign came to depend on Jackie's efforts to counter Pat Nixon's Republican-cloth-coat image — efforts that more often than not included Caroline. In magazine layout after magazine layout, Caroline was shown napping, beaming at her parents, hugging her stuffed animals, or simply gazing in wide-eyed wonder into the camera lens. "She was," Jacques Lowe said, "a *phenomenally* photogenic child." Conspicuously absent was Maud Shaw, who was careful to stay out of the range of photographers. Jackie actually told *Life* that she raised Caroline without the help of a nanny. "If Jack proved to be the greatest president of the century and his children turned out badly," she proclaimed, "it would be a tragedy."

In the closing days of the campaign, Jack pleaded with his wife to join him in New York City for a final campaign push. Jackie's doctors, fearing for their patient and her unborn child, urged her to defy her husband and stay home with Caroline. But ultimately the candidate's wife relented. "It's the most important time of Jack's whole life," she said. "I should be with him."

Jackie once again showed off her linguistic abilities, speaking Spanish to crowds in Spanish Harlem and Italian in Little Italy. The climax of the campaign trip — a ticker-tape parade through New York's fabled "Canyon of Heroes" — almost turned tragic when Jackie, now eight months pregnant and riding on the back of an open car with her husband, was nearly catapulted to the pavement by adoring fans.

Jackie, assuming that she might be confined to Hyannis Port as the end of her pregnancy drew near, sent in her absentee ballot even before the grueling trip to New York. But on Election Day — November 8, 1960 — Jackie showed up at Boston's West End library to smile for the cameras as Jack cast his vote. Then they were off to Hyannis Port to await the results.

Once they were in the house, Jackie asked

her husband to sit down in his favorite wing chair. Caroline, she said, had a surprise for him. The little girl, her curly blond hair held in place by two powder blue ribbons, rocked on her heels and began to speak as her mother looked on expectantly from the sidelines:

"My candle burns at both ends;
It will not last the night;
But ah, my foes, and oh, my friends —
It gives a lovely light!"

Jack clapped his approval. "Wonderful, Buttons!" he said.

"Wait, there's more," Jackie interrupted.

Caroline cocked her head, took a deep breath, and started again:

"Safe upon the solid rock
    the ugly houses stand:
Come and see my shining palace
    built upon the sand!"

That Jackie would choose to teach Caroline to memorize Edna St. Vincent Millay's "First Fig" and "Second Fig" — two poems that rail against those who choose the cautious life — seemed oddly prophetic. But to Caroline it would be one of her sweetest childhood memories. "I remember his delight," Caroline later recalled, "and my own."

That night, the family watched the election results on television, although even more up-to-the-minute, precinct-by-precinct results were coming in over the thirty phone lines installed on Papa Joe's sunporch. In the beginning, it appeared as if Jack would win in a landslide, but as the night progressed and the returns came in, Nixon gained ground.

At 4:00 a.m., with the results still see-sawing between Kennedy and Nixon, Jack went upstairs to join his wife in bed. "Wake me," he told Pierre Salinger, "if anything happens."

Jack woke a little before 9:00 a.m. and was again soaking in the bathtub when his daughter burst into the room. "Daddy, Daddy!" Caroline yelled. "You won! You won!" As it turned out, JFK adviser Ted Sorensen had awakened him with the news minutes before. But Daddy wasn't about to dampen Caroline's enthusiasm.

"I won? Really?" he said.

"Yes, Daddy," she replied with a nod. "You won!"

"Does that mean I'll be president?"

"Yes." More nods. "Miss Shaw told me to call you 'Mr. President' now."

Later Jack put on a gray suit and a red polka-dot tie, then joined Caroline and her mother for breakfast. But an hour later, Illinois and Minnesota were placed in the undecided column, and though Jack was holding on to the slimmest of leads, it was anything but certain that Richard Nixon would concede. Caroline watched as the mood among the grown-ups careered from jubilant to tense and back again. While Daddy and his friends sat staring at the television, Mommy drifted upstairs. The tension was palpable, even to a child. Maud Shaw helped Caroline into her coat and took her outside to scamper about on the grass.

Finally Nixon spokesman Herb Klein appeared to congratulate Jack on his victory. Out of 69 million votes cast, the Democrat had won by 118,550 — fewer than one-fifth of 1 percent. Notwithstanding the excruciating back pain that had plagued him his entire adult life, Jack stepped outside into the brilliant sunshine, grabbed Caroline, and gave her a piggyback ride. Then, carrying her in his arms, JFK went over to the scores of reporters and photographers waiting for him on the lawn. Still holding Caroline, he answered reporters' questions while Jackie walked off toward the beach virtually unnoticed.

Caroline returned with her parents to Georgetown, where Secret Service agents had already cordoned off the block around the N Street house. Reporters and onlookers waited, sometimes for hours, to catch a glimpse of the newly elected president and his family. Caroline, until this point largely sheltered from the outside world, now heard perfect strangers call out her name whenever she left the house with her nanny or even pressed her nose to her bedroom window.

"It was quite a scene," Salinger recalled. "And Jackie hated it. Caroline had a very sunny disposition, but even at that age, she had to notice how unhappy all the hoopla made her mother. Jackie felt her privacy was being invaded, and to some extent she resented Jack for that."

Jackie was equally upset about the havoc occurring *inside* the Kennedy household. The house on N Street served as headquarters for the precocious and spirited Kennedy transition team during the two-and-a-half-month period between Election Day and Jack's inauguration on January 20, 1961. While key advisers like Dean Rusk, Robert McNamara, Ted Sorensen, McGeorge Bundy, and Pierre Salinger seemed to take up almost permanent residence at the house, Jackie charmed the scores of political luminaries who came to seek favors or advice, or just to pay their respects.

Yet Jackie made no secret of her displeasure to Jack. "I can't stand this chaos, Jack," she finally said within earshot of Salinger. "It's driving me crazy."

The President-elect was not impressed. "Oh, for God's sake, Jackie," he replied, "all you have to worry about right now is your inaugural-ball gown."

Years later, Caroline would speak movingly of the private moments she shared with her parents. But she seldom talked of the cyclonic forces that swirled around her mother and father from the very beginning — of standing on the sidelines with her nanny while towering grown-ups crowded in, demanding and consuming most of her parents' time and attention. She also witnessed — and would grow to adulthood remembering — the tensions between her parents that stemmed from their life in the proverbial fishbowl. "Caroline was always around," Lowe recalled. "She was always a very bright, inquisitive child — you'd glance over and she'd be very quietly soaking it all up. Jack and Jackie were loving, attentive parents, but they were also very headstrong people. He would blow up and forget about it ten minutes later. She could hold a grudge forever. When things weren't right between them, Caroline could sense it. Everybody could."

Once again, Daddy was disappearing for long stretches — most often to Palm Beach, where he went over his cabinet choices with his father as both men relaxed by the pool. Jack returned to Georgetown to spend Thanksgiving with his wife and daughter, but only with the proviso that he return to Palm Beach immediately after dinner.

Jackie was just three weeks away from delivery, and she was under strict doctor's orders to stay home — preferably in bed. Given her history, the likelihood that something might happen was far from remote. Jackie begged her husband not to leave her side at this critical point in her pregnancy. "Why can't you stay here until I have the baby?" she asked him as Caroline looked on. "Then we can all go down together."

JFK was unmoved. After all, he was preparing to take office as President of the United States. "Caroline had arrived on time," Jack's friend Bill Walton said, "and he saw no reason to think anything would be different this time around."

That night, Jack departed for Florida aboard the *Caroline*. The plane's namesake, meanwhile, was whisked off to her room by Maud Shaw, but not before witnessing her mother break down in tears. An hour later, Shaw was tucking Caroline into bed when she heard a scream. She ran, with Caroline in hot pursuit, to Jackie's room and found her sitting on the edge of her bed clutching her stomach. There was blood on the bedspread. Jackie and Shaw reassured Caroline and told her to go back to bed. Frightened, Caroline slowly walked back down the hall to her room.

Shaw grabbed the phone and called Jackie's obstetrician, John Walsh. Ten minutes later, Caroline's mother was racing toward

Georgetown University Hospital in an ambulance. At the same time, Jack was in high spirits aboard the *Caroline*, smoking a cigar and chatting about his new cabinet and how it was shaping up. Once word of Jackie's condition came over the radio, he was "stricken with remorse," said his aide Kenneth P. O'Donnell, "because he was not with his wife."

As soon as the plane touched down at the West Palm Beach airport, Jack phoned Dr. Walsh. Jackie, Walsh informed him coldly, was in the process of being prepped for an emergency cesarean. Jack did not inquire about Caroline; there was no need. The President-elect correctly assumed that his little girl remained at home, being comforted and reassured by Maud Shaw. This would be only the first of several crises the matronly English nanny would confront with the Kennedys in the coming years. Shaw always watched as Caroline said her bedtime prayers, but tonight she asked the little girl to say a special prayer for "your mommy and your little brother or sister." Caroline, climbing back into bed and clasping her hands together tightly, eagerly obliged.

This time, Jack wanted to get back to Washington as fast as humanly possible. Since the DC-6 press plane that trailed the *Caroline* was actually capable of flying at much higher speeds, he commandeered it for

80

the flight home. En route, he clamped on the cockpit headphones and waited.

It was just past 1:00 a.m. when news crackled over the radio that Jackie had given birth by cesarean section to a six-pound, three-ounce boy. Both mother and child were healthy and resting comfortably. Salinger made an announcement over the public-address system, and reporters aboard the plane began cheering. The President-elect, who only moments before feared that he might lose both his wife and their baby, lit up a cigar and bowed deeply.

In truth, mother and child were still in guarded condition. John Fitzgerald Kennedy Jr. would spend the first six days of his life in an incubator. It would be months before both would fully recover from the effects of the emergency cesarean. The day after the baby's birth, Kennedy family nurse Luella Hennessey wheeled Jackie in to see him in his incubator. As they made their way down the hospital corridor with their Secret Service detail, a photographer burst out of a storage closet. A fusillade of flashbulbs went off before Secret Service agents confiscated the film.

Now Jack was determined to make up for not being there when Jackie most needed him. With Caroline in tow, Jack visited his wife and newborn son three times a day. "Now, that's the most beautiful boy I've seen.

Maybe," Jack joked, "I'll name him Abraham Lincoln."

The atmosphere at Georgetown Hospital, recalled *Life* magazine reporter Gail Wescott, was "buoyant and joyous, almost carnival-like. Security was minimal, and President-elect Kennedy would wave from his wife's hospital room and then stop and talk with us all when he came downstairs. Back on N Street, we took marvelous pictures of him wheeling Caroline in her stroller. It was innocent and exhilarating. It did not seem that anything could ever go wrong."

Indeed, Caroline was the new darling of the White House press corps. As her father met with the men who occupy the most powerful positions in government, Caroline made faces behind the backs of reporters, slid down banisters, careered around the room, or simply tugged at her daddy's sleeve.

No one was happier during this time than Caroline, who turned three just two days after John Jr.'s arrival. "She was told the baby was her birthday present," Maud Shaw said. "Caroline thought for a long time after that he *belonged* to her." She was so convinced of this, in fact, that at the time she referred to him as "my baby."

John Jr. was one week old when Caroline accompanied her father to the hospital for the baby's christening. Jack was wheeling mother and infant toward the hospital chapel when suddenly they spotted a pack of photographers waiting for them at the other end of the corridor. "Oh God, don't stop, Jack," Jackie pleaded. "Just keep going." But JFK, not unaware of his young family's powerful appeal, paused just long enough for pictures to be taken of the newest edition clad in Daddy's forty-three-year-old baptismal gown.

The day she was to be released from the hospital, Jackie grudgingly acquiesced when Jack pleaded with her to go on an introductory White House tour with outgoing First Lady Mamie Eisenhower. On December 9, 1960, Jack and the rest of his family flew back to Palm Beach aboard the *Caroline*. As soon as they arrived at Joe Kennedy's mansion on North Ocean Boulevard, the President-elect resumed his poolside discussions with his father over who should people the top echelons in the new administration. Caroline spent every available moment with her new brother. "They were awfully cute together," said family friend Chuck Spalding. "Caroline was totally smitten with John."

Jackie, meanwhile, suffered a setback as a result of her grueling White House tour; the new First Lady would spend the next two weeks in bed. Caroline's brother took an even more dramatic turn for the worse. "John's health really wasn't doing so well," she later said. "There was, thank God, this brilliant pediatrician in Palm Beach who really saved his life, as he was going downhill." John Jr. was, it turned out, suffering from an inflammation of the lung's hyaline membrane — the same respiratory ailment that would eventually claim the life of another Kennedy child.

Just two days following John Jr.'s recovery, Richard P. Pavlick drove his car to the Kennedy estate at Palm Beach and watched as the President-elect stepped outside en route to Sunday mass at St. Edward's Church. Pavlick had seven sticks of dynamite in his car and intended to crash into Jack's limousine as it pulled out of the driveway.

The self-styled suicide bomber had his foot poised over the gas pedal when Jackie and Caroline suddenly appeared. They were trailed by nurse Luella Hennessey, who cradled John Jr. in her arms. Pavlick, suddenly overcome by the sight of the Kennedy children, simply drove away. Pavlick's macabre plot was exposed three days later, after he was arrested for driving while intoxicated. Convicted of attempted murder, he was sentenced to a prison term.

When told of Pavlick's scheme, Jackie was understandably upset. "We're nothing," she said, pulling Caroline to her side, "but sitting ducks in a shooting gallery."

Over the next month in Palm Beach, Jackie would spend much of her time in bed trying to regain her strength while Jack threw his already frazzled transition team into high gear. Adding to the controlled chaos, Caroline now routinely upstaged her father at press conferences. At one briefing in Palm Beach, a bemused Arkansas Senator J. William Fulbright looked on as Caroline, clad in pajamas and robe, hobbled around in her mother's size-ten-and-a-half stiletto heels. "I want my daddy!" she announced. The President took Caroline's arm and led her out of the room while the reporters roared with laughter. At another press conference, she zoomed between correspondents' legs on her tricycle.

When she could summon the strength, Caroline's mother touched base by phone with her old friend Letitia Baldrige, whom Jackie had hired to be her social secretary. Jackie told Baldrige, previously employed as publicity director for Tiffany's, that she had come away from her tour with Mamie thinking that the Executive Mansion looked like "the world's greatest monument to bad taste. And the furniture — positively atrocious!"

Vowing to transform the executive mansion into a showcase of American furnishings and art, Jackie returned to Georgetown on January 14 — alone. She told Jack that he and the children would have to remain behind in Palm Beach because she was not well enough to oversee the move and help the children settle into their new home at the same time. A top priority: preparing the nurseries for Caroline and John on the second floor of the White House — as well as a schoolroom-cum-playroom in the third-floor solarium.

By the time Jack arrived in Washington on January 18, the house on N Street looked much like any house on moving day. The walls had been stripped bare, and everywhere there were cartons and packing crates brimming with personal effects. Jackie, who with the help of New York interior designer Sister Parrish had marshaled a battalion of experts to restore the White House, now sat cross-legged on the floor, trying to decide what stayed behind and what accompanied the Kennedys to their new home.

Still feeling the effects of John Jr.'s birth, Jackie insisted that the children continue to remain with their nannies in Palm Beach. Now the mere thought of having her husband and his omnipresent entourage under foot was enough to send her over the edge. At his wife's request, the future president promptly moved into the home of his Georgetown friend and neighbor Bill Walton.

The next day, the nation's capital was struck by a full-blown blizzard. It was to be a white inauguration, the coldest in history. At noon on January 20, 1961, thirty-one-year-old Jackie looked on proudly as Jack placed his hand on the Fitzgerald family Bible and took the oath of office from Chief Justice Earl Warren. At that instant, Jack, age forty-three, became the youngest elected president in U.S. history, the first Roman Catholic to hold the office, and the first chief executive born in the twentieth century. Caroline and her brother, still in balmy Palm Beach, sat with their nannies, watching the entire spectacle on television.

That night, the handsome young President and his dazzling First Lady made it through three of the five scheduled inaugural balls before Jackie called it quits. "I just crumpled," she said. "All of my strength was finally gone." Jack continued without her, quickly rendezvousing with his friend Paul "Red" Fay and Fay's date, the striking blond actress Angie Dickinson. "He was the killer type," Dickinson later said of Caroline's father, "a devastatingly handsome, charming man — the kind your mother hoped you wouldn't marry."

At 4:00 a.m., the new President finally went home to the White House. That first night in the White House, Jack and Jackie slept apart. With Jackie already fast asleep in the Queen's Room (given the name because, over the course of White House history, five queens had slept there), Jack crept across the hall and crawled into Abraham Lincoln's huge, ornately carved rosewood bed.

Rather than resenting her husband for partying until dawn while she coped with the aftereffects of John's difficult birth, Jackie blamed herself "for not participating more in those first shining hours with Jack. But," she added, "at least I thought I had given him our John, the son he had longed for so much. . . ."

The First Lady was pleased to learn that Caroline's and John's toys had been stashed away in the closet of White House Chief Usher J. B. West. "We'll bring them out as soon as the children's rooms are ready." The toys were actually the first things to arrive from the Georgetown house, surreptitiously carried in while the Eisenhowers were still very much in residence.

Flying in the face of reality — and the fact that her children would always be cared for by nannies and governesses — Jackie vowed that Caroline and John would have something approaching a normal childhood. "I want my children to be brought up in more personal surroundings," she said. "And I don't want them to be raised by nurses and Secret Service agents."

In truth, Jackie was less worried about Caroline and her brother being harmed physically than by the notion that they might be scarred emotionally. "It isn't fair to children in the limelight to leave them in the care of others and then expect that they will turn out all right," she said. "They need their mother's affection and guidance and long periods of time alone with her. That is what gives them security in an often confusing world."

The President and First Lady were waiting at the airport to greet them when Caroline and John finally arrived from Palm Beach on February 4, 1961. Fashion-conscious Jackie had called down the night before and instructed Maud Shaw what to dress the First Daughter in for her capital-city debut — white coat, white stockings, and a matching white hat. Thrilled to see her parents in person for the first time in weeks, Caroline squeezed between them for the limousine ride to her new home. Jackie, wearing a wool coat, leather gloves, and one of the pillbox hats that had already become her trademark, held a blanket-swathed John Jr. in her lap.

"There's your new home, Caroline," Jackie said as the car pulled up to the White House gates. The grounds of the executive mansion were still blanketed with snow.

"Pretty grand, eh, Buttons?" her father added. Caroline stood up, pressed her nose against the car window, and stared openmouthed. "Wow," she gasped. "It's very big."

As soon as Secret Service agents opened the rear doors of the presidential limousine, Caroline scampered out — and headed straight for the snowman that had been built at the edge of the driveway. The snowman had buttons for eyes, a carrot nose, and wore a big white panama hat. The President grinned as his daughter, who had spent the last two months in the eighty-degree Florida heat, playfully poked the snowman in the stomach.

Even before she saw the family quarters, Caroline offered her opinion of her new house. "There's so much room to play," she said to a delighted Pierre Salinger. "And a great big garden, too!"

Jack took Caroline by the hand and, with Jackie still holding John Jr., led his daughter down the main hall of the family residence. Opposite the Yellow Oval Room, with its doors opening onto the Truman Balcony, were the children's rooms. Not the slightest trace was left of the Eisenhowers' motel-modern decor. The color scheme in Caroline's room was white and pink, with a white canopy bed, matching rosebud linens and drapes, stuffed animals, a Grandma Moses painting on the wall, and rocking horses. Later an elaborate dollhouse would dominate the room — a gift from one of Jackie's most ardent admirers, French President Charles de Gaulle.

Between Caroline's room and John's blue-and-white nursery was the small, strategically situated room of their nanny. "Maud Shaw won't need much," Jackie wrote in a memo to J. B. West. "Just find a wicker wastebasket for her banana peels and a little table for her false teeth at night."

The same could not be said for Jackie, whose chandeliered blue-and-green French provincial bedroom was strewn with leopardskin throws. In the President's bedroom, separated from his wife's by a walk-in closet containing their stereo system, stood Harry Truman's huge mahogany four-poster, an upholstered Carolina rocker, and — out of concern for JFK's ongoing back problems — a heating pad kept within reach on the nightstand.

The vast, impersonal "Family" Dining Room on the main floor was anything but suitable for a young family. To get around that problem, Jackie designed a kitchen and a markedly cozier dining room just steps from the West Sitting Hall where the family congregated. Everywhere were the paintings, flowers, and family photographs that reflected Jackie's understated sense of style. "She turned this drafty, cold, old place," Tish Baldrige said, "into a warm environment for a family overnight."

During the family's first few weeks in the White House, Caroline was encouraged to explore. Wandering into the basement, she encountered a worker who asked what her father was doing.

"He's upstairs with his shoes and socks off," she answered, "doing nothing."

The family gradually settled into a routine that seldom varied during their thousand days in the White House. While the President and the First Lady seldom saw each other before noon, Caroline spent time with both of her parents nearly every morning the family was in residence. Daddy, who was invariably up by 8:00 a.m., consumed a hearty breakfast — coffee with cream and at least three teaspoons of sugar, two soft-boiled eggs, bacon, toast, and orange juice. Then it was into the tub, where he read memos, cables, and the morning papers.

Daddy was usually propped up in bed in his bathrobe when Maud Shaw brought both children in to say good morning. After the kids kissed their father, he went in the dressing room to change while they sat on the floor watching cartoons. At 9:00 they switched to TV exercise pioneer Jack LaLanne, and the President clapped along as Caroline imitated LaLanne's routine of jumping jacks, lunges, and squats. Later Little Brother would become part of the act.

Once he was dressed in a suit picked out by his valet, George Thomas, the President took Caroline's hand and asked her to walk him to the Oval Office. Once behind his desk, JFK kissed his daughter good-bye, and Caroline was off to the little school Jackie had set up for her children as well as the six-teen offspring of White House staffers and a few particularly close friends. Along the way, Caroline (and, when he was old enough to toddle along, John) dropped in to see Mommy, who ate breakfast on a tray in her room.

The invitation-only White House School, by definition the most exclusive early-learning institution in the country, boasted two emi-nently qualified teachers — Elizabeth Boyd and Alice Grimes — and kindergarten and first-grade curricula that included arithmetic, French, American history, and hygiene. Caro-line's mother personally picked out the colors for the school uniforms: red, white, and blue.

Around noon, Jackie often joined Caroline and John in the "High Chair Room," watching as they gobbled down hot dogs or hamburgers prepared by the White House chef. Then Caroline went back upstairs to school, and Jackie would take it upon herself to bring John for a walk in his stroller.

The President, meantime, was taking the first of his two daily nude swims in the White House pool. Finishing up at 2:00 p.m., he would put on a bathrobe and repair to the family quarters for a private lunch with his wife. The next two hours were sacrosanct for the First Family. During this time, the doors to the second floor were sealed. No visitors, no phone calls, no messages, not even servants were allowed upstairs. Even the sounds of children were nowhere to be heard; by this time, Maud Shaw had put both Caroline and John down for their afternoon naps.

Creatures of habit, Jack and Jackie seldom varied their lunch menus. Dining on trays in the living room, Jackie would have her favorite midday fare — a grilled-cheese sandwich — while Jack usually opted for a medium-rare hamburger. Afterward both retired to their separate beds for a nap. George Thomas, who had strict orders to wake the President at 3:30 p.m., did not always find them sleeping separately. Caroline's parents, her uncle Yusha Auchincloss observed, "had a very close, very romantic relationship. . . . Technically they had separate bedrooms, but they slept together. There was a lot of laughter. They enjoyed each other. They had *fun*."

Caroline knew early on that Daddy took lots of showers — he took his third of the day right after his afternoon nap. Dressing in a fresh suit — he would wear at least three in any given day — JFK returned to the Oval Office.

Just a few yards away, just outside the windows of Daddy's office, Jackie spent part of the afternoon watching as Caroline and John cavorted in the play area she had specially designed for them. Following the First Lady's sketches, White House carpenters installed a leather swing, a barrel tunnel, a rabbit hutch, a trampoline concealed by evergreens, and a treehouse with a slide. Jackie had a difficult time preventing Caroline from trying to push her baby brother down the treehouse slide "carriage and all."

The first thing Caroline pushed down the slide was not John but their aptly named dog Pushinka, a gift to the family from Soviet Premier Nikita Khrushchev. John later would say this single event — Caroline teaching the hapless Russian dog to go down the treehouse slide — would form his earliest childhood memory.

The same carpenters who built the play area also built doghouses for Pushinka and Charlie, the Welsh terrier the Kennedys had brought with them from Georgetown. They were joined by Wolf, an Irish wolfhound given to the President by a priest in Dublin, and then by Clipper the German shepherd, a gift to Jackie from her admiring father-in-law.

Caroline's cat, Tom Kitten, was eventually given away — the President was so severely allergic to cats that Tom Kitten's mere presence in the family quarters made it difficult for him to breathe. "Caroline was very understanding, and didn't make a fuss at all," Jackie later recalled. "She loved Tom Kitten, but when we explained how sick he made Daddy, she understood completely."

To a lesser extent, Daddy was also allergic

to dogs and horses. But so long as the animals kept their distance, he tolerated his children's growing menagerie. Before long, there were pens for the guinea pigs, ducks, lambs, and Zsa Zsa the beer-guzzling rabbit. Caroline's favorite pet, a canary named Robin, lived in her room with the children's hamsters, Bluebell and Marybell. When Robin died, Caroline gave the bird a funeral and buried it on the White House grounds. Not long after, when the Shah of Iran visited the White House, Caroline took the hand of his wife, the Empress Farah Diba, and led her to Robin's tiny grave.

The most famous Kennedy pet of all — Caroline's pony, Macaroni — was not about to take up residence on the second floor. Jackie, an expert equestrienne, had a stable constructed that was big enough for Macaroni and Leprechaun, the pony she acquired for John. It quickly became evident, however, that John was even more allergic to horses than his father was.

After their afternoon play period, Caroline and John usually ate dinner around 5:30, and once again Mommy sat with them, talking over what they'd learned in school that day. "I know I'm her mother and I shouldn't boast," Jackie told Chuck Spalding, "but Caroline is a very smart little girl. She is already reading at three, and over dinner she bubbles over with excitement about what happened that day in her little class in the solarium. . . . Of course, I shouldn't be surprised if she's precocious. Caroline is Jack's daughter, after all."

Caroline's vocabulary was already extensive, and she learned how to pronounce the names of foreign leaders — from Haile Selassie to Konrad Adenauer — with relative ease. The President's daughter did not brook any baby talk or condescension. One day Pierre Salinger pointed to a "Moo cow" standing in a field.

"No," she said dismissively, "that's a Hereford."

Caroline was eager to please her parents and her nannies alike, and rarely disobeyed adults. And she expected no less exemplary behavior, even from her brother. Whenever the baby banged his spoon on the table, spit out food, or threw a tantrum, Caroline rolled her eyes. "There he goes again," she said in an exasperated tone. Often she took it upon herself to discipline him. "Now, John," Caroline would say, "be a good boy and eat your cereal." But John was not quite so compliant as his big sister. "John is a bad squeaky boy," she complained to her grandmother Rose, "who tries to spit in his mother's Coca-Cola and has a very bad temper."

While their mother chatted with Caroline and John over their dinner, Jack left his office and took his second swim of the day before changing into yet another freshly pressed suit. Around 6:00 p.m., Jackie joined him for daiquiris in the Yellow Room. In the absence of any formal functions downstairs, they usually dined with close friends like Ben and Tony Bradlee and Charlie and Martha Bartlett. At the time, Bradlee wrote for *Newsweek*, and Bartlett was the Washington correspondent for the *Chattanooga Times*. The Bartletts, in fact, were responsible for bringing the future President and First Lady together in the first place, arranging for Jack and Jackie to get to know each other at a small dinner party in the Bartlett home in 1952. (Jackie later thanked the Bartletts for their "shameless matchmaking.") By way of after-dinner entertainment, they would often screen a new film in the White House theater. Jack and Jackie, as it turned out, did not share the same taste in movies. "My mommy always watched cowboy movies with my daddy," Caroline would say a few years later, "because my daddy always liked cowboy movies. My mommy doesn't like cowboy movies *at all*, but she watched them because she loved my daddy."

Caroline was also old enough to realize that it was Mommy, not Daddy, with the highbrow tastes. Under Jackie's guidance, the Kennedy administration celebrated culture to an unprecedented degree. The world's greatest classical musicians, stars of the Metropolitan Opera and the Royal Ballet, and Shakespearean actors were among those invited to the East Room to perform before visiting heads of state.

"Mommy loves the ballet," Caroline told one visitor to the White House, "and so do I. Daddy claps, but I don't think he really likes it. He makes faces when he thinks no one is looking."

To be sure, JFK's tastes ran more to show tunes, Peggy Lee, and sometimes even Elvis. Ted Sorensen, one of the architects of the New Frontier, remembered that his boss "had no interest in opera, dozed off at symphony concerts, and was bored by ballet." Jackie sighed to friends, "The only song Jack really likes is 'Hail to the Chief.' "

One evening in 1962, Caroline was watching television in her room with Maud Shaw when Jackie came in with Leonard Bernstein. The legendary composer/conductor was one of the guests at a small dinner party the President and First Lady were giving for Igor Stravinsky, and before the dinner started, he wanted to catch the opening of one of his famous Young People's Concerts.

"So I sat with Caroline and Maud Shaw watching," Bernstein later recalled, "and I remember very well Caroline sitting, hypnotized by this program and just thrilled with every moment. We were sitting holding hands, and she was wrapped up in the concert, and then she suddenly looked up at me with this marvelous clear face and said, 'I have my own horse.' Now, that really brought me down to earth, so that moment I turned off the set and rejoined the others."

Sometimes Caroline and John provided the evening's entertainment. Even with nannies and nurses — not to mention valets, butlers, secretaries, and Secret Service agents — around to maintain a semblance of order, visitors to the White House residence were invariably treated to a glimpse of the high-spirited Kennedy kids. As they stepped off the elevator one evening, several of the President's dinner guests were met by the sight of a stark-naked Caroline racing toward them, being chased by a mortified Maud Shaw. "She practically knocked us over," said one guest. "Then she looked up with these huge eyes, looked back at her nanny, and shot off down the hall."

The President, told of the incident a few moments later, seemed delighted. "Buttons?" he said. "Hmm. Sounds like John's rubbing off on her."

And vice versa. Just like Caroline before him, John came running as soon as he heard his father clap and call his name. *Look* photographer Stanley Tretick, who would go on to snap John and Caroline dancing around the Oval Office and hiding beneath their father's desk, said that the President usually called his son's name twice — "John, JOHN" — before the boy showed up. "So," Salinger explained, "everyone started calling him 'John-John.' " Everyone, that is, except the other family members. To his parents and to Caroline, he was always simply "John."

As far as the Secret Service was concerned, however, none of these familiar names applied. To the agents assigned to guard the First Family, the President's daughter was neither Caroline nor Buttons. Her code name was Lyric, while her baby brother was Lark. Daddy and Mommy: Lancer and Lace.

The First Lady was, in fact, very precise about what she expected from the men assigned to protect her children. For example, "Mrs. Kennedy feels strongly, though there are two children to protect, it is 'bad' to see two agents 'hovering around,' " wrote the head of the Secret Service Children's Detail (better known within the agency as the "Kiddie Detail") in a confidential memo to Secret Service Chief James J. Rowley. "If Mrs. Kennedy is driving the children, she still insists the follow-up car not be seen by the children. . . .

"Mrs. Kennedy is adamant in her contention that the agents must not perform special favors for John Jr. and Caroline or wait upon them as servants," the memo continued. "Agents are not to carry clothes, beach articles, sand buckets, baby carriages, strollers, handbags, suitcases, etc., for Caroline and John Jr., and the children must carry their own clothing items, toys, etc. . . . The agent must drift into the background quickly when arriving at a specific location, and remain aloof and invisible until moment of departure. . . .

"Mrs. Kennedy is inclined to believe that the agents are doing too much for the children, and feels it is bad for the children to see grown men waiting upon them. The agents must demand that Caroline pick up her own discarded clothes, shoes, toys, accessories, etc."

Even if it meant that she would have to take personal responsibility for her children's safety, Jackie was willing to do it rather than have them treated "like hothouse orchids." At the seashore, for example, she insisted that she be her children's first line of defense. "Drowning is my responsibility," she insisted, adding that the Secret Service "is not responsible for any accident sustained by the children in the usual and normal play sessions." These were, she wanted it understood, "the sole responsibility of Mrs. Kennedy."

The Secret Service agents reluctantly agreed to give the First Lady some leeway at the beach. "We could still watch from a distance without her even knowing we were there," said one. "If one of the children had wandered out too far or been knocked over by a wave — even with their mother standing a foot away — three agents would have come swooping out of the dunes to rescue them."

In truth, much of the burden fell to Maud Shaw, who rarely left the children's side. Caroline was never the challenge her brother was. "John was never afraid of the water," said Shaw, who would dry and dress John after a swim and then turn to do the same for Caroline — only to turn again and see John heading into the surf fully clothed. "Then I'd just have to take him back to the house dripping wet, his little feet squelching in their shoes."

What concerned the Kiddie Detail most, aside from the ever-present specter of a Lindbergh-style kidnapping, was Caroline's affinity for horseback riding. When it was suggested that the agents follow Caroline on horseback whenever she took off on Macaroni, Jackie objected strongly.

Caroline was, her mother told them flatly, "a better rider than the Secret Service agents. In fact, Caroline would probably be safer riding with other children than she would be with a Secret Service agent who has a very limited knowledge of horses."

Moreover, Jackie told the Secret Service that as a child she had broken her collarbone falling off a horse, and that the occasional spill went with the territory. "I expect Caroline to have her share of riding spills and accidents. How else will she learn?"

Caroline's father, though no horseman himself, shared his wife's philosophy. He was, after all, from a family that encouraged risk taking — sometimes with tragic results. Once, while Caroline was riding Macaroni at Hyannis Port, JFK watched from the porch as the horse stumbled, hurling the little girl to the ground. One of the agents assigned to watch the children, Joseph Paolella, ran toward Caroline, but the President did not budge from his rocker. Rather than checking to see if his daughter was injured or offering words of sympathy, JFK shouted, "Caroline, get up! Get back on the horse!"

When she heard the story, Jackie approved. "You don't even have to ride to know that old saying about conquering fear," she said. "You know — if you fall off a horse, the best thing to do is get right back up again."

Even inside the White House, keeping up with Caroline was an exhausting proposition. Secret Service agents were always hot on her heels when she pedaled furiously down White House corridors or dashed from pillar to pillar firing off her cap pistol.

If Jackie grudgingly tolerated the agents who shadowed her children, she openly resented the incursions on her privacy from the public and press. "I can't bear all those people peering over the fence," she said. "I may abdicate." As for photographers stalking

104

her children, Jackie had a way about her, said Stanley Tretick, "that strikes terror in your heart. . . . She was a tough babe." Not that she was totally averse to publicity; magazines like *Look* and *Life* and the *Saturday Evening Post* were welcome to do stories on Caroline and John — so long as Jackie exerted control.

Over the thousand days the Kennedys occupied the White House, these controlled glimpses of the First Family would melt the hearts of the American public — and remain as some of the most enduring images of the era: Caroline riding Macaroni on the White House lawn or sitting in a horse cart with her mother at bucolic Glen Ora, the Kennedys' rented Virginia hideaway; Daddy clapping along as Caroline and John whirled around the Oval Office. Then there were shots of Caroline and John showing off their Halloween costumes to delighted White House staffers and to Daddy, who dissolved in hysterics.

John was a cute enough toddler at this point, and would eventually eclipse his sister in the public eye. But now, at the height of what would later be known as Camelot, the public could not get enough of the irresistible, blue-eyed, blond-banged, crinoline-wearing Caroline. "Not since Shirley Temple zoomed into international fame," wrote one reporter of the President's only daughter, "has one child received so much international coverage in so short a time."

"Jackie didn't want Caroline and John-John to be treated like stars," Tish Baldrige concurred. "But of course they *were* stars. The American people just fell in love with them."

As much as such statements horrified Jackie, the President "saw a photo op behind every tree," Baldrige said. Agreed Jacques Lowe, "The kids were a great asset for his administration. He was proud of them. He wanted to show them off. It got to be a game between the two of them — the President and Jackie — with me stuck in the middle."

In one instance Lowe was summoned to the Oval Office. JFK told him to "take some pictures of Caroline" and hand them over to the President's friend Ben Bradlee at *Newsweek*.

"You know I can't do that, Mr. President," Lowe protested, explaining that the First Lady strictly forbade any photos of Caroline "running around the White House."

"Then don't tell her," Kennedy said matter-of-factly.

Lowe followed the President's orders, and as predicted, Jackie hit the roof. The President, as he always did under such circumstances, played dumb.

Tretick found himself in a similar spot when he was assigned by *Look* to do a story on the family of Jack's sister Eunice and her husband, Sargent Shriver, and their young family. As part of the story, Tretick covered the clan's Fourth of July celebrations at Hyannis Port in 1961. Jackie ordered him in no uncertain terms not to take any photos of Caroline, who cavorted with her cousins on the sprawling lawns of the compound. But when Tretick took shots of Caroline despite her orders, Jackie refused to give the go-ahead. After waiting a year, the magazine ran them anyway — and Jackie blasted the President for letting it happen. JFK, enraged because this time she unleashed her fury on him directly, passed the sentiment on to Tretick.

But no one caught more heat from Jackie than Pierre Salinger. "From the moment she set foot in the White House," Salinger said, "she wanted to keep them out of the spotlight. She made this abundantly clear to me on many occasions. Whenever a photo was taken of Caroline or John that she hadn't signed off on, I could be certain to catch hell for it."

When a photograph of Caroline astride Macaroni hit the papers, an angry Jackie dashed off a note to the press secretary. "They have had all the pictures of Macaroni they need," she wrote. "I want no more — *I mean this* — and if you are firm and will take the time, you can stop it. So please do. What is a press secretary for — to help the press, yes — but also to protect *us*."

After a lull, another photo of Caroline — not on horseback but simply playing on the White House lawn — was picked up by the Associated Press. "Now if they get away with this," Jackie wrote to Salinger, "I am afraid they will start in full force again — so could you berate the fotog. . . ." Meantime, she continued, "guards should be told to watch out for people through grilles — The guards at the gate could have stopped this — If necessary one can patrol up & down outside by S.W. gate. . . . They should watch for people there — climbing on cars to take pictures etc."

On yet another occasion, Salinger was about to bawl out the press for photos of the children that had somehow been taken on the grounds of Camp David, when he realized who the culprit was. Stanley Tretick had given Salinger's ten-year-old son, Marc, a tiny camera, told the boy how it worked, "and then," said Salinger, "how to smuggle it out when he was done snapping candid photos of Caroline and John."

Unauthorized photographs were only the tip of the iceberg. "Few things upset Jackie more," Salinger said, "than the idea that somebody might be making money off the Kennedy name." When a Caroline doll started popping up in toy-store windows around the country, Jackie shot off another one of her memos to the man Tish Baldrige referred to as "Poor Pierre." The First Lady complained, "they are now selling *Caroline* Christmas dolls — with wardrobe. . . . Can you do something about this?" She went on to say that the Ideal Toy Company was trying to "pressure" her into endorsing an official Caroline doll, with the proceeds going to charity. "I'd rather have a doll a month than endorse one," Jackie said. "But this is irritating — so please do see what you can do."

Even before they moved into the White House, Caroline was aware of her mother's distaste for reporters and photographers. However, the little girl was anything but shy when it came to having her picture taken. "Even as a two-year-old, sometimes John-John would tell you off, or even take a swing at you or kick at you," said Lowe. "He was constantly hearing his mother refer to photographers as pests or far worse, and so he caught on. But Caroline was always sweet and polite and just delightful. She would just keep right on playing if a candid shot was called for, or sit absolutely still if you wanted her to pose. John-John could seem spoiled and out of control, but never Caroline."

Grandma Kennedy agreed. "I don't think she's spoiled," Rose said of Caroline. "She's too young to realize all these luxuries. She probably thinks it's natural for children to go off in their own planes."

But Caroline also knew by now that hers were no ordinary parents. Her life of dolls, toys, ponies, and tea parties on the South Lawn would be counterpoint to the elements of power, glamour, and crisis that would come to define the Kennedy era.

Indeed, it should have come as a surprise to no one — least of all Jackie — that her only daughter would be treated like a princess. From their first triumphant European tour, when JFK introduced himself as "the man who accompanied Jacqueline Kennedy to Paris," to the sixty-six dazzling state occasions they presided over with regal aplomb, the vibrant young President and his beautiful First Lady were the closest thing America had to royalty.

"When they appeared at the top of those stairs," veteran *Washington Star* reporter Betty Beale said of the First Couple's entrances at state dinners and formal receptions, "they were a glorious-looking, stunning couple — almost beyond belief. . . . It was more a royal court than an administration."

Like any other little girl whose parents were about to have a grown-up evening, Caroline watched spellbound as Mommy put on her lipstick, fastened her earrings, and checked her look one final time in the full-length mirror. Sometimes Jackie let her daughter galumph around the room in her pumps, or she let her try on Jackie's pearls and her opera-length gloves before sending her off with a kiss on the cheek and an affectionate pat on the behind. Caroline would trace her own classic fashion sense — and her early lack of confidence when it came to her appearance — back to these early memories of her mother preparing for yet another lavish affair. "She was always so beautiful, so perfect," Caroline would tell a college friend years later. "It wasn't just me — everyone thought that. I wanted to be exactly like her, and of course there was no way I could even come close. I mean, there was no way *anyone* was going to come close."

While it was clear to Caroline that Daddy was the principal star of the family, Mommy gave her plenty of reason to be proud — and more than a little intimidated. Like the rest of the nation, Caroline sat glued to the TV when her mother gave the first televised tour of the White House on February 14, 1962. At the time ranking as the most-watched prime-time broadcast in the history of the medium, the show gave Americans a chance to see the results of Jackie's ambitious restoration project.

The following month, Caroline's mother set out on her first overseas solo tour as First Lady. From her audience with Pope John XXIII in

Rome, Jackie traveled to India, where she fed pandas, sailed down the Ganges, jumped horses with New Delhi guardsmen, watched a cobra fight a mongoose, and, with her sister Lee along for the ride, loped about atop an elephant named Bibi.

With more than sixty photographers and reporters tagging along, Jackie dominated the news for three weeks. Her daughter followed her every step of the way in the press. "Miss Shaw, look!" Caroline yelled with pride and amazement as she pointed to yet another photo spread, this one in *Life*. "Mommy and Aunt Lee are riding an *elephant!*"

Historian Theodore H. White appreciated how JFK used his wife "to enhance American prestige. . . . No one could excite crowds here and abroad like Jack and Jackie Kennedy."

For all the global adoration lavished on her, Jackie never seemed aloof or remote to Caroline. In fact, the most glamorous First Lady in history was, said J. B. West, "never more animated and happy" than when she was at home playing with the children.

This was particularly true on holidays, when Jackie made certain her kids shared in all the experiences that shaped the typical American childhood. Like millions of other parents, she helped them cut out and color heart-shaped cards to give to their classmates on Valentine's Day, dyed Easter eggs with them in the kitchen, and decorated the White House Christmas tree with them.

One holiday presented more of a challenge than the others. On Halloween night, 1962, presidential adviser Arthur Schlesinger Jr. opened the door of his Georgetown home to find several goblins hopping up and down. "After a moment a masked mother in the background called out that it was time to go to their next house. The voice was unmistakably Jackie's." With the Secret Service lurking just out of sight, she and Lee — both wearing orange-and-black sacks with eyeholes over their heads — were escorting Caroline (dressed as a witch) and her cousins on their trick-or-treat rounds. "[Former Secretary of State] Dean Acheson was the next stop."

Daddy took as much if not more pleasure in the company of his children. He often dropped in on Caroline and her classmates at the small school Jackie had set up for them in the third-floor solarium. "He would be up there to see the children constantly. He would go to the South Lawn and play with them and talk to them, and they would all troop into his office whenever he gave the signal" — clapping his hands and calling their names. "So the house was full of children morning, noon, and night. You never knew," Baldrige added, "when an avalanche of young people would come bearing down on you — runny noses, dropped mittens in the hall, bicycles. . . ."

Not that Caroline or John ever interfered with affairs of state. "The children could be playing all over him," Baldrige recalled, "and he could still be conducting a conference or writing a speech."

When they had his full attention, JFK loved to tell the children stories that he invented on the spot — about Maybelle, the orphan who lived alone in the forest, an ogre named Bobo the Lobo, and a shark that existed on a steady diet of people's socks.

As with all new parents, holidays took on added meaning for Jack. He watched as Caroline, wearing a dress adorned with a pair of dancing poodles, threw up her hands in wonder at the lighting of the White House Christmas tree. When it was time for Caroline to send her Christmas list to Santa Claus, he had the White House switchboard put a call through to the North Pole instead.

"Miss Shaw! Miss Shaw!" Caroline shrieked as the ran toward her nanny. "I just talked to Mrs. Santa Claus! I left a whole list of presents for me and John!"

Jackie was thrilled that her husband had chosen to play such a hands-on role in their children's lives. She reveled in the fact that on some days Caroline and John would "even have lunch with him. If you told me that would happen, I'd never have believed it. But after all, the one thing that happens to a president is that his ties to the outside world are cut, and the people you really have are each other."

Although he had the typical Ivy League aversion to public displays of affection, no such rules applied to the way he interacted with his children. Despite his bad back and a wide range of other health problems, JFK routinely tossed Caroline and John into the air, tickled them, and joined them in every children's game from peekaboo and leapfrog to hide-and-go-seek. "He was enjoying his kids," said official White House photographer Cecil Stoughton. "He played with them in that marvelous way that some people have and some people don't."

JFK had an easy rapport with Caroline but at times was frustrated by his inability to understand John's baby talk. In those instances, Caroline served as her little brother's interpreter.

What made Jack's transformation from urbane, emotionally detached bachelor to doting dad even more remarkable was the fact that his own parents were anything but overtly affectionate. Relying on a platoon of nursemaids and governesses to help with her brood of nine, Rose Fitzgerald Kennedy was a cold and unforgiving presence in the lives of Jack and his siblings. "She was never really there when we needed her," Jack later said. "My mother never really held me and hugged me. Never! Never!" Joe was not much better. He was keenly interested in his children's progress in school and on the playing field, but Jack also remembered him as being "stern" and "brusque" as a dad. The boisterous one-big-happy-family facade notwithstanding, there was little real intimacy among members of the clan.

Yet as grandparents, Joe and Rose were far more accessible. While Rose would never cease to be intimidating to her children as the family matriarch, she was far less so with their children. Caroline was a particular favorite — in part because, unlike her unruly cousins and her little brother, Caroline managed to be both spirited *and* obedient. "Caroline was just the best little kid," Hyannis Port neighbor Larry Newman recalled, "and of course her grandmother really appreciated that." In her unforgettably quavering voice, Rose "would go straight to her and tell her how pretty she was in her new dress, and ask her all about what games she liked, what books she was reading. . . . They would have real conversations — you could see there was a connection there."

Larger-than-life Grandpa Joe also doted on Caroline — and on Caroline's mother. "When the President's father came to visit," J. B. West said, the First Lady "danced down the halls arm in arm with him, laughing uproariously at his teasing." Agreed Secret Service Agent Ham Brown, who was assigned to protect Joe, "Jackie and Joe were buddies. She loved him, and he admired her, respected her." As for Caroline, "He would come up to her and lean down and say, 'Ah, you're going to be a great beauty, just like your mother!'"

Caroline had been there the night her pregnant mother began hemorrhaging and called out for help, but she had never seen Jackie weep. Not until December 19, 1961, when seventy-three-year-old Grandpa Joe suffered a massive stroke that left him paralyzed on his right side and only able to utter the word "no" over and over again. "It made an impression on Caroline," Baldrige said, "to see both her mother and her father so upset about Joe."

From then on, the man who was responsible for putting Caroline's father in the White House would be confined to a wheelchair. Although he drooled and his face was contorted, Grandpa Joe was included in all White House functions. Caroline would watch as her mother sat next to Joe, making one-sided conversation, helping him with his food, dabbing at his chin with a napkin.

At first Caroline complained that she couldn't understand her grandfather when he tried to speak. "Grandpa keeps saying 'No.' Did I do something wrong?" But in time, Caroline learned to follow her parents' lead and, like them, pretend to understand what the "no, no, no"'s meant. "It was very touching," said Evelyn Lincoln, JFK's long-time private secretary. "Caroline knew just to act as if nothing was wrong. A lot of the time she talked about how her brother was misbehaving. That was a favorite topic of hers." With good reason. While Caroline sat patiently at her grandfather's side, John usually dashed around the room, crashing into furniture and knocking over glassware.

For her part, Jackie was considerably better equipped to share affection with her children than Jack was. For all his wanton philandering, Black Jack Bouvier lavished attention on Jackie and Lee. But Jackie's socially ambitious mother was every bit as chilly to her daughters as Rose Kennedy had been to her children. The difference was that, unlike Rose, Janet treated her grandchildren no differently. "Mrs. Auchincloss was not," said Jacques Lowe, "the warm and cuddly grandma type."

Jackie would credit her mother with being a strict disciplinarian — just as Jack once called *his* mother "the drill sergeant" — and with setting high standards for her daughters. By the same token, almost from birth, Caroline had been expected to be exceptionally well behaved. The same rules, however, did not apply to her baby brother.

According to his friend George Smathers,

JFK "was absolutely determined to spoil John from the beginning. He could not deny that boy anything. If the President was having a cabinet meeting or talking to some head of state, it didn't matter — he'd stop everything if John came skipping into the Oval Office."

Jackie didn't mind. She hadn't, as Smathers pointed out, expected JFK to be such an "adoring, affectionate father." In fact, it soon became clear that both the President and First Lady were willing to cut John considerably more slack than they did Caroline — a sign of favoritism that rankled, among others, Maud Shaw.

"Mrs. Kennedy insisted that Caroline be well disciplined and not fawned over," the nanny said. "But once John was old enough to walk, there was no doubt that he was the center of attention." Indeed, Shaw increasingly found herself having to spend time with the ever-demanding John-John, often at Caroline's expense. Whenever he accomplished any task — from brushing his teeth to dressing himself — it was Shaw's approval that John sought. "Miss Shaw, I'm your big boy!" he would boast, and the nanny nodded in agreement. "I'd always say, 'Yes, John, you are my big boy.' But if Caroline was around, she'd sometimes give a little smirk or shake her head in annoyance."

On one occasion, when Jackie returned home after a trip to New York, she walked past Caroline to give John a hug. "Then she turned to Caroline, almost as an afterthought," recalled Shaw, "and said, 'Oh, Caroline. Lovely to see you.' I thought, 'Why didn't she hug Caroline like she did John?' "

Caught up in the White House social whirl, Jackie, who had once taken such pains to teach her daughter poetry, suddenly found herself with little time to devote to Caroline. At one point, Caroline approached Nanny Shaw and asked her to fill the void. "Oh, Miss Shaw," she said, "I wish you would come back on your days off and read to me. Mommy's too busy to read."

"It really hurt me," Shaw recalled years later, "that Mrs. Kennedy didn't have the time to sit down and read to her for just a little bit." Touchingly, Caroline now referred to the ever-present Maud Shaw — a mother figure in the lives of both Kennedy children — as her "bestest friend."

Miss Shaw may have been Caroline's "bestest friend," but she was not the only White House staffer the First Daughter came to depend on. The Secret Service agents assigned to the Kiddie Detail spent far more time with the children than either of their parents did; it was their job, after all, to be a constant and reassuring presence. Over the years, both children, but Caroline in particular, formed emotional attachments to these surrogate father figures — and those ties would only grow stronger in the coming years. Tellingly, one night Caroline awoke from a nightmare and cried out not for her mother or even Nanny Shaw but for Secret Service Agent Lynn Meredith. "That really upset Jackie," recalled Agent Joseph Paolella. "She mentioned it next day to the chief of the Secret Service, and he sent around a memo telling the guys not to get quite so close to Caroline." The prohibition did not apply to John, presumably because Jackie felt he was too young to have affection withheld from anyone.

If there was any resentment on Caroline's part at the time, no one recognized it. She did, however, occasionally play the part of the bossy big sister. Rose Kennedy's secretary, Barbara Gibson, remembered that Caroline was "always after him, 'John, do this' and 'You're not supposed to do that, John.' "

One of John's favorite pastimes at the beach was building sand castles, then kicking them to smithereens. When Caroline took it upon herself to do the demolition work, however, John ran to Maud Shaw screaming, "Cannon [he had difficulty pronouncing Caroline] stepped in my castle!"

"Peace could only be restored," Nanny Shaw remembered, "if I got down on my hands and knees and helped construct another, bigger, better castle." Which he would then kick down before Caroline could.

Accustomed to being the center of attention, John made every effort to reclaim the spotlight if it looked as if Caroline might steal it. One week Caroline harassed nearly everyone she came in contact with by demanding answers to the riddles she had learned.

Frustrated, John finally blurted out to Nanny Shaw, "I know a riddle, too."

"Yes, John, and what's your riddle?"

The little boy paused a minute, then shouted, "Um . . . apples, giraffes, and alligators!"

"I'm afraid you've stumped me," Miss Shaw replied. John, satisfied with this outcome, would then scamper off to tell his sister.

Since the President and the First Lady had an agreement never to argue in front of the children, neither child seemed aware of the tensions in the marriage that stemmed from JFK's flagrant womanizing. When Jackie whisked Caroline and John off to the Loudoun Hunt horse show in Virginia, they had no way of knowing that it was to prevent them all from being embarrassed at the sight of Marilyn Monroe purring "Happy Birthday, Mr. *Pre-si-dent*" to Daddy before the assembled multitudes at Madison Square Garden. While New York and Washington power circles buzzed with speculation about the relationship between Monroe and the President,

Caroline proudly watched her mother win a third-place ribbon at the horse show.

Mom's attempt at subterfuge was not entirely successful. When they returned home to Washington, Caroline saw television footage of a cleavage-baring Marilyn at JFK's Madison Square Garden birthday gala. "Who's the pretty lady singing to Daddy?" she asked innocently as Maud Shaw looked on nervously. Jackie, smiling inscrutably, turned off the set and told her daughter that it was time for bed.

Caroline and John spent most of July with their mother on Cape Cod. But Jackie's world was rocked again that August by Marilyn's untimely death at age thirty-six. The public at large, stunned by the news, mourned the passing of Hollywood's reigning sex symbol — another victim, it was said again and again, of a cruel industry. But the public also remained blithely unaware of the President's relationship with the tragic sex symbol — not to mention the follow-up affair she had with presidential brother Bobby Kennedy.

Jack, however, was reacting to the death in a way that confirmed his wife's worst suspicions. Brother-in-law Peter Lawford, who had introduced Monroe to the President, was burning up the lines to the White House. There was real concern that J. Edgar Hoover's FBI had managed to get hold of the audiotapes of Marilyn making love to both Kennedy brothers.

Jackie knew damage control when she saw it. Angry at her husband for humiliating her, she fled with Caroline, John, and twelve Secret Service agents to Ravello, the village on Italy's Amalfi coast where the Radziwills had rented a clifftop villa. The paparazzi followed in droves, snapping away as the First Lady went water-skiing, shopped, read, and simply roamed the narrow village streets. Undaunted, she took Caroline to an ice-cream party with local children at the villa of an American friend. "I remember Caroline had a wonderful time and that all the Italian kids loved her," said one of the other children at the party. "I don't think the paparazzi bothered her at all — she grew up thinking that was just part of life."

But back home, Daddy was seething over rumors that Jackie had extended her Italian idyll from two weeks to four because of her interest in another Radziwill houseguest, the good-looking and fatally charming Fiat chairman, Gianni Agnelli. When the AP ran shots of Jackie and Agnelli swimming together off the auto tycoon's yacht, the President fumed. A LITTLE MORE CAROLINE, he said in a cable fired off to his wife after the photos ran, AND LESS AGNELLI. The next day, JFK picked up the papers to see photos of Jackie and Agnelli scuba-diving together.

Later that year, whatever differences Jack and Jackie may have had suddenly seemed trivial. On the morning of October 16, 1962, the President was informed that U.S. intelligence had determined that there were Soviet offensive missiles in Cuba.

The outside world was unaware of the growing crisis at this stage, but Caroline noticed that something was not quite right. Daddy was not available to spend time with them, Mommy was smoking more than ever, and there were men — Pentagon and State Department officials, trying to keep their presence at the White House under wraps — sleeping on cots downstairs. As he contemplated the growing possibility of global thermonuclear war, JFK's mask of confidence slipped off for a moment. "We've already had a chance," he told Jackie. "But what about all the children?"

Thirteen days after Caroline's father ordered a naval blockade, Russian ships carrying missiles toward Cuba turned back. The standoff ended one of the most dangerous confrontations in history.

Caroline could not comprehend what had happened, but there was no mistaking the sudden change in her parents' mood. As the world breathed a collective sigh of relief, Jackie immersed herself in plans for a joint party to celebrate her children's birthdays — Caroline's fifth and John's second. The birthday girl, wearing a party dress, a crucifix, and a pink ribbon in her hair, gobbled down a large portion of creamed chicken. Then, with the help of their mother, Caroline and John blew out the candles on each of their birthday cakes.

The Marine Band provided the entertainment, and at one point John grabbed a pair of maracas and joined in. Once Caroline finished playing with the dolls and coloring books she had been given, she and John joined their guests for cartoons in the White House theater.

With JFK's popularity still soaring in the wake of his handling of the Cuban Missile Crisis, Jack and Jackie were euphoric that Christmas of 1962. At the Kennedy estate in Palm Beach, they immersed themselves in the holiday spirit, surrounding themselves with family and friends. As Grandpa Joe, Rose, and all the aunts and uncles looked on, the leader of the free world rolled around on the White House floor with John and Caroline. Later, everyone settled in to watch Caroline play the Virgin Mary in a family production of the Nativity.

That following spring, the First Family tried to escape to their country hideaway in Glen Ora, Virginia, whenever possible. During one of those weekends at Glen Ora, Maud Shaw searched the house, but Caroline was nowhere to be found. Venturing outside, she called Caroline's name. No reply. Ten minutes later, the nanny and three Secret Service agents were scouring the grounds in a frantic search for the President's daughter.

"We are going to have to search down by the ponds," one of the agents told Shaw, who by now was so terrified that she nearly burst into tears.

Then a small voice called out. "Miss Shaw! Miss Shaw!" The nanny, overcome with relief, watched as Caroline climbed out of a chicken coop. That did not, however, prevent Shaw from giving the little girl what the nanny later described as "a hard smack on the bottom."

Now openly weeping, Shaw shouted, "You naughty girl! Never, never hide from me again!"

"But I wasn't hiding from you," Caroline said, pointing to the coop. "I was playing with my dollies in the little house."

Shaw, shaken and more than a bit ashamed, hugged Caroline tight.

Already for all intents and purposes the perfect young lady, Caroline had no trouble learning how to curtsy in preparation for the April 30, 1963, state visit of Luxembourg's Grand Duchess Charlotte. She also took a hand in teaching her brother the correct way to bow.

Just to make sure everything went off without a hitch, Maud Shaw promised both children cookies and ginger ale as a reward after they greeted the grand duchess. Growing impatient, John threw a tantrum just as his mother was introducing her son to their royal visitor. Hurling himself to the floor, he refused to move until Miss Shaw was summoned to cart him off. Caroline, meanwhile, rolled her eyes in exasperation — and executed her curtsy perfectly. She got her cookie and ginger ale, and gloated when John did not. "You were very naughty, John," Caroline scolded him. "*That's* why you don't get a cookie."

Ballet may have bored the President, but he did not hesitate to attend the recital Caroline put on with the other students of her White House kindergarten in May. Jackie came up with the theme — a tribute to the White House chef — and designed the costumes: leotards and homemade paper toques blanches. With Caroline stepping boldly out front, the dozen or so children danced while holding serving trays — and the President led the audience in spirited applause.

There was little doubt that Jack's favorite time with Caroline was the one-on-one time they spent together. One particular Memorial Day would come to haunt Caroline. After laying a wreath on the Tomb of the Unknown Soldier at Arlington, Jack took a stroll with Caroline on the cemetery's lush grounds. They were both struck by the view of the Potomac and Washington beyond.

"Who lives there, Daddy?" she asked, pointing to the stately hilltop mansion overlooking Arlington.

"That's the Lee Mansion," he answered. "A very famous Civil War general named Robert E. Lee lived there a long time ago." From that point on, whenever she was being driven through the streets of Washington, Caroline would search the horizon until she spotted it. "When Caroline was very little," Jackie later said, "the mansion was one of the first things she learned to recognize."

That spring day at Arlington also left an impression on the President. "You know, Buttons," he told her as they gazed out over the capital, "I could stay here forever. . . ."

By May 1963, Jackie had already explained to Caroline and John that they would soon have a baby brother or sister. After a miscarriage and a stillbirth, Jackie was determined not to take any unnecessary risks. With John and Caroline never far away, Jackie holed up in a rented beach house on Squaw Island. The Squaw Island house, a short drive from Hyannis Port, was bigger, more opulent, more secluded, and significantly quieter than their home inside the Hyannis Port compound.

On August 4, they cruised Nantucket Sound aboard the presidential yacht *Sequoia*, Jackie puffing away on cigarettes while Caroline and John kept an eye out for the mythical sock-devouring shark their father liked to talk about.

Three days later — August 7, 1963 — Caroline spent the morning doing what she loved best: horseback riding, at stables not far from their Squaw Island house. But on the drive home, Jackie was not feeling well. Caroline knew that it was too early — the baby was not due for another five weeks — but her mother was experiencing sharp labor pains.

"Don't worry, Caroline," Jackie reassured the little girl, whose worry was clearly evident on her face. "Mommy will be fine. The baby will be fine."

Her obstetrician, Dr. John Walsh, met her at the house and summoned a helicopter to take the First Lady to the military hospital at Otis Air Force Base. For the first time, Caroline saw her mother panic.

"Please hurry!" she pleaded with Walsh. "This baby mustn't be born dead!"

Caroline and John watched from the house with Nanny Shaw as the helicopter landed on the back lawn, then waved good-bye as it took Jackie off to the hospital. "Your mommy is going to be fine," Shaw reassured them. "But I think we should say a prayer for her, and for the baby."

At 12:52 p.m., Jackie gave birth by cesarean section to a four-pound, ten-ounce boy who was immediately placed in an incubator. The base chaplain, aware that the infant's future was in doubt, baptized the boy Patrick Bouvier Kennedy, after Jack's paternal grandfather and Black Jack Bouvier.

Jack arrived at the hospital forty minutes later. Dr. Walsh met the President at the door and took him aside. Patrick, Walsh informed him, suffered from a severe respiratory condition involving the lung's hyaline membrane. It was, in fact, the same condition shared by John and his stillborn sister.

As soon as the ambulance carrying Patrick left for Boston, the President rushed to Squaw Island to be with Caroline and John. Once again at Miss Shaw's urging, Caroline had been praying for her mother and her baby brother. Now she lit up as she saw her father's motorcade pull up to the house. The President leaned down and drew both children to them. He saw no reason to upset them. "Patrick has a little problem breathing and has to go to a hospital in Boston where they can make him better," Jack told them. "Mommy is fine. Everything is going to be okay."

Less than an hour later, JFK returned to the hospital to make sure his wife was all right, then flew on to Boston. But Patrick's condition worsened, and that night he was moved to Harvard's School of Public Health and placed in an oxygen chamber. Jack checked on the baby four times that day, helicoptered back to Otis to report to Jackie, then returned to spend the night with Patrick in the hospital.

America, transfixed by the unfolding drama, was stunned when, at 5:00 a.m. on August 9, Patrick died. "Oh, Jack, oh, Jack," Jackie sobbed, her words fully audible to the doctors and nurses standing just outside the door. "There's only one thing I could not bear now — if I ever lost you."

At the Squaw Island house, it was left to Maud Shaw to break the news to the children. Caroline had been eagerly anticipating the arrival of another little brother and, in her bossy big-sister way, lectured John on the care, feeding, and sleeping habits of infants.

"I have some bad news, children," Shaw said. "Do you remember what your daddy said about Patrick not being able to breathe? Well, the doctors tried to help little Patrick, but it was just too hard for him. He's with the angels now."

Caroline looked pensive for a moment. "Miss Shaw," she said, "Patrick is still my baby brother, right?"

"Yes," she answered. "He is still your baby brother."

"Then I think," Caroline said, folding her hands in prayer, "we should ask God to take care of him in heaven."

"Caroline was so quiet, so composed,"

Shaw marveled. "And the rest of us all had red eyes from crying."

Two days after Patrick's death, Jack picked up Caroline in his white Lincoln convertible and drove her to visit her mother at the hospital. Jackie brightened when she saw Caroline, her blond hair back in a ponytail. The little girl wore sneakers and a paisley sundress, and was holding on tightly to a bouquet of black-eyed Susans.

Jackie would spend a full week recuperating in the hospital, and was too drained physically and emotionally to attend Patrick's funeral. Jackie's mother, sister, and half brother Jamie joined Bobby, Teddy, and New York's Cardinal Spellman at the small service conducted by Cardinal Cushing. Later, at Brookline's Holyhood cemetery, the President broke down again as Patrick's coffin was lowered into a grave next to Caroline's stillborn sister. "Good-bye," he said. "It's awfully lonely down there."

Jack worried about Jackie, but he also fretted over the children. "He knew how sad Caroline was going to be," Jamie Auchincloss said, "and he wanted to try and offset that in some way." By way of distracting Caroline and John, the President showed up at the Squaw Island house with a cocker spaniel puppy. As the children squealed their approval, Daddy informed them that the puppy's name was Shannon.

The day Jack escorted their mother home from the hospital, Caroline and John ran outside to greet her. "Look, Mommy," Caroline said, holding up the newest member of their canine family. "The puppy's name is Shannon." Not to be overlooked, the rest of the pound — Charlie, Clipper, and Pushinka's puppies Butterfly, Blackie, White Tips, and Streaker — also crowded the front lawn, clamoring for attention.

A handful of friends showed up at Hammersmith Farm on September 12 to join with Caroline's parents in toasting their tenth wedding anniversary. The couple, brought together by Patrick's death, was more affectionate than they had ever been before. "When their emotions do surface, it is especially moving," said Ben Bradlee. Caroline noticed the difference. "There was a tenderness between her parents that she really hadn't seen before," said Pierre Salinger. "It made an impression on her. You could see the little gears in her head turning as she watched them embrace."

But JFK was still concerned about Jackie's mental state after this latest tragic loss of a child. Lee Radziwill had been trying to think of ways to cheer her sister up when Greek shipping magnate Aristotle Onassis offered the use of his fabled yacht *Christina*. Lee had "a sort of romance going with Onassis," the President's secretary, Evelyn Lincoln, recalled. To be sure, there were rumors that Lee intended to divorce Prince Stanislas ("Stas") Radziwill and marry Onassis. After much deliberation, Jack reluctantly agreed to let his wife go along on the grounds that a cruise of the Greek Isles might, in Evelyn Lincoln's words, "do her some good." For appearances' sake, the President sent Undersecretary of Commerce Franklin D. Roosevelt and his wife, Suzanne, along as chaperons.

Initially Onassis, fully cognizant of how it might look if he were photographed vacationing with the wife of the President of the United States, had not intended to go along on the cruise. But Jackie insisted that he come. "It would have been too cruel," she said, to take advantage of Onassis's hospitality and "not let him come along. I just couldn't have done that."

Less thought, it seemed, had been given to what impact Jackie's sudden departure might have on Caroline. It had, after all, been scarcely a matter of weeks since Patrick's death. Yet Jack took care to explain to Caroline that her mother needed a vacation, and he sought to fill the void with extra play sessions in the Oval Office.

Although Caroline did not accompany her mother this time, Jackie's voyage aboard the *Christina* seemed reminiscent of her earlier interlude with Gianni Agnelli. As the Aegean cruise progressed, Onassis lavished attention on Jackie — this time at her sister's expense. When he gave Jackie a spectacular ruby-and-diamond necklace, Lee wrote to Jack in mock indignation, "All I've got is three dinky little bracelets that Caroline wouldn't wear to her own birthday party!"

After weeks of island-hopping, swimming, and dancing to bouzouki music aboard the *Christina*, Jackie returned to Washington on October 17, 1963. Caroline, John, and their father were at Dulles International Airport to greet her. "Oh, Jack," she said, throwing her arms around him, "I'm so glad to be home!" On the ride to the White House in the presidential limousine, Caroline squeezed between her parents while John snuggled up to Mommy. Jackie, still very proper in her white satin gloves, tickled John until he dissolved in hysterics.

"Be careful, Mommy," Caroline cautioned. "He just had something to drink."

Now that she was back at the White House, Jackie made Caroline's religious instruction a top priority. In part, she was motivated by the cosmic questions Caroline had been posing since Patrick's death. Why would God let a baby die? What was heaven like? Will we see Patrick there someday? But even before Patrick's birth, Jackie, who was far more devout than her husband, had begun the search for a suitable Catholic school. In

May, she had dispatched Miss Grimes, the headmistress of Caroline's little White House school, to the Georgetown Visitation Academy — a cloistered convent — to see if it might take on Caroline and her six Roman Catholic classmates.

Teaching catechism at the academy was Sister Joanne Frey of the Mission Helpers of the Sacred Heart. "Caroline would have stood out even if she wasn't the President's daughter," Frey said. "She was exceptionally well spoken for someone her age, and completely unspoiled." When Sister Joanne asked her pupils to tell a story using pictures cut out of magazines, Caroline proudly showed Frey a picture of a woman cradling an infant and a child of five or six. "This is Mommy," Caroline said as she pointed to the woman, "this is me, and this would have been Patrick, my baby brother. He's in heaven."

"There were moments like that," Sister Joanne said, "when Caroline would catch you off guard with her innocence. It really kind of took your breath away. Everyone had gone through the tragedy of Patrick's death; the experience was still fresh in people's minds. What could you say?"

It was not at all unusual for Jackie to show up at the classes, the very existence of which were unknown to the public at the time. It seemed strange to Sister Joanne that the classes remained undetected for the entire eight months that Caroline attended them. "The limos in front of the building were obvious," Sister Joanne said. "It was apparent to anyone who cared to notice that something was going on. But the press never discovered we were there."

Sometimes John accompanied Jackie and Caroline to class. One day in October 1963, Caroline's little brother marched noisily into the classroom with his make-believe rifle — a stick — over his shoulder. "He thinks he's a soldier," sighed an exasperated Caroline, "and he doesn't even know how to salute." Sadly, one month later Caroline stood next to their mother while her brother snapped off a salute that would melt the hearts of millions.

On November 13, 1963, General Maxwell Taylor stood in full dress uniform on the White House balcony with the children, waiting for the President and First Lady to arrive. Bundled up against the cold, Caroline and John sipped tea poured for them by White House butlers. Once Jack and Jackie appeared, the seventeen hundred underprivileged children and their families who had gathered on the South Lawn to hear the kilted Black Watch pipers broke into applause.

John squirmed in Mommy's lap, then jumped up to peer over the wrought-iron railing. Caroline, meantime, was content to snuggle up against her father, her arm around him.

JFK had always loved the plaintive wail of bagpipes, and of all the pipers, the famous Black Watch Regiment was his favorite. "They're wonderful, aren't they, Buttons?" he said.

"Yes, Daddy," Caroline answered, always eager to please her father. "And very loud."

For this most celebrated of all First Families, it was the last time they would be together in public. Eight days later, Maud Shaw brought Caroline and John to say good-bye to their parents. "Mommy's going, too?" Caroline had asked. After all, Jackie rarely accompanied the President on his trips around the country.

JFK first hugged Caroline, whose eyes widened when he said he and Mommy might encounter some real live cowboys on this trip. Then he knelt down to give John a kiss and an affectionate pat on the bottom. Caroline waved as Mommy and Daddy left the White House — for Dallas.

Those poor children.

— Ethel Kennedy,
on learning from her husband that
JFK had been assassinated

Your father's death had been
a tragedy for the Nation,
as well as for you. . . .

— Lyndon Johnson,
in a note he wrote to Caroline on the
night of the assassination

My mommy cries *all the time.*

— Caroline

4

Sitting in the backseat of a station wagon, her favorite pink teddy bear in her lap and her small suitcase at her feet, Caroline was lost in conversation with her friend as she headed for her very first sleepover. The friend's mother was driving; an unmarked black sedan with a single Secret Service agent brought up the rear.

Music had been playing on the car radio when, jarringly, a man's voice interrupted the broadcast. "We have a news bulletin. . . . This just in — President Kennedy has been shot. I repeat, the President has been shot in an apparent assassination attempt in Dallas, Texas. . . ." The driver scrambled to turn off the radio. She checked out the children in the rearview mirror and, since both girls were still talking about their sleepover plans, assumed that Caroline had not heard the shocking news.

Yet Buttons *had* heard. The driver glanced

in her rearview mirror again and signaled to the agent in the black sedan. Within moments, both cars had pulled over to the side of the highway. The rear passenger door opened, and the agent leaned inside. "Caroline," he said, "we're going to have to turn back. Could you come along with me?" Bewildered, the little girl grabbed her suitcase and climbed out of her friend's station wagon and into the black Ford.

As the Secret Service agent raced toward the White House with his precious cargo, an anonymous driver recognized the President's daughter sitting in the front passenger seat of the unmarked car. Apparently believing that Caroline was being kidnapped, he gave chase. The agent, not sure of his pursuer's intentions, took evasive action and radioed back to the White House that he was being followed. The First Daughter, who in keeping with the custom of the time was not wearing a seat belt, held on for dear life.

Once Caroline arrived safely back at the White House, she was greeted by a visibly shaken Maud Shaw. To the nanny's surprise — and relief — Caroline asked no questions and gave no indication of what she knew. For the moment, JFK's daughter was content to read a book — and wait for someone to tell her what was going on.

More than a thousand miles away at Dallas's Parkland Memorial Hospital, Mommy was walking toward Dr. Marion Jenkins, head of Parkland's anesthesiology department. Jackie's pink wool suit was splattered with gore, and she was still wearing her white kid gloves. "She then with her right hand handed me a good-sized chunk of the President's brain," Jenkins later recalled. "She didn't say a word. I handed it to the nurse."

Only minutes before, Caroline's parents exchanged one final glance in the back of the presidential limousine as the first shots struck Jack in the neck, severing his windpipe. Then Jackie watched the second bullet strike. He looked "puzzled," she would later say, "as if he just had a slight headache. I could see a piece of his skull coming off — this perfectly clean piece detaching itself from his head. . . ."

Caroline was still reading in her room at the White House when Jackie finally pushed her way past Head Nurse Doris Nelson and into the room where her husband lay dying. She sank to her knees on the blood-covered floor and prayed, but at 1:00 p.m. one of the attending physicians, Dr. Kemp Clark, told Jackie her husband was dead. A sheet was pulled over the President's face, but Jackie pulled it back down. His eyes were open. His mouth, she later recalled, "was so *beautiful*." Then Jackie startled the medical staff by kissing his foot, leg, thigh, chest, and finally his lips. "She didn't," Dr. Jenkins recalled, "say a word."

Back in Washington, Uncle Bobby assumed the grim task of calling family members with the awful news. When all the Kennedys knew — except for Caroline and her brother — Bobby then called Lee Radziwill at her home in London.

Grand-mère Janet Auchincloss (Jackie insisted that Caroline and John use French when referring to their grandparents) had just returned from a round of golf and was resting at her mansion in Washington when Bobby called. Jackie's famously meddlesome mother made the unilateral decision to have the children brought to her house on O Street to spend the night. (Mrs. Auchincloss would later claim that, as Jackie returned home with Jack's body and newly sworn-in President Lyndon Baines Johnson aboard Air Force One, an unidentified person had called and instructed her to pick up the children.)

Caroline was playing with John in the living room of their grandmother's house when Jackie's sixteen-year-old half brother, Jamie Auchincloss, rushed in. "Of course, before I got to my parents' house, I assumed that they had been told," Jamie said. "But it became obvious very quickly that that wasn't the case." The children were, he said, clearly "expecting to spend a playful late afternoon with their Uncle Jamie."

"Uncle Jamie! Uncle Jamie!" John shouted as he flew his helicopter around the room. Caroline was more composed. Whenever he saw them, it was inevitable that they would talk about all the fascinating and important things Daddy and Mommy were up to. "Caroline was pretty mature for her age," Jamie said. "But of course she was most interested in talking about how Mommy rode an elephant, or how Daddy was going to send a man to the moon. . . ."

This time, rather than talking to Caroline and John about their parents, Jamie "steered them away from the subject, although I'm sure with all the excitement, Caroline knew something was up."

It would have been hard for a child as observant as Caroline not to notice that something was amiss. While she and John played on the floor with Uncle Jamie, a half dozen Secret Service agents had gathered around the television set in the kitchen.

Jamie did his best to shield his niece from the painful truth; there would be a lifetime of grief ahead of her. "I thought, Why tell her now? Why not let her have a few more hours of blissful innocence?" When, without warning, Caroline dashed into the kitchen for a cookie, the Secret Service men hurried to block the screen, but too late. Returning to Jamie and her brother, "Caroline's mood had changed," said Jamie. "She turned very quiet."

While Caroline and John played with Jamie at their grandmother's house, a stunned nation watched as the coffin bearing their father's body was taken off Air Force One and loaded into a waiting hearse at Andrews Air Force Base. Their mother still refused to leave Daddy's side, sliding along with Bobby into the back of the hearse.

From Andrews, the hearse drove forty minutes to Bethesda Naval Hospital in Maryland, where an autopsy was to be performed. When Jackie arrived, she was met by friends and family — Defense Secretary Robert McNamara, the Bartletts, and the Auchinclosses among them. They listened numbly as Jackie, still "amazingly calm," as one of those present put it, relived the day's events again and again.

Grand-mère Auchincloss was taken aback when Jackie suddenly asked where the children were. It was the first time Jackie had mentioned Caroline and John since their father's life had ended over eight hours earlier.

Janet Auchincloss reassured her daughter that the children were fine. "They are with Jamie at our house," she said, fully expecting her daughter to be reassured.

Yet Jackie was anything but pleased.

"The best thing for them," Jackie insisted, "would be to stay in their own rooms with their own things so their lives can be as normal as possible." Jackie then shook her head, and for the first time since arriving back in Washington, raised her voice in anger. "Mummy, my God, those poor children. Their lives shouldn't be disrupted now, of all times!"

Back at the Auchincloss mansion, Maud Shaw was told of the change in plans. "Come on now, Caroline," said Miss Shaw, "gather up your toys. John, you, too. It's time to go back to the White House. Your mommy is going to be coming home soon."

Jamie Auchincloss watched as Caroline and John took Miss Shaw's hands and climbed into the government limousine that would take them to the White House. "I knew their lives had been changed forever," he said, "but then, so had everyone's."

When Caroline and John walked into the second-floor family quarters of the White House, Ben and Tony Bradlee were there to greet them. They had decided to check in on JFK's beloved children but were uncomfortable with the fact that, all these hours after the shots were fired, Jack's children still had not been told. "I'm going to do it," Ben told his wife.

Tony refused to let him. "No, no you're not," she objected. "That's not our decision to make."

If he could not tell them, Bradlee reasoned, then at least he could entertain Jack's children. He read John story after story until, exasperated, he told the little boy to chase him around the house. While a delighted John pursued Bradlee around the Yellow Oval Room, Caroline sat reading. She knew that something was being kept from her, but she was still not quite sure what.

At about the time Tony Bradlee was restraining her husband from breaking the news to Caroline and John, Janet Auchincloss was asking the only person who mattered. "Who do you want," Janet asked her daughter bluntly, "to tell the children?"

For a moment, Jackie pondered the idea of waiting a few days to tell them herself. Bobby had decided not to tell Joe right away — it might kill the old man, he reasoned — and maybe she could wait until she was out of this fog of unreality that enveloped her. John was no problem — he was too young, really, to comprehend any of this. But Caroline was another matter. What if she turned on the television, which was likely to broadcast little if anything else for weeks, or talked to one of her young friends?

Someone would have to tell them, but Jackie could not bear the notion of sitting Caroline down and telling Jack's adored Buttons that she would never see him again. Caroline's mother had so much to deal with; this was one onerous task she had to hand to someone else — someone who would not collapse from the strain of performing it, as

Jackie feared she would.

No-nonsense, dependable-to-a-fault Maud Shaw had broken the news of Patrick's death to Caroline and John, and she was as close to them as any family member — closer, in some ways. Caroline was scarcely a week old when Miss Shaw came to the hospital to care for her while Jackie recuperated from her cesarean. While Caroline's parents pursued their hectic public lives, it was plump, proper, yet earth-motherly Miss Shaw who was the one constant presence in their lives.

From the moment she heard that shots had rung out in Dallas, Miss Shaw correctly feared that Jackie would ask her to be the one to tell the children. She was close to Caroline and John — too close. It would break Miss Shaw's heart to tell them, every bit as much as it would break their mother's heart.

Shaw walked up to Secret Service agents, the Bradlees, anyone who was at hand and pleaded that someone else — anyone else — take it upon himself to tell the children. "I haven't the heart to tell them," she said again and again, her tone growing more and more desperate. "Why can't someone else do this? I can't . . . I can't . . ."

Miss Shaw steeled herself with a cup of tea and tucked John into his crib — he was not yet quite old enough to sleep in a bed — said good night, and tiptoed out. She mentioned nothing of his father; the consensus was that he was too young to understand even if she did tell him, so she might as well wait until morning.

The nanny felt she should take just the opposite approach with Caroline. "It's better for children Caroline's age to get a sadness and a shock before they go to sleep at night," Shaw later explained to Jackie. "That way it won't hit them hard when they wake up in the morning."

As she did every evening, Miss Shaw stood by while Caroline put on her pink pajamas and brushed her teeth, and pulled back the covers of the canopy bed so the little girl could climb in. Then, as she often did, the nanny sat down on the edge of the bed while Caroline settled in, her favorite pink teddy bear on the pillow beside her.

This time, however, Miss Shaw seemed uneasy. She took Caroline's hand in hers, and the little girl could see that her nanny's eyes were welling up with tears.

"What's wrong, Miss Shaw?" she asked softly. "Why are you crying?"

"I can't help crying, Caroline, because I have some very sad news to tell you," she said. "Your father has been shot. They took him to a hospital, but they couldn't make him better. He's gone to look after Patrick. Patrick was so lonely in heaven. He didn't know anyone there. Now he has the best friend anyone could have. And your father will be so very glad to see Patrick."

Given the way she had couched the news, Miss Shaw was surprised at how quickly — and how strongly — the little girl reacted. She instantly burst into tears. "But what will Daddy do in heaven?" she asked, choking back sobs.

"I am sure God is giving him enough things to do, because he was always such a busy man," Nanny Shaw said. "God has made your daddy a guardian angel for you and for Mommy and for John."

But Caroline could not be comforted. She had already had to deal with Patrick's death, and more than most children her age — Caroline's fifth birthday was only days away — she understood something of the finality of it. Nanny Shaw remained with Caroline, stroking her hair as she cried into her pillow for more than an hour before succumbing to sleep.

Miss Shaw did not sleep that night; her unenviable assignment was only half done. At eight-thirty the next morning, she went into John's room and gently woke him. She had agonized over the best way to tell the little boy that his father wasn't coming home, and decided that it would do no good to mention that the President had been shot. JFK had actually worried that his son was too fond of toy guns, of the military trappings that surrounded life at the White House, and Miss Shaw did not want to frighten or upset John any more than necessary.

"John," she said softly, "your father has gone to heaven to take care of Patrick." And yes, he took his "big plane" with him.

John looked up into her eyes and cocked his head slightly. "I wonder," he said, "when he's coming back."

Down the hall, Caroline was stirring awake. She'd had nightmares before, but the one last night was the scariest ever. To make things even stranger, Miss Shaw, who had always come to comfort her when she had a bad dream, was actually part of the dream this time.

Staring at her from the foot of the bed was the stuffed giraffe Daddy had given her for her last birthday. Caroline climbed out of bed, grabbed the giraffe, and — as she did every morning — ran down the corridor toward Daddy's room. John was in hot pursuit.

Caroline turned the knob, pushed the heavy wooden door open, and for a split second saw someone in Daddy's bed. "Daddy!" she squealed. But as the door swung back farther, it revealed not one but two people — *Grand-père* and *Grand-mère* Auchincloss — sitting up in bed. Asked by Jackie to stay overnight in Jack's room, they had understandably found it impossible to sleep.

Caroline's smile melted. Newspapers were spread out on the bed, and on top of the pile was the *New York Times*, with the President's black-bordered portrait covering the entire front page.

"Who is that?" Caroline asked as she held on tight to her giraffe.

Shaking her head, Grandma Auchincloss sighed, "Oh, Caroline — you know that's your daddy."

She stared at the picture for what seemed to Janet like an eternity. Then she looked up. "He's dead, isn't he?" Caroline said. "A man shot him, didn't he?"

Janet could only gaze in wonder at her grandchild. "Her little face was so extraordinary," she later said of her granddaughter. "It's hard for Caroline to . . . she's a very, very affectionate little girl, and she's a very thoughtful child."

Father John C. Cavanaugh, a former president of Notre Dame University, arrived that morning at the White House to say mass for a small gathering of family and friends. Maud Shaw, meanwhile, had helped Caroline and John dress, and at 9:45 a.m. she brought them both to Jackie's bedroom. Until this moment, Jackie had not been able to face them.

Jackie hugged Caroline and John, then grasped their hands and walked them downstairs. Too young to attend mass in the East

155

Room — mourners were seated on folding wooden chairs facing the President's flag-draped coffin — the children watched with Miss Shaw from the Green Room next door. Staring at the President's coffin, Caroline tugged at her nanny's sleeve. She did not see how her father could fit into such a small box. "Daddy's too big for that," she said. "How's he lying? Are his knees under his chin?"

Caroline then asked if she could see her daddy one more time. But Jackie did not want the children traumatized by the sight of their father's body — particularly after Jack's trusted friend Bill Walton warned Jackie that the mortician had made JFK look "like a waxworks dummy, something you'd see at Madame Tussaud's." Jackie, unwilling to put her husband on display in such a manner, ordered that the coffin stay closed.

Also watching from the sidelines were Uncle Jamie and Aunt Janet (Jamie's sister and Jackie's half sister), who scooped the children up after the mass and spirited them away to spend a few hours playing with their German shepherd and *Grand-mère*'s poodle at nearby Manassas Battlefield. Caroline and her brother took turns walking the dogs — John shrieking with joy as he tried to hold on to the leash, his sister hot on his heels.

Unfortunately, dogs were not permitted on the battlefield. Without warning, an angry park ranger appeared, waving his arms and shouting as he ran toward the children. As he got closer, the park ranger recognized Caroline and John and stopped in his tracks. Then, overcome, he began to weep.

Following the mass, White House usher J. B. West walked Jackie over to the Oval Office for one final look before her husband's things were packed up. With "eyes like saucers," as West put it, she memorized everything in the room — right down to the small white-and-gold-embossed leatherette picture frame that held photos of herself, Caroline, and John. She picked up the triptych, studied the photos, then sadly placed it back on Jack's desk.

That night, Jackie opened a note the new President had written to Caroline just hours after her father was gunned down. "Your father's death has been a great tragedy for the Nation, as well as for you," he wrote, "and I wanted you to know how much my thoughts are of you at this time. He was a wise and devoted man. You can always be proud of what he did for his country. Affectionately, Lyndon B. Johnson."

LBJ also scrawled a note to John. "It will be many years before you understand fully what a great man your father was," Johnson wrote. "His loss is a deep personal tragedy for all of us, but I wanted you particularly to know that I share your grief — You can always be proud of him."

Jackie sat both of her children down and read Johnson's letters to them. Then she told Maud Shaw to fetch pencils and paper for the children. "You must write a letter to Daddy now," she told Caroline, "and tell him how much you love him."

Caroline pressed down hard on the paper with her pencil as she covered the page with large block print: DEAR DADDY, WE ARE ALL GOING TO MISS YOU. DADDY, I LOVE YOU VERY MUCH, CAROLINE. Jackie then asked her son to write something. Below his sister's writing, John scribbled a large X.

Not long after she finished writing her letter to Daddy, Caroline watched her mother greet a familiar guest to the family living quarters. Manhattan-based Dr. Max Jacobson had hopped a flight to Washington as soon as he heard the first news bulletin. Jacobson had been to the White House dozens of times, and Secret Service agents had standing orders to escort him to the second-floor residence as soon as he arrived.

This time, Jacobson spotted Caroline and stopped to ask her how she was doing, before being ushered in to see the First Lady. The wild-eyed doctor with the big black medical bag was something of a mystery to Caroline; she noticed that whenever her parents felt very tired or sad, Dr. Jacobson would drop by, and suddenly they were back to being themselves — vital, active, and full of fun. But Jackie was careful not to reveal too much to her daughter; Dr. Jacobson's treatments were always administered behind closed doors.

Jackie and the President had long relied on these injections from Dr. Feelgood — amphetamines (mostly Dexedrine) mixed with steroids — to get them through the day. Jacobson's potent "cocktails" were perfectly legal; at the time, the medical community viewed both drugs as harmless and nonaddictive. Jackie rolled up the sleeve of her black mourning dress and looked the other way as Jacobson injected a stronger-than-usual dose into her veins.

Even Jacobson's critics acknowledged that, without the added pharmaceutical help, Jackie would have crumbled. Caroline, who never actually witnessed her mother receiving the injections, would nonetheless notice that Dr. Jacobson seemed to be everywhere over the next few days — never introduced to anyone, seldom uttering a word, but always at hand in case Mommy needed him.

No one, however, would be more heavily relied on than Uncle Bobby. Drained of emotion, in the words of Ben Bradlee "almost catatonic," Bobby would literally be at Jackie's elbow for the next few days. "She relied on him totally," Spalding said, "and so

159

did the kids. Caroline in particular had always been close to Bobby, and even though he was in total shock, he showed tremendous tenderness toward them."

The next morning, before JFK's body was to be taken to lie in state in the Capitol rotunda, Jackie and Bobby went to the East Room to see him one final time. The lid was opened, and Jackie slid two letters — Caroline's and one Jackie had written her husband the night before — inside, along with two personal items she had given Jack: a treasured piece of scrimshaw and a pair of gold cuff links. Bobby added a gold PT-109 tie clip Jack had given him, a silver rosary, and a clip of his own hair.

Then she walked into Pierre Salinger's office and sat down. Salinger later described her as looking "almost ghostly" as she began to talk.

"Pierre," she said, "I have nothing else to do in life but help my children deal with this terrible problem, the effect of their father's assassination, to bring them up well, and see that they become decent, caring, and intelligent people. I have to make sure they survive."

At about the same time, in the basement of the Dallas County Jail, a local nightclub owner named Jack Ruby bolted from the shadows and shot accused assassin Lee Harvey Oswald. Ruby's avowed motive: to spare Jackie the ordeal of a trial, and to avenge Caroline and John.

That evening, a little more than ten minutes after Oswald was pronounced dead, the eyes of millions were on the Capitol Rotunda. Surrounded by Supreme Court justices, senators, cabinet members, diplomats, generals, admirals, and family members, Jackie and Caroline led a nation in mourning. That day Jackie had wanted her children to look like children; unlike their cousins, who wore black, Caroline and John were outfitted in matching blue coats, white ankle socks, and red shoes.

Although he managed to follow his father's casket up the Capitol's thirty-five steps alongside Jackie and Caroline, once inside, John grew fidgety. Miss Shaw responded quickly, whisking the boy into an office down the hall. In the rotunda, meanwhile, Jackie leaned down and whispered to her daughter, "We're going to say good-bye to Daddy now, and we're going to kiss him good-bye and tell Daddy how much we love him and how much we'll always miss him."

Mother and daughter, both wearing white gloves, approached the bier, sank to their knees, took the flag that covered the coffin in their hands — and pressed it to their lips.

Such gestures were a small but significant part of the spectacle that Jackie sought to stage in her husband's memory. She had relied on her own highly developed sense of style and showmanship to transform the White House of Ike and Mamie into an American Versailles. Now she wanted her husband's state funeral to reflect what she perceived to be his greatness — and the magnitude of the nation's loss.

On the eve of her husband's state funeral, Jackie dined with Bobby and Lee in the West Sitting Room while Pat and Peter Lawford, Eunice and Sargent Shriver, Robert McNamara, longtime Kennedy aide Dave Powers, and a few others were seated in the family dining room. One last-minute addition was Aristotle Onassis, kept under wraps because of his long history of shady business dealings. It would be four years before the press learned that Onassis had been dining inside the White House just forty-eight hours after the assassination, a guest of the President's widow.

Caroline and John ate that night, as usual, in the High Chair Room. Once they had bathed and dressed in their pajamas, the children were escorted by Miss Shaw into the Family Sitting Room to say good night to the adults. According to their nanny, what Caroline witnessed that night — a traditionally raucous Irish wake — "obviously confused her." It did not surprise the little girl that her mother, eyes red and swollen from crying, was still quiet and subdued. But her aunts and uncles and those grown-ups who had been closest to Daddy behaved in quite a different manner.

"We all laughed and sang and carried on with great hilarity," said Lem Billings. Ted, who like most of the others in the room was thoroughly soused, led everyone in several choruses of "When Irish Eyes Are Smiling." Dave Powers told stories about his boss that had everyone roaring with laughter. "People were shrieking with laughter, crying with laughter," Peter Lawford said. "Everybody was up, drinking and smiling and trying to make the best of it. Not being Irish, I tried to get in the swing of it, but I was thoroughly destroyed."

Even Jackie, now running on cigarettes and adrenaline, laughed at Dave Powers's tall tales of Jack's early days campaigning for Congress in Boston. The sight of her children standing in the room in their pajamas, however, brought her quickly down to earth. Caroline and John kissed their mother good night and then toddled off to bed.

It was only then that Maud Shaw realized that, in all the confusion, everyone had forgotten that the next day — Monday, November 25 — was not only the day of JFK's funeral. It was John's third birthday. Since Caroline turned six just two days later, Jackie suggested that there be a joint party midway between the two dates.

Still, Caroline did not want her brother's actual birthday to go unnoticed. The following morning, Miss Shaw and Caroline sang "Happy Birthday" to John over breakfast. Then he merrily tore through the wrapping on two gifts — yet another toy helicopter from Caroline and a book about planes from his nanny.

The rest of the day would be burned into Caroline's memory — and the nation's psyche — forever. While she and John waited at St. Matthew's Cathedral, Mommy, Uncle Bobby, and the other Kennedy grown-ups walked behind JFK's coffin as it made its way from the White House to the cathedral on a caisson drawn by six gray horses. Caroline would later comment on how beautiful they were, though her favorite was Black Jack, the traditional "riderless horse" that trotted behind the coffin. Following Jackie and the family was a cortege made up of dignitaries from 102 nations, including Great Britain's Prince Philip, Ethiopian Emperor Haile Selassie, French President Charles de Gaulle, Israel's Golda Meir, and West German Chancellor Ludwig Erhard.

For Caroline, the sounds that day were no less memorable — especially the plaintive, haunting rhythm of the muffled drums that accompanied the procession. "Those drums!" Pierre Salinger remembered. "I don't know anyone who was alive then who doesn't remember that sound. I understand the memory of those drums bothered Jackie for years. It must have had the same effect on Caroline."

Once the cortege reached St. Matthew's, Jackie sat between her children as Cardinal Cushing began the Latin mass. Halfway into it, Cushing switched to English: "May the angels, dear Jack, lead you into paradise. . . ."

With that, Jackie finally broke down. Caroline turned to her mother. "You'll be all right, Mommy," she said. "Don't cry. I'll take care of you." Then Caroline, who had been given a handkerchief by Maud Shaw before leaving the White House, reached up to wipe away her mother's tears.

Not wanting to upset the children any more than they undoubtedly already were, Jackie quickly pulled herself together. "Caroline — she held my hand like a soldier," Jackie said not long after. "She's my helper. . . ."

When it was time to say a silent prayer, Caroline turned to her mother again — this time for advice. "What kind of prayer should I say?" she asked.

" 'Please, God, take care of Daddy,' " Jackie suggested. "Or 'Please, God, be nice to Daddy.' "

Moments later, Caroline and John stood on either side of their mother outside St. Matthew's, looking on as the flag-covered coffin departed on its final three-mile journey over the Potomac to Arlington. Then Jackie, her tears hidden behind a long black veil, told John to say good-bye to his father, and the little boy snapped off the salute that would melt hearts for generations to come. Caroline, still holding her mother's hand and engrossed in the mass card she had been handed inside, paid no attention.

Scarcely forty-five minutes after lighting the Eternal Flame atop her husband's grave, Jackie was greeting dignitaries in a White House receiving line. Nanny Shaw took an exhausted John upstairs, but Caroline was too old — and too anxious — for an afternoon nap. Jackie wanted her daughter to be suitably occupied, and before she took her place at the head of the receiving line, she suggested Caroline do some work in her religion book before heading off to catechism class.

For the time being, however, no one knew exactly what to do with Caroline. Seeking to distract her, one of Caroline's favorite bodyguards offered to take her for a ride. She put on a little trench coat her mother had bought for her just days before and headed out. For what seemed like an eternity, they drove aimlessly around the city until Caroline had an idea.

As expected, Sister Joanne Frey had already been alerted to the fact that Caroline would not be attending class that day. While Sister Joanne was preparing for the other students' arrival, however, Caroline and her Secret Service agent suddenly appeared in the doorway. She looked, Frey observed, "so lost and alone."

"Sister, I know I'm early," Caroline said, "but we were just riding around, and we didn't have anyplace to go."

"Oh, I'm glad you're here," Sister Joanne said brightly. "I have so many things to do to get the class ready — you can help me!"

Caroline unbuttoned her trench coat, offering the nun a glimpse of a silver-dollar-size medallion hanging around her neck. Before Frey could ask what it was, Caroline quickly pulled her coat closed in front of her. "I've got something to show you," she said coyly, and this time she whipped open her coat to reveal the gold medallion.

"Oh, that's very, very nice, Caroline," Sister Joanne said.

"Haile Selassie gave it to me," Caroline muttered offhandedly.

Opening her religion book, she apologized again. "My mommy had lots of things to do, and I know I'm not supposed to, but she told me I could go ahead a few pages and work in my religion book. I'm sorry. Everybody else was so busy. I just needed something to do."

The nun fought back tears. "Of course it's fine, Caroline," she said.

That afternoon, Jackie and Grandma Rose were having coffee in the Yellow Oval Room when Caroline raced up to her mother with a question. "Mommy, did they love Daddy?" she asked.

"Oh, yes, they loved Daddy," Jackie answered without hesitation. Rose Kennedy, who by now had lost three of her nine children, nodded in agreement.

"No, Mommy," Caroline shot back, "they couldn't have loved Daddy. If they had loved him, they wouldn't have done what they did to him."

Jackie had no ready answer; this was one of the questions that would keep her up nights for years to come. Caroline's grandmother squirmed nervously on the couch.

It turned out that Caroline wasn't finished. "Mommy," she asked tentatively, "do they love you?"

"Well, I think so," Jackie replied, "at least some." Now it was clear what this was all about. Caroline feared that the same thing that happened to Daddy might happen to her mother. Jackie, mistakenly believing that this would probably be the one and only assassination that would touch her family, had rushed to reassure her daughter. But instead Caroline seemed more confused than ever.

"Maybe I should have told you that not

everybody loved Dad," Jackie continued. "Many more loved Daddy than loved me. But I think some of them love me, too."

It was obvious from the look of bewilderment on Caroline's face that this was not the answer she had hoped for.

"After all, not everybody loved Jesus, did they?" Jackie added.

That seemed to do the trick, and Caroline zipped off to the family dining room, where John's birthday party was in full swing. Mommy had decided that, while they would still have a joint party for the children later on, she could not deny her son the joy of celebrating his birthday. "We need a party," Jackie said to Maud Shaw, "on this day more than any other, don't you think?"

But even at her brother's party, Caroline could not escape the fact that this was a mournful day. When Dave Powers led the revelers in a selection of Irish songs, Uncle Jamie put his arm around Caroline. "Emotions were strained to the very limit," Jamie recalled. When Powers burst into "Heart of My Heart," one of Jack's favorites, Bobby was overcome and fled the room in tears.

"John was too young to get what was going on, but Caroline understood," Auchincloss said. "That is one major difference between Caroline and John: He was so young that he was just blissfully unaware, really. But Caroline got it. She got it. . . ."

Thankfully, Caroline was spared knowledge of another clandestine mission undertaken at Jackie's request. The President's young widow wanted her stillborn daughter and son Patrick reburied next to their father at Arlington. After the infants' bodies were disinterred, they were flown aboard the *Caroline* to Arlington. That night, illuminated only by the flickering light of the Eternal Flame, Jackie, along with Jack's brothers and Jamie Auchincloss, buried the children in a brief secret ceremony. "It was incredibly touching," Auchincloss recalled. His sister "wanted to bring them all together again, and she did."

Two days after her father's funeral, Caroline arrived with her mother and brother at Hyannis Port to spend Thanksgiving with the rest of the Kennedys. It was Caroline's birthday, but Jackie felt that — unlike John — her daughter was mature enough to wait until the planned joint celebration, now postponed until December 5.

While Caroline played with her cousins, Jackie spent an hour with Grandpa behind closed doors. Although Bobby and the others had summoned the courage to tell Joe the previous Sunday, the mere presence of Jackie and the children unleashed another torrent of grief among the staff. "Tears everywhere," said Secret Service Agent Ham Brown. "Secretaries, nurses, Secret Service agents. We were all a mess."

Again Caroline soaked it all in. "She was a very observant child," Brown said. "Nothing got past her."

As people did in millions of American homes that Thanksgiving, Caroline and John sat at the children's table, where their less well behaved cousins made rude faces and teased one another. The following evening, Mommy summoned a short, bespectacled *Life* magazine writer named Theodore White to Hyannis Port. With Caroline and John tucked in bed upstairs, Jackie sat curled up on the living-room sofa, sharing every gruesome detail of her husband's murder with a wide-eyed White.

By the end of the three-and-a-half-hour interview, Jackie had sown the seeds of a myth that would shadow Caroline and her brother for the rest of their lives. While they slept soundly, their mother drew a parallel between JFK's thousand days in office and the legendary kingdom immortalized in JFK's favorite musical, *Camelot*.

"There was never any question that Jackie knew *exactly* what she was doing," White later observed. "She wanted Jack to be viewed by future generations as a sort of storybook hero. But I'm not sure she considered what burdens that placed on JFK's children."

On the eve of their departure from the

White House, Jackie threw the promised joint birthday party for Caroline and John. There was a big cake with candles — six for Caroline and three for John — music, games, and presents. The guests of honor took turns ripping through the wrapping paper to get to their gifts. John's favorite was a model of Air Force One; Caroline's was yet another stuffed bear.

The next day, a White House limousine pulled up in front of then–Undersecretary of State Averell Harriman's seven-bedroom red-brick house on Georgetown's N Street, just a short walk from where the Kennedys once lived. Caroline stepped out, then her mother and brother. Uncle Bobby and Aunt Ethel were close behind, pursued by photographers. When Jackie bade Bobby and Ethel good-bye at the door a half hour later, flashbulbs popped. "We will stay here," Jackie told Caroline, "until we can find a house of our own. But it has to be just right for us."

In the meantime, Caroline got a crash course in French impressionism from her knowledgeable mother. Everywhere in the Harriman house there were breathtaking works by van Gogh, Monet, Manet, Cézanne, Toulouse-Lautrec, and Matisse. Caroline nodded appreciatively as Jackie skipped from one masterpiece to the next, and when it was all over she asked if she and her brother could go outside and play. Soon two Secret

Service agents were standing guard at a local park as Caroline and John bobbed up and down on teeter-totters.

The Secret Service would, in fact, continue to watch over JFK's young family. At that time, the law provided that Caroline, John, and their mother would receive protection for two years. The period was later extended to a presidential widow until remarriage or death, and to the children of ex-presidents until age sixteen.

They could not, however, protect Jackie and her children from the prying eyes of the public. Crowds of the curious formed on the street outside, and once again Jackie complained of feeling as if she were "on display, like some carnival freak." She also worried that Caroline was crumbling under the pressure.

To provide Caroline with some sense of continuity, Jackie insisted that her daughter be allowed to continue attending the White House school until Christmas break. "It would be cruel," Jackie said, "to yank her away from her teachers and all her little friends at the very moment she needs them most."

But to the teaching staff, it was obvious that Caroline was, understandably, suffering terribly. "Caroline looked ghastly," said her French teacher, Jacqueline Hirsh. "She was so pale and her concentration broken. She comprehended the assassination fully, absolutely. You could see that it was on her mind, that it was rough on her. But she never did complain, never."

To make matters worse, both Caroline and her brother came down with chickenpox and were confined to their beds. As was to be expected, Caroline followed Maud Shaw's directions to the letter. Her brother was another matter. "I used to go out of the room," Shaw said, "and wait outside his door, knowing full well what he was going to do. I would hear his little feet padding across the bedroom carpet, the door would open ever so slowly, then his head popped 'round the door, his face bright with mischief."

It was inevitable that the holiday season this year would be wreathed in melancholy. There would be no phone calls to the North Pole this Christmas — Daddy was no longer there to tell the White House switchboard operators to imitate Mrs. Claus. Instead Caroline wrote a letter to Santa asking for a Nancy Nurse doll. Jackie wanted the White House Christmas pageant to go on as usual, and Caroline showed up at the White House every day to rehearse her role as an angel. More often than not, Mommy, sometimes wearing riding clothes, dropped by to check on the pageant's progress. When it was held, everyone — the Auchinclosses, the Kennedys, and family friends — showed up and cheered and sang Christmas carols. But without her father, Caroline would later say, her childhood holidays would never be the same.

Just as they had done every other year, Jack's little family joined the rest of the Kennedys in Palm Beach for Christmas. While decorating the tree on Christmas Eve, Caroline suddenly turned to Jackie with a question about her father. "Will Patrick be looking after him in heaven?" she asked.

Jackie, taken off guard by the question, tried to think of a suitable answer, but before she could, John piped up with a query of his own. "Do they have fish chowder in heaven?" Everyone — Jackie, Joe, Rose, and the Kennedy uncles and aunts — laughed. Fish chowder was something of a Kennedy family obsession — and Jack was the biggest chowder fanatic of all.

Caroline, however, was failing to see the humor in much of anything. It was obvious to even the casual observer that she was no longer the carefree "Buttons" she had been. "She seemed to age before our eyes," recalled Joe Kennedy's private nurse, Rita Dallas. "Children seldom clench their fists, but her tiny hands were always knotted."

Her mother hoped that Caroline's mood would change after Christmas, when the family moved out of the Harriman mansion and into the fourteen-room town house Mommy had bought for $175,000 at 3017 N

Street. Jackie had wanted to make the transition to their new lives as easy as possible for the children. Toward that end, she showed decorator Billy Baldwin photographs of their rooms at the White House and asked him to re-create them down to the tiniest detail.

At first, the strategy seemed to work. Caroline beamed when she saw her room for the first time. "Look!" she said, running up to her canopied bed, then to her toy box. "Everything is just like it was!" Instinctively, she grabbed the stuffed giraffe her father had given her and hugged it. "Now we're really home."

But Jackie had not taken into account the basic floor plan of their new house and how it made it easier for the curious to literally peer in on their lives. Unlike the Harriman mansion, here all the rooms that faced the front — including the dining room, living room, and several bedrooms — were plainly visible from the street. "If Jackie felt like a prisoner before," said Jacques Lowe, "now she felt like a caged animal." To thwart the Peeping Toms, she kept the curtains drawn twenty-four hours a day.

Jackie told Baldwin that she found all the attention lavished on Caroline and John "very upsetting . . . the world is pouring terrible adoration at their feet, and I fear for them. How can I bring them up normally?"

It didn't help that Jackie herself was now

descending in a downward spiral of despair. To a friend, she confessed, "I'm a living wound. I'm dried up — I have nothing more to give, and some days I can't even get out of bed. I cry all day and all night until I'm so exhausted I can't function. Then I drink."

Millions of Americans, so impressed by the incredible strength she displayed during her husband's funeral, recognized the haunted look in her eyes when she appeared on television to thank the public for its support. She was seated in a leather club chair in Bobby's office at the Justice Department; still glued to his sister-in-law's side, he stood in the wings offering moral support.

"The knowledge of the affection in which my husband was held by all of you has sustained me," Jackie said in her trademark breathless whisper. "The warmth of these tributes is something I shall never forget," she said. "Whenever I can bear to read them . . . All his bright light gone from the world . . ." Once the cameras were turned off, Bobby looked around the room. Several crew members were clearing their throats and furtively wiping away tears with their sleeves.

Fortunately for John, his mother shielded him from the pain she was going through. Even as she sank deeper and deeper into depression, Jackie made certain that male members of Jack's inner circle — Dave Powers, Ben Bradlee, and Uncle Bobby chief among them — were always on hand to roughhouse with the slain President's three-year-old son. Consequently, he remained oblivious to Mommy's heartache.

Yet Caroline was all too aware of what was going on inside the house on N Street. Of all the Kennedy cousins, she had been the most introspective, sensitive, and perceptive. Sister Joanne Frey had spotted those traits early on. During a field trip to St. Joseph's Church in Washington, the nun pointed out a statue of St. Thomas More and asked Caroline and her classmates if anyone could identify him.

Caroline looked the statue over for a moment and said, "I don't know who the man is. But I know he probably lived hundreds of years ago and is wearing the robes of an Englishman in office."

Sister Joanne Frey was impressed that six-year-old Caroline was able to recognize a sixteenth-century cleric, but she was not surprised. "Her mother read to her a great deal," she said. "They were always skipping way ahead in the text. She was a very, very bright little girl."

That, Frey said, was Caroline's problem. "After her father died, she picked up on everything that was going on around her." Caroline was "very much attuned," the nun said, "to her mother's pain."

At home, that pain was impossible for her to miss. "You could be walking down the hall," said one Secret Service agent, "and hear Mrs. Kennedy weeping in her room." Maud Shaw remembered walking into the dining room with Caroline, only to see Jackie sitting with her head down on the table. "She looked up," Shaw said, "and tears were streaming down her face. Caroline pretended not to notice."

Other times, Caroline took it upon herself to comfort her mother. She would often sidle up to Jackie and give her a reassuring hug or climb into Mommy's bed and stroke her hair lovingly until, exhausted, they both fell asleep.

It was a heavy burden for a little girl to bear. During one catechism class in late January 1964, Sister Joanne was telling the story of Mary Magdalene when, without warning, Caroline blurted out, "My mommy cries all the time."

Sister Joanne paused for a moment, then picked up where she left off. "And so Mary Magdalene bathed the feet of Christ, and —"

"My mommy cries all the time," Caroline said again, unwilling to let it go. "My mommy cries *all the time*."

Again Sister Joanne tried to stick to the day's lesson. But when it became clear that Caroline needed to talk, the nun finally put her book down and listened to what the child had to say. The other children, all of whom had been instructed by their parents to be especially nice to Caroline, hung on every word.

"After my daddy died," Caroline explained, "my mommy is always crying. I go and get in bed with her and tell her everything is all right and tell her to stop crying. But she doesn't. My mommy is always crying. . . ."

What struck Sister Joanne was the fact that Caroline herself seemed calm, very much in control. "Caroline wasn't crying when she said this — she didn't even seem that emotional," Frey said. "She just had to tell somebody what was happening behind closed doors. It was a cry for help. Obviously the poor little girl didn't know what to do." For her part, Sister Joanne was "completely lost for words. What could I possibly say to her?"

Jackie and the children were spending one chilly weekend in early February at Hyannis Port when Joe's nurse, Rita Dallas, spotted Caroline strolling on the beach. She was alone — except for the presence of a Secret Service agent in the distance — and lost in thought. "Caroline stopped and sat down on the sand," Dallas observed, "and stared out over the water, and it was just so heartbreaking to see this little girl looking so lost."

Then Jackie materialized "out of nowhere," said Dallas, and joined Caroline. Suddenly there was a stiff wind blowing in off the Atlantic, and Jackie folded her arms around her daughter to fend off the cold.

That first year after the assassination, Jackie could scarcely hold herself together, much less prevent her kids from being hurt. But Rita Dallas pointed to that gray, drizzly day at the beach as an example of how, in the long run, Jackie would protect and nurture her children to adulthood. Jackie shielded Caroline "until the sharp pain had settled into a dull, eternal ache. She set an example for her, and as the years passed, the little girl was able to pick up the task of living."

As much as she mourned for her mother's loss, Caroline was feeling her own. Yet it was not in her nature to reveal too much of herself to anyone. "When she was small," Maud Shaw later said, "Caroline was capable of holding her feelings tight inside her — and it took careful coaxing to find out what was wrong."

Caroline was incapable of concealing her feelings entirely, however. During one family dinner, she pulled at one end of a wishbone and her teenage Aunt Janet held the other. "Can I wish for anything I want?"

"Anything," Aunt Janet said.

"I want," Caroline said firmly, "to see my daddy."

Every time I see her,
I want to go somewhere and cry.

— *Bobby Kennedy,*
on Caroline

She is vulnerable to hurt.

— *Maud Shaw,*
Caroline's nanny

The other girls keep telling me how
lucky I am to be Caroline Kennedy,
and they keep staring at me.
Isn't that silly? I'm just the same
as anyone else, aren't I?

— *Caroline,*
age ten

At nine years old,
she had memorized the entire
"Charge of the Light Brigade."
I was still trying to manage limericks.

— *John*

5

It is Lincoln's Birthday, 1964, and Sister Joanne has three pictures to show to her catechism class. Every time she holds one up, she asks her pupils to identify the president. The first is George Washington, followed by Abraham Lincoln. Then Sister Joanne holds up a portrait of JFK.

"Who can tell me who this is?" Sister Joanne asks. Sitting in the second row, Caroline, Frey will later remember, "was just *vibrant,* but she didn't say anything."

Then the other children begin shouting "That's Caroline's daddy! That's Caroline's daddy!" And Caroline "just sat there," said Sister Joanne, "beaming with pride."

Caroline was, by all accounts, becoming progressively less withdrawn. That St. Patrick's Day, Sister Joanne had just finished teaching another class when Caroline walked up to her and gestured toward a magazine on her desk with her father on the cover. She asked

Frey if she could take the periodical home. "My mommy saves every picture she can find of my daddy. She told me that whenever I see one, I should bring it to her. Then she puts them in these big books. I don't know why, but it makes her smile."

Later that day, Sister Joanne was driving home when she spotted Jackie in Washington's Rock Creek Park. Frey rolled down her window and called out to her. Jackie walked up to the car — there were no Secret Service agents in sight — and as she got closer, it was obvious to Sister Joanne that Caroline's mother had been crying.

"Caroline told me about the picture of my husband you showed in class," Jackie said. "I'm looking forward to seeing it."

As she drove away, Sister Joanne now had a better understanding of all that Caroline had been going through. "Seeing her mother so lost and confused, it must have been so terribly hard on Caroline," she said. That day at Rock Creek Park, Frey had been given a rare candid glimpse of "the *real* Mrs. Kennedy — alone, sad, completely devastated."

But "as sad as Jackie looked," Chuck Spalding said, "Bobby looked even worse." The one person who could understand the depth of her grief, Bobby devoted himself to his brother's widow and her children. Nearly every day, Jackie took her son and daughter to Hickory Hill to play with Bobby and

Ethel's tribe of eight. In the process, Uncle Bobby became a surrogate father to Caroline and John. "They think of Hickory Hill," Jackie said, "as their own home. . . . Bobby wants to look after his brother's children."

Not that she wanted her children to grow up like Bobby's. One evening, she returned home from a day with the Kennedys at Hyannis Port and flew into a rage. "She was fuming," said Secret Service Agent Bob Foster, "about how boisterous they all were. She said they were a pack of gorillas, and told John and Caroline that she expected them to behave with more self-restraint and less like animals in a zoo."

Bobby's desire to step into his big brother's shoes may have stemmed, at least in part, from his nagging suspicion that he may somehow have contributed to his brother's death. As attorney general, Bobby had decimated the ranks of organized crime, sending to jail many of the same underworld figures who had secretly supported his brother's presidential ambitions.

At the same time, the Mob, acting on instructions from the CIA and as a special favor to Jack, had made several ill-fated attempts on the life of Fidel Castro. According to Mob boss Johnny Rosselli, who was executed after telling his story to veteran Washington columnist Jack Anderson, Cuban dictator Fidel Castro hired mafioso Santo

Trafficante to take out a contract on the life of the President. Lyndon Johnson came to believe the conspiracy theory ("Kennedy tried to kill Castro, but Castro got him first," he told ABC's Howard K. Smith years later), and so did several Kennedys — Ted among them. But Jackie never questioned the findings of the Warren Commission or the commission's ultimate conclusion that Oswald acted alone. "What did it matter what they found out?" she asked. "They could never bring back the person who was gone."

Jackie's children would eventually have divergent views on the Lone Gunman Theory. In his thirties, John began looking into the evidence and became increasingly convinced that his father may have been the victim of a conspiracy. Caroline, like her mother, would spend her life looking the other way. "To dredge all that up, to relive all those painful moments, why on earth would she want to do that?" Jacques Lowe said. "Remember, John didn't have that clear picture in his mind of those days — the sheer horror, as well as the sadness — but Caroline certainly does. It could never be just an intellectual exercise for her."

In the immediate wake of her dad's murder, Caroline turned to the one male figure who most reminded her of him. Whenever she was at Hickory Hill, Caroline would cling to her uncle in much the same way she had to her father. "Bobby had always been Jack's pit bull," said a former Kennedy family employee. "He was the enforcer of the family, and he had plenty of enemies. Lyndon Johnson was just one of the many people who absolutely hated him. But at home with Caroline, Bobby was this warm and fuzzy guy. He did all the things with her that Jack did — toss her into the air, wrestle with her on the floor. She'd sit for hours in his lap. They really loved each other."

The arrangement had Jackie's blessing. If there were any Father's Day activities at school, Bobby showed up for Caroline. She, in turn, showed her report cards to Uncle Bobby. Her artwork during this period was invariably inscribed "To Uncle Bobby" and brought to him for his approval. He referred to Caroline as "my pal," but he could not bring himself to call her "Buttons."

"Let's face it," Kennedy friend Chuck Spalding said, "Bobby was in every way the logical choice to be a surrogate father for Jack's kids. To Caroline, it must have been very comforting to have him around reminding her of her father — the way he sounded, the body language, the hair, those teeth!"

There was never any question in Jackie's mind that only Bobby could replace Jack in her children's lives. Early that spring of 1964, she asked him to legally adopt them — a move that would have given Bobby and Jackie equal status as the children's guardians. Ethel, never a great fan of her famous sister-in-law, vetoed the idea.

Caroline was also aware of how much her mother relied on Uncle Bobby and how her mood brightened whenever he was around. That March, Caroline and John accompanied their mother on a ski holiday in Stowe, Vermont. There they were joined by Uncle Bobby, Uncle Teddy, and their families. When the press surged toward Jackie, Caroline was shoved to the ground. "How," Jackie later asked, "do you explain *that* to a child?"

From Stowe, Jackie and Bobby left — sans Ethel — to spend a week with Lee and Stas Radziwill in Antigua. Before long, rumors were rampant that the special bond between Caroline's mother and her beloved uncle was developing into something more than friendship. "She relied on him for everything, and he adored her," Spalding said. "There was definitely an intimacy there."

But it was not enough to overcome the fact that Jackie felt that her life, or what remained of it, was no longer her own. The crowd outside her Georgetown home seemed to grow bigger and more aggressive with each passing day.

Jackie fled this atmosphere whenever she could, taking Caroline and John with her. On May 29, 1964 — what would have been

Jack's forty-seventh birthday — Caroline placed flowers on her father's grave and then knelt beside her mother and prayed. A mob of tourists, held back by police barricades, took pictures and called out their names. It was the beginning of what would become an annual ritual. "She would take the children to the grave on the anniversary of the President's birthday," Tish Baldrige said. "Not his death, his birthday. She believed in celebrating life, not death."

Following a mass at St. Matthew's Cathedral — the site of her father's funeral — Caroline flew north with her mother and brother to Hyannis Port. "Caroline looked so sad whenever she got here," said their neighbor Larry Newman. "Then her little face just lit up when she saw her grandparents and her cousins."

Short excursions aside, Lee Radziwill was determined to once and for all tear her sister away from the circus atmosphere that prevailed in Washington — and all the painful memories of her days as First Lady. She lobbied to have Jackie move to New York, whose infinitely more blasé inhabitants were more likely to let her live her life in relative peace. Lee even took the first major step by buying an eleven-room co-op of her own at 969 Fifth Avenue, only a few blocks away from Steven and Jean Kennedy Smith and Pat and Peter Lawford, as well as several Auchincloss and Bouvier relatives.

After several apartment-hunting trips, Jackie plunked down $200,000 for a five-bedroom, five-bath, fifteenth-floor apartment at 1040 Fifth Avenue. Camping out at the nearby Carlyle Hotel alone — Caroline and John remained in the care of Maud Shaw back in Georgetown — Jackie then spent several months and $125,000 renovating the place.

On June 19, 1964, Caroline was at home in Georgetown when her mother got the call that tragedy had struck the Kennedys once again. Ted had insisted on flying to Springfield, Massachusetts, in a storm to accept his party's nomination for a second Senate term. Jackie sank into her chair as Bobby told her that Ted's small plane had crashed, killing the pilot and Ted's aide. Ted had survived with a broken back.

Jackie reassured Caroline that her uncle would be fine, but it was impossible to conceal her own fear and despair from her intuitive daughter. "Just as things seemed to be getting back to normal," Pierre Salinger said, "they had the rug pulled out from under them. A child becomes fearful when bad things keep happening for no apparent reason."

Fortunately, Jackie was now able to reassure Caroline that Uncle Bobby would continue to be close at hand after they moved to

New York. Jack's younger brother intended to run for the Senate from that state if Lyndon Johnson failed to pick him as his running mate in 1964.

One week after Teddy's plane crash, Bobby posed for the cover of *Life* with a half dozen little Kennedys crawling all over him. Everyone appeared to be overjoyed, with the notable exception of Caroline, who perched on Uncle Bobby's lap with a forlorn expression on her freckled face.

That September, Jackie, Caroline, and John made the move to New York — but not before Jackie, determined to start fresh, axed two key members of her entourage. She told her longtime secretary, Mary Gallagher, "Well, since my life is all changed . . . I guess I really won't be needing you anymore."

The other dismissal would be harder on Caroline. She had grown particularly attached to one of the Secret Service agents assigned to guard the family — so attached that Jackie began to worry that Caroline might prefer him over Uncle Bobby. Reluctantly, Jackie asked that the agent be reassigned — and gave him their Welsh terrier Charlie as a token of their affection.

Jackie viewed her return to New York as a homecoming and was eager to introduce Caroline and John to the delights of the city where she grew up. For the time being, however, they remained at the Carlyle while the finishing touches were being put on the Fifth Avenue apartment.

The Carlyle was familiar territory to Jackie. Jack, who maintained a sprawling suite there for years, came to consider the place his home away from the White House — so much so that he had a special bow window constructed to accommodate a breakfast nook. This distinctive architectural figure — the only one of its kind at the Carlyle — juts out of the building's north side.

Jack was fond of the Carlyle for other reasons that were not known to his young widow at the time. Beneath the hotel was a labyrinth of tunnels that enabled the President to walk undetected to the nearby town houses of some of New York's wealthiest and most beautiful women.

Although she and the children had yet to move into their new apartment, Jackie was eager for Caroline and John to start their new lives in New York. On September 15, Jackie and Pat Kennedy Lawford walked Caroline and Pat's daughters, Sydney and Victoria, to their first day of school. All three Kennedy girls were enrolled at the exclusive Convent of the Sacred Heart. The school, which Caroline's grandmother Rose had attended more than a half century earlier, was situated at Ninety-first Street, just a few blocks up Fifth Avenue from their new apartment. Sydney Lawford, who was a year older, grew especially close to Caroline. They were, Maud Shaw said, "more like sisters than cousins." (John would not be enrolled at St. David's, another elite private school in the neighborhood, until the following February.)

After school, Caroline changed out of her white-collared uniform — Sacred Heart students were also required to wear white gloves — and into a summer dress for a family outing in Central Park. At one point the former First Lady, somewhat incongruously attired in a double-breasted white wool suit, climbed into a boat with her children and proceeded to row them around the lake. All the while, their fellow New Yorkers pretended not to notice.

It was not until mid-November — two weeks after Bobby vanquished incumbent New York Senator Kenneth Keating at the polls — that Caroline, her brother, and their mother finally moved into their new home. "It was Jackie's haven, her refuge," said Tish Baldrige. "And a magical place for any child to call home."

The apartment at 1040 Fifth would be the epicenter of Caroline's world for the next two decades, and it would remain largely unchanged during all that time. To ease the transition for the children, Jackie filled their new home with furnishings from their family quarters at the White House.

The minute the private elevator opened onto the apartment's long, mirrored entrance hall, Caroline recognized the marble torso of a Roman god displayed on a table between two yellow porcelain jardinieres. The marble torso, along with a half dozen ancient busts scattered about the living room, were part of the antiquities collection started by Caroline's father.

As Jackie led her children through the apartment for the first time, Caroline pointed to the drawings, paintings, and furniture that had decorated their Georgetown house and, before that, the White House. There were Louis XVI chairs and white sofas in the living room, along with John Singer Sargent's *Venetian Girl* displayed on an easel.

Jackie was proudest of the red-walled dining room, with its marble fireplace, bookcases, inviting overstuffed couches, and black baby-grand piano. Whenever visitors came to 1040 Fifth, Caroline took it upon herself to escort them to the dining room and point out a world map covered with colored pins. "My daddy went to all those places when he was president," she would tell them. "That's a lot of places." Like everyone else who set foot in the apartment, Caroline was most captivated by the view of Central Park and the reservoir, and the ships plying the Hudson River in the distance.

Although she and her mother had collected

hundreds of pictures of her father over the past ten months, Caroline noticed that her father's image was nowhere to be found here. The exception: a single silver-framed photograph on the dresser of Jackie's green-and-white corner bedroom. From here, Caroline would later be able to look down on another reminder of her father: the Metropolitan Museum's glass-enclosed Temple of Dendur, which Jackie would choose when Egypt offered to give one of its ancient ruins to the United States in memory of JFK.

Caroline's watercolors and drawings, along with John's finger paintings and doodles, were also proudly displayed — along with family snapshots on a bulletin board in the kitchen. "It was obviously," said one early visitor, "nothing even approaching what you could call an average American home. But when you walked into the kitchen and saw the photographs and Caroline's art so proudly displayed, you realized maybe they weren't so different after all."

For Caroline, the transition to life in New York was difficult. Although Miss Shaw was still a reassuring presence, she missed the friends she had made at the White House school. She also found it hard to make new ones in New York. When several fellow Sacred Heart second-graders failed to invite Caroline to their birthday parties, Jackie phoned one of the mothers and asked if there was some reason the late President's only daughter had been excluded.

Once she managed to catch her breath, the woman explained, "*Of course* we'd love to invite Caroline, but we all felt it might be presumptuous of us to ask."

"Oh, no!" Jackie said. "She's just a little girl. Please invite Caroline to everything! She's dying to come!" Within days, Caroline raced home with invitations to several parties and play dates. She was most excited by the chance to spend the night at the home of one of her new friends — a chance to at last have that first sleepover that had been so long delayed since the day of her father's assassination. Caroline would not be like any other guest, however. For security purposes, a Secret Service agent would be stationed in the hall outside the host's apartment.

Jackie was surprisingly open when it came to inviting other children into her home. "Quite often," Maud Shaw recalled, "we invited children we met in the park home to the Fifth Avenue apartment for dinner. Mrs. Kennedy was very good about that. I always used to ask her beforehand, of course, but her reply was always the same. 'Certainly they can come,' she would say. 'I leave it to you. I like the children to have new friends. It's good for them.'"

Kathy Bouvier was not surprised that her

cousin would invite virtual strangers for dinner, if that was what made her daughter happy. "She had a desire," Bouvier said, "that Caroline be brought up in a healthy and positive way."

In addition to her newfound popularity at school, Caroline reveled in the fact that she and her family could walk the streets without being harassed. Jackie and her children "couldn't go anywhere in Washington without being mobbed," said her friend Truman Capote. But New Yorkers, he added, ignored Jackie, Caroline, and John "the way they ignore everyone else."

No one was more pleased than Jackie with the obvious improvement in Caroline's state of mind. At a weekend party in Westchester a few months earlier, Jackie had confided to Kitty Carlisle Hart that she worried about her children and what impact losing their father at such an early age might have. "I had lost my husband [playwright Moss Hart] only a year earlier, and I know how it feels to suddenly be left alone with young children," Hart said. "There was kinship between us. I could sympathize. I harbored many of the same fears and anxieties she did about whether our children would be emotionally scarred — and what we could do about it." At the time, it quickly became clear that Jackie was far from being past the shock of her husband's murder, going over the grisly details "over and over and over again. . . . She was a woman possessed."

More than anything, Caroline's mood was tethered to that of her mother. Jackie was no longer crying herself to sleep, and for the first time in months, she could get through an entire day without mentioning Daddy's name. "The black cloud had lifted," Pierre Salinger said, "so they could start to get on with their lives." Mommy still spent several hours a day sorting through thousands of letters from friends and strangers alike offering words of condolence. But she also set aside time to take Caroline and John to the Central Park carousel, to the World's Fair (where Caroline proudly showed off two missing front teeth to reporters), to the circus, and to their favorite hangout, Serendipity off Third Avenue, for butterscotch sundaes.

Caroline was not prepared, however, for the outpouring of grief that would surround the first anniversary of her father's death, or how that would send Mommy into an emotional tailspin. Wherever she went, Caroline saw black-bordered photographs of her father in store windows, on the sides of buses, at newsstands, and on television. She realized that the ubiquitous reminders would be too much for her mother; soon Mommy was crying herself to sleep again.

Jackie became so depressed during the weeks leading up to November 22, 1964, she now confessed to former deputy defense secretary and longtime friend Roswell Gilpatric that she even considered taking her own life. "I have enough sleeping pills to do it," she told him. Gilpatric knew it was an empty threat. "Of course she wouldn't," he said, "because of the children."

When the anniversary finally did arrive, Jackie took Caroline and John to a playground in Central Park. Then, while Secret Service agents watched over her children, Jackie found an out-of-the-way bench. There, she later told a friend, she spent the afternoon "crying my eyes out."

"Everyone who loved her was very much concerned," said Gilpatric, who took turns with other friends inviting her out. These dinner parties, which invariably took place in town houses or Upper East Side apartments, were always limited to two or three couples — "never more than that," said frequent escort George Plimpton, a friend since her days as a debutante. According to Plimpton, Jackie — whatever the depths of her own despair — made a "valiant" effort to maintain a cheerful facade for Caroline and John.

"She was absolutely devoted to her children," Plimpton said, "and even with all that had happened, she made sure they had a happy life. I always adored Caroline. She was really a very, very special person. Whenever I could, I'd drop in to read her a bedtime story. When I was a boy, I loved *Treasure Island*, but when I read it to her, she'd be out by the time I got to the second page."

Now that Uncle Bobby was ensconced in New York as that state's newly elected senator, Caroline saw him even more frequently than she had in Washington. Moreover, at the age of seven, she may well have recognized that her mother and her uncle now enjoyed an especially warm and tender relationship, not unlike the love between her mother and father.

Although Jackie had dated other men since the assassination — including Gilpatric and Marlon Brando, with whom she had a brief affair in January 1964 — her only significant relationship was with Bobby. A favorite meeting place was the bar of the Sherry-Netherland Hotel, where Peter Lawford and journalist Taki Theodoracopulos shared an apartment. "Lawford was telling me at the time," Taki said, "that Jackie was sleeping with Bobby."

Jackie leased a house near Bobby's summer rental in Glen Cove, Long Island. There, according to Bruce Balding, who owned the stable where Jackie kept her horses, "many people often saw Jackie and Bobby off by themselves, heads together, or looking fondly at each other in various hotels in the area, so they got the idea."

Caroline got the idea as well. "Caroline

would come to the stable with her mother, and Bobby would be there," said another Glen Cove horse owner. "Jackie seemed very affectionate with him, and Caroline seemed perfectly happy with that."

By Christmas, 1964, Jackie, with Uncle Bobby's help, had somehow managed to bounce back. The next day, Jackie hustled Caroline and her brother off for a ski vacation in Aspen, again with Uncle Bobby. There were two more ski trips in early 1965 — to the Catskills and then to New Hampshire — with Caroline and John throwing snowballs at each other and struggling to make it down the bunny slope while photographers gleefully captured it all on film.

Caroline, like most of her Kennedy cousins, was already proving to be something of a natural athlete. While her mother watched from the sidelines, Caroline took the inevitable spills without complaint. "John whined quite a bit back then," said a family friend, "but never Caroline. She was always the little trouper of the family."

Caroline made her first trip abroad in May 1965, when she accompanied her mother and John on a trip to Runnymede, the meadow beside the Thames where the Magna Carta was signed in 1215. On this spot, Queen Elizabeth was to dedicate Great Britain's memorial to JFK in the presence of the martyred President's young family.

Caroline had been carefully instructed by Maud Shaw on the proper way to curtsy when she was introduced to the queen. With uncles Bobby and Teddy looking on proudly, Jack's daughter executed the move flawlessly. Seated between Jackie and her mother during the long ceremony, however, the little girl struggled in vain to stifle a yawn. After tea with the queen at Windsor Castle, Maud Shaw was just happy that both children had managed to get through the afternoon "without spilling tea on Her Majesty or otherwise causing an international incident."

Their royal obligations out of the way, Caroline and John moved into Aunt Lee's house in Regents Park and spent the next few days behaving like any other tourists. They had their pictures taken with the unblinking cavalrymen at Whitehall and watched the changing of the guard at Buckingham Palace. At the Tower of London, a bemused Caroline held an executioner's ax. But after John climbed into the barrel of an ancient cannon, Caroline took one look inside and shook her head in disgust. "A bit dirty," she said, pointing to several centuries of accumulated grime. Before they left England, Caroline and John posed for the artist Cecil Beaton. Jackie was impressed with how much John resembled his father as a boy and how Beaton managed to convey the ineffable sadness in Caroline's huge blue eyes.

Nanny Shaw was, of course, always around to hold the children's hands as they crossed the street, watch over them as they played, and make sure they were properly taken care of. She had been as much a mother to Caroline as Jackie had — and that is why Jackie abruptly fired her. Caroline was told that Miss Shaw would not be accompanying the family back to the United States because she wanted to spend some time in England with relatives. In truth, Jackie believed that Caroline had grown too close to Nanny Shaw, and because of that she was being let go after seven years of service with the Kennedys.

Shaw was crushed. "I loved Caroline very dearly, and I loved her for a very, very long time," she said. "When I came home [to England], I wept a great deal because I felt that the way her mother lived, Caroline would not get the security I gave her."

Returning to New York, Caroline watched as her mother plunged headlong into the city's frenzied social whirl. Only months before, she'd spent most nights sobbing in her room. Now life for Jackie was an unremitting series of parties, balls, concerts, and benefits. Night after night, before she was tucked into bed, Caroline would peek in on Mommy to see what she was wearing. On one occasion, *Addams Family* creator Charles Addams sat in the living room waiting to escort Jackie to a fund-raiser when Caroline came out to say hello. "Then her mother walked in, and, as usual, she was just dazzling," Addams said. "She was wearing this very sleek white dress, with a diamond necklace and matching earrings. Just spectacular."

The urbane, normally sardonic Addams told Jackie she looked like a queen. "I've seen a queen," Caroline chimed in, "and my mommy looks better. *Lots.*"

The second anniversary of the assassination hit Mommy again, though this time she seemed to recover more quickly. One evening, Jackie kissed Caroline good night and disappeared. When Truman Capote returned home to his UN Plaza apartment that night, he found Jackie, who had been let in by an understandably awestruck doorman, sitting there alone. The two sat in his living room and talked until sunup.

Now that she fluttered from one glittering social event to another, Jackie's face was back in the papers — and the public appetite for gossip about her was more insatiable than ever. Reporters sifted through her garbage, and photographers crouched behind parked cars at 1040 Fifth to score a photo of the kids as they left for school.

Jackie responded by cracking down on the people who worked for her. On pain of immediate dismissal, no one was to reveal even the most inconsequential details of Jackie's life — and she felt even more strongly about anyone who uttered a word about Caroline and John. No one was to know who Caroline's friends were, what toys and games she liked best, what foods she preferred, or her tastes in music, films, and television.

In her zeal to protect her children's privacy, Jackie inadvertently chipped away at what little sense of continuity and security they possessed in their daily lives. Secret Service agents were replaced on a more frequent basis than they had been so that Caroline would not become too attached. Every week, Caroline saw a different limousine driver behind the wheel; Jackie also had them rotated on a regular basis so that none would be too knowledgeable about the family's schedule. In addition, the drivers were told not to speak to Caroline — or anyone in the family, for that matter — unless spoken to.

Caroline was fond of her new piano teacher, but the woman mentioned her job in passing to a man who turned out to be a reporter. The piano teacher was fired the next morning. After school each day, Caroline liked to amble into the kitchen to chat with the cook. But when the cook made the mistake of mentioning to a reporter friend that her boss had dieted away twenty-five pounds, she was summarily sacked. The young chef who replaced her, Annemarie Huste, announced her plans to write a cookbook —

and within hours was told to pack up and leave. When it came to writing books, even the children's now-departed surrogate mom was not exempt from the wrath of Jackie. When she learned that Maud Shaw was writing her memoirs, Jackie threatened to sue unless she was given approval of the final manuscript — which she was.

To be sure, a few familiar faces remained — most notably Tuckerman and Providencia "Provi" Paredes, who had been Jackie's maid since 1955. But Mommy's frenetic social schedule and her distrust of those around her contributed to Caroline's growing sense of anxiety. "I've never known anyone," said Uncle Jamie, "who cut people off with such ease. The phrase 'out of sight, out of mind' was invented for Jackie." Caroline had already lost her father. "The way her mother dispensed with people, Caroline must have found it all bewildering — and more than a little scary."

Jackie had her own methods for coping with stress. One of the most effective involved jumping onto a horse and taking off into an open field. Jackie replaced her weekend retreat on Long Island with a leased farmhouse in Bernardsville, New Jersey, so she could ride with the exclusive Essex Hounds Fox Club. Following her mother's fearless example, Caroline learned to jump hedges and fences on the way to becoming an accomplished rider in her own right.

Like everyone else, Caroline was amazed at her mother's energy — though she had no way of knowing that it was being fueled to some extent by the amphetamines still routinely supplied by Max Jacobson. Certainly the pace Jackie maintained — and that her children were forced to keep up with — was daunting.

In addition to the weekends spent riding in New Jersey that winter of 1965, there were trips to Antigua — where Caroline snorkeled in the clear waters of the Caribbean — as well as more ski outings to Sun Valley, Stowe, and Gstaad in Switzerland. On their return, Jackie and the kids stopped off in Rome for an audience with Pope Paul VI, then swooped down to Argentina. Jackie, thrilled that her daughter shared her passion for horses, took the opportunity to introduce Caroline to some bona fide *caballeros*.

Even when Jackie did not take her children along on her adventures, Caroline followed her mother's progress in the papers. Traveling to Spain in May 1966 for Seville's famous *feria*, Mommy was photographed wearing a *peineta*, or high comb, and a white lace mantilla as she rode in a carriage through Seville. The next day, she was sidestepping through the streets of the city on a white stallion. When she attended the bullfights, all three matadors ignored Princess Grace of Monaco, who sat nearby, and offered their first kill to Jackie. Back in New York, Caroline rushed home from school waving a copy of the new *Life*. Mommy — astride her stallion in leather chaps, ruffled shirt, and crimson jacket — graced the cover. Caroline's priorities were obvious. "I wonder," she asked one of the Secret Service agents, "whose horse that is."

Once home in the United States, Jackie kept a longstanding promise to Caroline. On May 28, mother and daughter teamed up to compete in the annual horse show in New Vernon, New Jersey, not far from their weekend home. They took second place.

It was only a matter of weeks before the family embarked on yet another adventure — this time with Uncle Peter Lawford and his children for a seven-week sojourn in Hawaii. Caroline and John stayed with their mother at a beachfront house near the base of Diamond Head, while the Lawfords were encamped not far away at the Kahala Hilton.

Caroline and John hooked up with three local boys and, with Jackie's blessing, found out firsthand what their Hawaiian counterparts did for fun. They went careering down mud slides, clambered over the rocks at the foot of Sacred Falls, and explored tide pools. At one point, Caroline, who proved to be just as intrepid as the boys, cut her feet badly on coral and had to be bandaged.

But it was John who, during an overnight trip to the big island of Hawaii, came closest to real disaster. "Be careful, John," Caroline warned her brother as he ran around the cooking pit that was being readied for a traditional luau. "You're getting too close. . . ." Then she screamed as he fell in. Before Secret Service Agent John Walsh could retrieve John from the fire, his arms, hands, and buttocks were badly burned. He was rushed to a nearby hospital, treated, and released after a few hours. "Are you all right, John?" Caroline asked him. Once he assured her that he was, Big Sister shook her head and said sternly, "You've really got to be more careful."

That July, Caroline was a flower girl at the wedding of her aunt, Janet Auchincloss, in Newport. It had been just thirteen years since throngs of well-wishers jammed the streets to see the rising star in the Democratic Party and his stunning young bride. Now the crowds were back — only this time to see the thirty-seven-year-old widow, named the world's most admired woman for the sixth year in a row. The bride, shoved aside by photographers jockeying to grab a shot of Jackie, cried into a handkerchief supplied by a sympathetic Lee Radziwill.

Caroline, her head ringed in flowers and clutching a bouquet, was surrounded by photographers as the wedding party tried to make its way from the church to several waiting limousines. While her brother scowled, Caroline fought back tears as they pressed in so tightly that the door to their car could not be opened to let them in. "She was clearly frightened," said one of the reporters assigned to cover the event, "and she had this pitiful, dazed 'why can't you leave us alone?' look on her face. At one point she stumbled, and somebody had to reach down and pull her up before she was trampled. A lot of us felt sorry for the kids and tried to pull everybody back so they could breathe."

Few people were as equipped as Caroline to cope with the demands of fame. Ever since she could print her name, Caroline was asked whenever she ventured out in public to sign autographs or pose for pictures. But her mother worried that such adulation carried with it too high a price — and too many risks.

Indeed. One Sunday, Jackie and Caroline held hands as they left their favorite neighborhood church, St. Thomas More on East Eighty-ninth Street. As they headed west toward Fifth Avenue, a woman lunged at Caroline and grabbed her. "Your mother is a wicked woman who has killed three people," the woman screamed. "And your father is still alive!"

At first Caroline struggled in vain to free

herself. After a few tense moments, Jackie and a Secret Service agent managed to pull the woman off, and she was carted away to Bellevue for observation. A year later, Jackie relived the terrifying moment for a friend. "It was terrible, prying her loose," Jackie said. "I still haven't gotten over that strange woman."

As always, the person Mommy turned to most often for comfort and reassurance was Uncle Bobby. Caroline's favorite times were still spent in the company of the man who most reminded her of her father. In May 1967, Bobby took Caroline on yet another adventure — this time a canoeing trip in upstate New York. She shared a tent with her cousins Kerry and Courtney Kennedy, then donned a hooded slicker and life preserver before paddling her way down North Creek.

Whenever Jackie worried that Caroline was becoming "too withdrawn," she relied on Bobby to raise the little girl's spirits — and her self-confidence. "We all owe so much to Bobby," she said. "I'd jump out a window for him."

Jackie had more than the usual cause for concern in early 1967, as she waged a legal battle to stop William Manchester from publishing his book *The Death of a President*. She had cooperated with the author initially, but now Jackie feared that many of the book's shocking, sometimes graphic details of the assassination and its aftermath would be deeply upsetting to the children — particularly Caroline.

The brouhaha between Jackie and Manchester dominated the news for weeks, and the impact on Caroline was predictable. "Jackie made a point of not talking about things like that with her kids," Salinger said. "But of course Caroline saw all the headlines and overheard everybody else talking about it. She was always a sharp cookie, and she knew when the buzz was about her family. It bothered her, absolutely. Would anyone want to have the details of their father's murder dredged up all over again?"

In her own quiet way, Caroline made the most of the front-page donnybrook. As she had done nearly every day since her father's funeral, Caroline cut out whatever photos of her father she came across. By this time, the walls of her bedroom were literally papered with images of JFK.

In May 1967, Jackie, determined to lift Caroline out of the doldrums, bestowed a singular honor on the nine-year-old. At Newport News, Virginia, President Lyndon Johnson craned his neck to watch, John squirmed, and Mommy applauded as Caroline smashed a champagne bottle across the bow of the aircraft carrier *John F. Kennedy*.

Already Caroline was seen as following in

her mother's footsteps as a trendsetter. Running a picture of Caroline at the carrier christening in her tight-waisted dress, *Women's Wear Daily* predicted that it heralded "the beginning of the end of the A-line."

Jackie saw the christening as a turning point in Caroline's life. "Caroline is old enough now to begin taking on the responsibilities of a young lady in her position," Jackie said. "As she grows up, the public will expect more from her. I realized that when she christened the ship, this was the beginning of a new kind of life for her that she'd have to learn about."

Not long after, Jackie threw a party but neglected to mention who or what it was for. As the guests arrived, they realized they all had one thing in common — they had young children, and they had all been asked to bring them. Those who showed up at the door of 1040 Fifth Avenue without a child were turned away.

It soon became apparent that Caroline, resplendent in a pink chiffon party dress with lace sleeves and a Peter Pan collar, was the star of the afternoon. "This party is sort of a farewell to part of her childhood," Jackie explained, "and a welcome into the world of a more grown-up young lady."

At one point during the affair, Jackie brought one of the parents, a State Department official, into the dining room where

Caroline was eating cake and talking to her friends. "You're a very charming little lady," the man said.

"Thank you," Caroline replied. "I hope you're having a good time tonight. I know my father would have wanted me to be a good hostess."

The man looked over at Jackie, but she was unexpectedly overcome with emotion and exited the room in tears. "She's so grown up already and so brave," she later said. "I'm glad she hasn't forgotten him. . . ."

Just a few weeks later, in mid-June 1967, Caroline and John went along with their mother on their first trip to Ireland. When they dropped in at Woodstown Beach in Waterford, dozens of reporters and photographers spilled out of two buses and hovered around the children. While John built sand castles, Caroline cavorted with several local children in the chilly waters of Waterford Harbor.

Unbeknownst to Caroline, she and her brother almost became orphans when Jackie went swimming alone a few days later, got caught in the undertow, and was nearly swept out to sea. John Walsh, the same Secret Service agent who had pulled John from the luau pit in Hawaii, would come to her rescue at the last minute. Although Walsh was particularly close to Caroline, Jackie — who recommended that he be cited for valor —

asked that Walsh not mention the harrowing incident to her daughter.

Caroline settled back into her school routine, as did John, now a second-grader at St. David's, a Roman Catholic school for boys on Manhattan's East Sixty-ninth Street. In contrast to her brother, Caroline took her schoolwork seriously — perhaps too seriously, her mother sometimes worried — and was a particular favorite of the nuns at Sacred Heart.

Jackie was proud of Caroline's academic accomplishments, but she also made it clear that she didn't want her children to be "just two kids living on Fifth Avenue and going to nice schools." From Uncle Bobby, in particular, they learned about the dark side of life in the city — about conditions in parts of Harlem and the South Bronx, where children their age endured winters without heat and Christmases without presents.

No sooner was she told about the plight of New York's poor children than Caroline devised a plan to do something for them. With her brother's full cooperation, she rounded up some of their best toys — and simply gave them away.

Jackie, too, was interested in exploring life outside the rarefied confines of her Fifth Avenue apartment. Leaving the children in the care of their new governess, Marta Sgubin, Jackie jetted off on excursions to Cambodia and Mexico that — at least in terms of the phenomenal press coverage — rivaled her days as America's most peripatetic First Lady. Caroline followed her mother's progress in the papers as Jackie globe-hopped from the fabled ruins of Angkor Wat to the Mayan pyramids on Mexico's Yucatán Peninsula.

Still too young at age ten to comprehend what all the fuss was about, Caroline also came across articles linking Mommy to several men — most notably Roswell Gilpatric and former British ambassador to the United States Lord Harlech. The one man who really was actively pursuing her mother with some success — bombarding her with letters and middle-of-the-night phone calls — was never mentioned in the papers as a serious love interest for the widow of the slain President. His name was Aristotle Onassis.

Bobby regarded Onassis as "a complete rogue on the grand scale," and rightly so. Through a series of highly questionable business deals, Onassis had parlayed an initial stake of sixty dollars into a half-billion-dollar shipping empire. Along the way, he romanced some of the world's most fascinating women, including Evita Perón, Paulette Goddard, and Joe Kennedy's longtime mistress, Gloria Swanson.

At age forty-six, Onassis had married Athina "Tina" Livanos, the seventeen-year-old daughter of Greek shipping magnate Stavros Livanos. That marriage came to an abrupt end eleven years later, when Tina caught her husband and the legendary opera singer Maria Callas in flagrante delicto aboard the *Christina*.

The flamboyantly temperamental diva — her wild-eyed tantrums were the stuff of opera legend — and the ruthless tycoon Onassis were a perfect match. Both had started at the bottom and, by sheer force of will and against seemingly insurmountable odds, somehow managed to claw their way to the summit of their respective fields. "They were exquisitely suited to one another," said Aileen Mehle, a close friend of both Onassis and Callas. "There was always this electricity between them — this spark." Whenever they were together, Mehle said, they spoke conspiratorially in Greek.

Callas would have become Mrs. Onassis as early as 1960, if it were not for the opposition of Ari's children by his first marriage. Alexander Onassis, twelve, and ten-year-old Christina made it known to their father and anyone else who would listen how they felt about Callas — "they hated her," said Ari's aide Johnny Meyer.

Now Ari ("Aristo" to his closest friends) had set his sights on the most famous woman in the world — and he saw as his chief rival Caroline's Uncle Bobby. "Onassis knew that he could never compete with Bobby as a father figure," Gilpatric observed. But once the senator from New York announced that he intended to run for president — an all-consuming process that meant Uncle Bobby would no longer be available to play the same role in the lives of Caroline and John — Onassis saw a clear path ahead.

Jackie was clambering over the ruins at Chichén Itzá with Ros Gilpatric when she learned that Bobby would run for president. Then Lyndon Johnson shocked his party and the world by declaring that he would not seek reelection.

There was no question in Jackie's mind that Bobby could win back the White House for the Kennedys, but at a terrible price. "Do you know what will happen to Bobby?" she later asked Arthur Schlesinger Jr. "The same thing that happened to Jack."

Caroline shared her mother's concern. After Dallas, Jackie had tried to reassure her daughter that more people loved the Kennedys than hated them. But Bobby had more than his share of enemies. This time, whenever Caroline asked her mother if she was worried about Uncle Bobby, Jackie promptly changed the subject.

Uncle Bobby was distressed, not by Jackie's dire warnings but by the possibility that she might actually marry "The Greek," as he disdainfully referred to Onassis. "For God's sake, Jackie," he pleaded, "this could cost me five states." Advised by Cardinal Cushing that it would probably not be wise to marry a divorced man twenty-nine years her senior, Jackie reluctantly agreed to put off making a decision — but only until after the election.

Caroline was at her desk at Sacred Heart on April 4, 1968, when one of the nuns came into class and whispered the horrible news in her teacher's ear: Martin Luther King had been shot to death outside his Memphis motel room. Caroline had met the civil-rights leader when she lived in the White House, and now Mommy was again trying to explain to her daughter why someone would want to murder a good man.

At first, Jackie only wanted to pay a private visit to King's widow at some future date; she felt she had mourned enough to last a lifetime. But Bobby, knowing full well the symbolic importance of having JFK's widow grieve alongside King's widow, urged her to attend the funeral in Atlanta.

Bloody riots swept the country in the wake of King's assassination and, coupled with the national division over the Vietnam War, gave the impression of a world spiraling out of control. Jackie did not want her children — Caroline in particular — to be overwhelmed by events. Marriage to a rich and powerful man, Jackie reasoned, would provide them with the financial, emotional, and physical security Jack Kennedy's children deserved.

Before she decided whether or not she would wed Onassis, Jackie wanted to give Caroline and John a chance to get to know him. That Easter, Onassis flew them to Palm Beach aboard his private jet. John warmed instantly to the genial, approachable Ari, who made a point of spending time with the children — and showering them with gifts.

A few weeks later, she left the children in New York and headed off with Ari aboard the *Christina* for a four-day cruise of the Caribbean. Caroline had already begun making inquiries about Mr. Onassis — Jackie gave strict orders that they were never to address adults by their first name, even though Ari had requested them to — asking point-blank if Jackie intended to marry him. Caroline had read that Mr. Onassis was already in love with someone else — a great opera singer named Maria Callas. What would she think? With this image of the jealous prima donna fresh in her mind, Jackie could scarcely enjoy her sojourn aboard the *Christina*; emotionally overwrought, she spent much of the cruise in her cabin trying to survive a violent bout of seasickness.

As she weighed the pros and cons of giving her children a Greek stepfather, Jackie could not overlook the fact that Onassis ranked only behind Howard Hughes and John Paul Getty as the world's richest man. She would never admit it to Caroline or John, of course, but money was the major consideration — particularly since she had been sending all her bills to Joe Kennedy, an arrangement that would last only as long as the Kennedy patriarch remained alive.

"As far as Jackie was concerned," Gore Vidal said, "the only thing better than a rich man was an obscenely rich man." As for Ari's looks, "He was short, squat, and very ugly," said one of his friends, writer Doris Lilly. "And do you think that mattered to Jackie one bit? Besides, Ari had something that went beyond looks. He was Zorba the Greek — full of life, full of fun."

Like Black Jack Bouvier, Joe Kennedy, and Jack Kennedy, Ari appealed to Jackie's lifelong love of pirates. "There was this element of danger," George Plimpton said, "that I think appealed to her." She worried, though, if marrying him would be the right thing for Caroline and John.

At home in New York, Jackie stayed true to her word to Bobby and kept her affair with Onassis private. She attended a number of high-profile affairs with her two favorite decoys — the escorts most reporters believed were serious marriage prospects — Ros Gilpatric and Lord Harlech.

At three-fifteen on the morning of June 6,

1968, Jackie finally switched off her television and headed for bed. She had been watching the returns from the crucial California primary and was finally satisfied that Bobby had won.

A half hour later, the phone rang. Lee and Stas Radziwill were calling from London, where the BBC was reporting that Bobby had been shot.

Caroline and John, tucked in their beds behind closed doors, slept soundly through their mother's screams. "No!" Jackie cried. "It can't have happened. No! It can't have happened!"

Jackie's prediction that Bobby would suffer the same fate as her husband came true in the pantry of the Ambassador Hotel in Los Angeles. Shortly after thanking supporters in the hotel ballroom, Bobby exited through the pantry. Lurking in the shadows was a young Palestinian named Sirhan Sirhan, enraged over the recent defeat of the Arabs by U.S. ally Israel in the Six-Day War. Sirhan fired six shots at close range, striking Bobby in the head, neck, and right side.

Jackie turned on the TV and watched in horror as footage of the chaos at the hotel — and of Bobby lying open-eyed in a pool of blood on the floor — aired again and again. Jackie arranged to take the first available flight to L.A., where Bobby lay in extremely critical condition at Good Samaritan Hospital. Before she left for the airport, she woke Caroline and John and told them what had happened. Caroline began crying, but Jackie reassured her that this was not the same as what had happened to Daddy — that Uncle Bobby was alive, and the doctors were doing everything they could to make him well. "That was more for my benefit than hers," Jackie later said. "I don't think Caroline believed a word of it."

They're like one soul.

*— One of Caroline's cousins,
on the relationship between
Caroline and Jackie*

6

Bobby lingered for hours, and the next day, at 1:44 a.m. Pacific time, he died with Ethel holding his hand. He was forty-two. As soon as she woke up that morning, Caroline was told that her beloved uncle was gone. Without her mother there, and with no one else to turn to, she went into her room — and cried alone.

In a bizarre reprise of Jackie's voyage from Dallas to Washington aboard Air Force One, she now joined Ethel and a handful of others aboard a government plane bearing RFK's body home to New York. The next day, June 8, 1968, the President and Lady Bird Johnson led the two thousand mourners who filed into St. Patrick's Cathedral to pay their respects to the slain senator.

Ethel, pregnant with Bobby's eleventh child, maintained her composure while Teddy delivered his moving eulogy to yet another martyred brother. "My brother need not be idealized," Teddy said, his voice beginning to quaver, "or enlarged in death beyond what he was in life, to be remembered simply as a good and decent man, who saw wrong and tried to right it, saw suffering and tried to heal it, saw war and tried to stop it. . . ."

Caroline and John stood by their mother inside the cathedral and, with several Kennedy cousins, took part in the mass. After the service, family and friends boarded the funeral train that carried Bobby's body from New York to Washington for burial at Arlington. More than 2 million people lined the 226-mile route to pay their respects. In yet another bizarre twist, several of Caroline's cousins watched in horror as two people who had come to bid Bobby farewell were killed by a passing train. The next day, with scores of gape-mouthed tourists taking snapshots just a few yards away, Caroline placed flowers on her uncle's freshly dug grave while John and her mother knelt on the grass and crossed themselves.

For Caroline, whose memory of their father remained agonizingly vivid, the events surrounding Bobby's death were nothing short of traumatizing. Yet Mrs. Kennedy was in no condition to try to console her daughter. Jackie was "just completely in shock," recalled Pierre Salinger. "It just defied belief that she — that we — would be reliving this nightmare."

The nightmare was no less vivid for Caroline. "Bobby's death was a huge shock to Caroline," Jamie Auchincloss said, "but she kept her feelings bottled up. She became more shy, more introverted, more withdrawn. It was a shame, really, because she had really just begun to come out of her shell — and this . . ." Caroline fell back on one of her old mechanisms for coping. Now she was cutting photos of Bobby out of newspapers and magazines and taping them on the wall next to those images of their father. "I think," Jackie later said, "it was Caroline's way of keeping them alive."

Caroline watched her mother's grief turn to anger — and to the realization that only by charting a course independent of the Kennedys could Jackie hope to guarantee her own children's safety. "I hate this country," Jackie declared. "I despise America, and I don't want my children to live here anymore. If they are killing Kennedys, my kids are the number one targets. I have the two main targets. I want to get out of this country!"

Jackie also craved seclusion, not only for herself but for Caroline and John. "As they get older, more and more photographers are going to start popping out from behind bushes," she told Pierre Salinger. "John is a boy, and he'll be able to handle it, but I'm worried about Caroline. She's so sensitive and, beneath it all, I believe more easily hurt.

231

She doesn't let on that anything's wrong, but she feels things deeply."

Perhaps no one was better equipped than Onassis to provide for the safety of Jack Kennedy's children. The family's four-man Secret Service detail was no match for Ari's seventy-five-member armed security force. As for Jackie's craving for seclusion, there were Ari's luxurious homes in Paris and Athens — not to mention his private island of Skorpios and, of course, the *Christina*.

The weekend following Bobby's funeral, Ari arrived with his daughter, Christina, at Hammersmith Farm. Jamie Auchincloss, assigned the task of showing her around Newport, remembered that Christina was "just a terrible pain. . . . Basically, she hated all things American." While Christina made no effort to disguise her loathing for Jackie, from the outset she regarded Caroline with big-sisterly affection. Christina, whom Callas once described as having "the look of a child marked for the nunnery," saw Caroline as a kindred spirit. "They both had too much fame and too much sadness heaped on them practically from the cradle," Doris Lilly said. "Christina must have recognized that in Caroline. She thought the little girl deserved to be happy."

Over the rest of the summer, Ari waged an all-out campaign to win over Caroline and John. They played tennis and fished together, and Ari routinely took them on shopping sprees to the Fifth Avenue toy store FAO Schwarz. Most important, he reminded Caroline and John at every opportunity that their mother was lonely and needed someone to take care of her.

Yet, like Jackie, Ari focused not on Caroline but on John. "Jackie worried that John needed a strong male figure in his life," one close friend of the family observed. "But I don't think she realized that Caroline needed a father as much if not more than John, especially at this time in her life. John was still this rambunctious little boy who really didn't remember his daddy, and Caroline was this sad, very sad and depressed preadolescent."

Still, Caroline had been a model student at Sacred Heart and was looking forward to returning in the fall. John, however, had proved himself to be quite a handful at St. David's. Although he made friends easily, John also responded to taunts from other students — "Your father's dead! Your father's dead!" several liked to chant — with his fists. John's studies suffered, and when it was recommended that he repeat first grade, Jackie transferred him to the equally tony Collegiate School across town on West Seventy-seventh Street. "My mother was very strict with me," John later said of Jackie, who was not above spanking her son if she felt the situation warranted it. "Caroline could do just about anything, but if I stepped out of line, I got a swat."

By late summer, Onassis had all but won over John and was making headway with the decidedly more reticent Caroline. At the same time, Jackie had convinced herself that marriage to Ari would provide her with the financial, physical, and emotional security she craved. In August, Caroline and John stayed behind in New York while Uncle Ted flew with their mother to Skorpios. It was there that the surviving brother of America's greatest political dynasty — and now father figure to no fewer than twenty-seven Kennedy cousins — hammered out the terms of a prenuptial agreement with Ari. Ultimately it would be left to Jackie's hard-bargaining financial adviser, Andre Meyer, to finalize the deal: $3 million for Jackie and a $1 million trust fund each for Caroline and John.

Even as the Kennedy and Onassis camps worked out the details of Jackie's marital contract, there was another crisis in the making closer to home. During one weekend at the house in Bernardsville, New Jersey, the Secret Service detail charged with protecting Caroline and John followed the wrong car turning out of the driveway and "misplaced" the children.

The mood at Secret Service headquarters in Washington verged on panic as agents frantically radioed one another in an effort to locate the two children. Their father and their uncle had both been murdered right under the nose of the Secret Service; was it possible that agents had somehow allowed JFK's children to be kidnapped in broad daylight?

Two hours had passed, and it was already dark when Jackie's New Jersey neighbor, Marjorie "Peggy" McDonnell, drove up to Jackie's relatively modest farmhouse. Caroline sat with her brother in the back. They had been playing with the McDonnells' eight children, and when no Secret Service detail showed up to bring Caroline and John home, McDonnell took matters into her own hands and did it herself — leaving her own eight children home alone in the process. The incident would be kept secret for decades, but Jackie would not soon forget. The day the Secret Service lost her children gave security-conscious Jackie just one more reason to marry Ari.

While Jackie was immersed in planning for her financial future, Caroline turned to the new mother figure in the children's lives — their new governess, Marta Sgubin. Dark-haired and slender, Sgubin was a Jackie look-alike who not only met the religious requirements for the job — she was a devout Roman Catholic — but also spoke five languages: English, French, German, Spanish, and Italian.

Caroline was having a friend stay over with her at Hammersmith Farm in Newport when she first met Sgubin, who arrived shortly before midnight after a storm delayed her flight from New York. "I didn't know which one was which," Sgubin later said of that first encounter, "and I looked at them and thought, 'I hope it's that one.' I'll never forget that. And that one was Caroline. So I felt I liked her the first minute I saw her."

After a two-week period of adjustment in Newport — "bicycle riding, going to the beach, and playing all kinds of outdoor games," Sgubin recalled — Caroline, John, and their new governess settled into their routine in New York. "Next to our mother," Caroline would concede years later, "Marta is the person John and I are closest to."

Yet no one could have prepared Caroline and her brother for the firestorm that lay ahead. When Doris Lilly, then a columnist for the *New York Post*, appeared on *The Merv Griffin Show* and predicted that Jackie and Onassis were about to wed, she was booed. Leaving the studio, she was shoved and heckled. "A Greek toad becoming the stepfather of John F. Kennedy's children? How dare I cast aspersions on *our* St. Jackie?"

Jackie shrugged off the criticism. Before the press got wind of her impending marriage, several friends pleaded with her to reconsider. "You're going to fall off your pedestal," one warned. "That's better," Jackie replied, "than freezing there." At lunch with Truman Capote, she grew exasperated over the notion that she should find someone more down to earth, someone more . . . American. "I can't very well," she sighed, "marry a dentist from New Jersey."

Despite Ari's presence in their lives, neither Caroline nor John knew that marriage plans were indeed being hatched. On October 15, the *Boston Herald* broke the story on its front page, forcing Jackie to hastily phone family members with the news. Rose Kennedy admitted to being "stunned" by this turn of events, not only because of the age difference but because Onassis was Greek Orthodox *and* divorced. Would their marriage, she wondered, be recognized by the Catholic Church? "I thought of Caroline and John Jr.," Rose added, "and whether they would learn to accept Onassis in the role of stepfather so that he could give them the guidance that children need from a man."

Still, Rose Kennedy was the only family member to offer Jackie unqualified support. Her own mother raged that Jackie was "getting back at me for divorcing her father. . . . I just know it."

Once Janet Auchincloss grudgingly agreed to make the formal wedding announcement,

Jackie finally sat Caroline and John down and told them that in a matter of days they would be getting a stepfather. "No one can ever replace Daddy, of course," she told them. "But Mr. Onassis is a good and kind man, and I'm sure that in time you'll learn to love him."

John later told a friend that he was "just fine with it" when informed that his mother was marrying Onassis. "He made her happy, and that was all that really mattered."

Caroline was a different matter. She was also fond of Onassis — he had, after all, been lavishing gifts and attention on both Kennedy children for months — and there was no denying that their mother was as happy as she had ever been since Dallas. But while Jackie had welcomed Ari into their tight little family unit, she had never mentioned the word "marriage" to the children — until now. "It was a terrible shock for Caroline," Jamie Auchincloss said. "She worshipped her father, and Bobby's death was still fresh in her mind. She was a terrifically well-adjusted and well-behaved kid, but this is a lot to pile onto a ten-year-old."

And that was even taking into account the global outpouring of hostility that followed. "Sad and shameful" were the words *France-Soir* used to describe the idea of Jackie's marrying Onassis. JACK KENNEDY DIES TODAY FOR A SECOND TIME, screamed the headlines in Rome's *Il Messagero*. JACKIE WEDS BLANK CHECK, blared one London paper, while West Germany's *Bild-Zeitung* proclaimed, AMERICA HAS LOST A SAINT.

Things weren't much better closer to home. "Anger, shock, dismay" were the words the *New York Times* chose to describe U.S. reaction to Jackie's wedding. Jack's old cronies charged that she'd gone "from Prince Charming to Caliban," while Aunt Lee, who had long had her sights set on Ari, screamed to Truman Capote, "How could she do this to me? How could this happen?!"

On October 20, a solemn-faced Caroline and her brother, both grasping slim white candles, flanked the bride and groom inside Skorpios's tiny Chapel of Panayitsa ("the Little Virgin"). JFK's children were among the twenty-two family members and friends invited to the ceremony. Standing with Onassis, who swayed noticeably, were his sister, Artemis, and half sister, Yerasimos, several business associates, and of course his children, twenty-year-old Alexander and Christina, now just eighteen. Among those on the bride's side of the aisle were Pat Lawford, Jean Smith, the Auchinclosses, as well as Lee and Stas Radziwill and their two children, Christina and Tony.

Just as he had when Black Jack Bouvier was too drunk to give away his daughter in marriage to Jack Kennedy, "Uncle Hughdie"

239

Auchincloss walked his stepdaughter down the narrow aisle. As Caroline and John stood by holding their candles, it was painfully evident that all of Onassis's Herculean efforts to win over JFK's children had not sufficiently prepared them for this moment. Caroline, in particular, looked "very somber and vulnerable," another guest observed. "A lot of people felt sorriest for her."

But Caroline was by no means the only sullen face in the wedding party that day. Christina (Ari called her *Chryso Mou* — "My Golden One") and Alexander, who had long held on to the hope that their mother, Tina, and their father might reunite, were heartbroken. Reporters noted that both looked more like they were attending a funeral than a wedding. "Ari's children thought Jackie was a gold digger — pure and simple," Onassis's friend Doris Lilly said. "They knew he wanted her because she was the ultimate trophy wife. It would not be overstating things to say they despised Jackie, and of course Caroline had to have recognized that."

Wearing gold robes and a long black beard, Greek Orthodox priest Polycarpos Athanassiou conducted the ceremony in Greek. Ari and Jackie, who towered four inches above the five-foot-five-inch-tall groom, were both crowned with wreaths of orange blossoms, which they exchanged. Then gold wedding bands were placed on their fingers, and these were also exchanged as a symbol of unity. While the bride and groom drank wine from a silver chalice, Athanassiou recited the wedding vows. Caroline looked at the priest with an expression that fell somewhere between apprehension and awe.

To complete the ceremony, Jackie and Ari walked around the altar three times. Then they did the "Dance of Isaiah," in which each tries to step on the other's foot first — a contest to determine who will have the upper hand in the marriage. Caroline's mother won.

Emerging in driving rain, the wedding party pushed past reporters to a gold-painted Jeep. With Ari at the wheel and a grave-looking Caroline sitting in her mother's lap, they headed for the reception aboard the *Christina*. Holding a glass of pink champagne, Jackie stepped out onto the deck with Caroline to greet a select group of reporters who had been invited on board. The new Mrs. Onassis shook hands, thanked the journalists for their good wishes, and then excused herself so she could return to her guests. "The entire time," said one of the reporters, "poor Caroline looked like the unhappiest kid in the world. She just looked, well, dazed."

It quickly became clear, however, that life as a stepchild of Aristotle Onassis would have its compensations. During the wedding reception, Ari presented his wife with $1.2 million worth of rubies and diamonds. Even Caroline perked up when she saw them. "Mommy, Mommy," she said, "they're so pretty! Are they real?" Onassis also gave gem-encrusted rings to Kennedy sisters Pat Lawford and Jean Smith, and a platinum-and-diamond ring to his disapproving mother-in-law. John and cousin Tony Radziwill each received $1,000 Swiss-made watches. Caroline and her cousins Sydney Lawford and Tina Radziwill were the last to open their presents. Each received a diamond bracelet.

From Georgetown and the White House to Hyannis Port, Palm Beach, and New York, Caroline had always lived a life of privilege. But being the stepdaughter of Aristotle Onassis added a whole new dimension to the word. For starters, there was the 325-foot *Christina*, with its crew of sixty that included two full-time hairdressers and two chefs. There was a ballroom, a grand piano in the glass-walled sitting room, a private screening room, a formal dining room, and an El Greco hanging in Ari's paneled study. Caroline was most impressed with the children's playroom, which had been decorated by *Madeline* creator Ludwig Bemelmans. While the adults partied into the night, nibbling on caviar and dancing to bouzouki music, Caroline dressed dolls in gowns made specifically for them by Dior.

In addition to the *Christina*, there was Ari's mansion in Montevideo, Uruguay, his pied-à-terre on avenue Foch in Paris, his seaside villa nineteen miles outside Athens at Glyfada, and, of course, Skorpios. Caroline was especially fond of Ari's island paradise, with its cypresses, fig trees, and bougainvillea. Here she and her brother hiked, swam, and sailed. And to make certain they did not grow bored, Ari bought a sailboat for Caroline, a speedboat for John, and Shetland ponies and mini-Jeeps for both of them.

Onassis, always sensitive to the wants and desires of the women in his life, overheard Caroline admire a particular horse and offered the owners twice what they had paid for it. Told that the animal was not for sale at any price, Ari did the next-best thing: He purchased the horse's parents and siblings for Caroline. Riding would, in fact, be one of Caroline's favorite pastimes on Skorpios — until Jackie decided the rugged terrain made it too dangerous. "We drive around in mini-Jeeps most of the time," Caroline later explained. "That's really the only way to get around."

Since Ari owned his own airline — Olympic Airways — they simply commandeered an Olympic passenger jet whenever they chose to travel abroad. Nevertheless, with the exception of one or two summer months spent on Skorpios, Caroline's life continued to revolve around the family's Fifth Avenue apartment, Hyannis Port, and the farmhouse in New Jersey. While John was continuing to get into fistfights with schoolmates who taunted him about his mother's marriage to Onassis, Caroline's Sacred Heart classmates made no mention of her new stepfather. "Caroline was always shy and quiet," said a former schoolmate, "and her cousins Sydney and Victoria, who were also at Sacred Heart, were very protective of her. My parents, like most parents, were shocked that Jackie married Onassis. But that just made everybody feel more sorry for Caroline."

Caroline continued to bring home A's and the occasional B-plus on her report cards, and to spend weekends riding to the hounds with her mother in Bernardsville. At first Ari was on hand at Bernardsville to watch her from the sidelines. But, growing bored and impatient, he invariably returned to the house, where he would spend hours deal-making on the phone.

"It was wonderful to see Ari with the children, and to watch how they reacted to him," George Plimpton observed. "He obviously got a charge out of being with Caroline and John." It was, said a longtime business colleague of Onassis's, "the kind of relationship he never really had with his own kids. When they were young, he was too busy to be bothered with childish things."

Indeed, Onassis occasionally took Caroline to their favorite hangout, Serendipity, for ice-cream sundaes, or for long walks in Central Park. But just as Jackie had focused most of her attention on her son, Onassis's one-on-one time was reserved almost exclusively for John. "Caroline is Caroline. She will do fine no matter what," Jackie told a friend. "But I worried about what would happen to John without a strong male influence in his life. He has that now." Among other things, Jackie said, she was concerned that without a father figure to guide him toward manhood, John would become "a fruit."

It was not in Caroline's nature to be jealous, particularly when it came to her little brother. But there was no question that Ari's first priority — aside from Alexander and Christina — was John. He showed up at Collegiate for school plays and soccer games and, though he was totally unfamiliar with American baseball, took John to watch the Mets play the Baltimore Orioles in the third game of the World Series.

For all Ari's efforts to bond with Caroline and John, neither child would ever call him "Dad." In fact, they would never call him "Ari." They would always refer to Jackie's second husband simply as "Mr. Onassis."

Caroline shared her brother's opinion of Onassis, though to a lesser degree. "Ari spent nowhere near as much time with Caroline as he did with John," said a former employee of the family. "That meant she could view things from a bit more of a distance. And Caroline always gave you the feeling that she was a little sponge, quietly taking in everything."

There was one thing that Caroline surely noticed — an aspect of the relationship between Jackie and Ari that stood in sharp contrast to the way Jackie and Jack behaved toward each other. Caroline seldom saw her parents display affection, in large part because JFK had a phobia about being touched. Their Hyannis Port neighbor Larry Newman remembered that Jack "was not a demonstrative person." But with Onassis, Newman said, "things were totally different. They'd hold hands, or they'd have their arms around each other . . . or they'd be *whistling*. And they'd kiss — something you never saw Jack and Jackie do. . . ."

Kitty Carlisle Hart was among the handful of friends invited to join the Onassises for their first Thanksgiving together at 1040 Fifth. Caroline dissolved in giggles as everyone tried to explain the intricacies of the purely American ritual to Ari. "They seemed, at least in that first year," said Hart, "to be very much in love with each other."

Yet from the beginning, Caroline and John — not to mention their mother — went for long stretches without seeing Onassis at all. Ari spent the vast majority of his time in Europe, and when he was in New York, he stayed at his own suite some twenty-four blocks to the south at the Pierre Hotel. Jackie was, he explained, "often at the other end of the world with her children — whom I should say I love very much. But they need time to get used to me, and I want to give them that time. They need time to understand that their mother has remarried and that I want to be their friend, and not replace their father, whom I admired so much. A father cannot be replaced, especially one like John Kennedy. I only desire that they consider me a best friend. That is another reason why I believe it is a good idea that Jackie has time alone with her children."

For Ari, these long periods apart also served another purpose. While Jackie and her children led their lives in the United States, Onassis was still free to spend time with Maria Callas in Paris.

None of this really mattered to Caroline. She already had two father figures in her life. One, Secret Service Agent John Walsh, was a constant presence. "He seems to be the father image she needs," a family friend told writer Jurate Kazickas. "He does so many things for her, like take her to the tennis courts and get those things for her that she needs. I think she is very close to him."

The other strong male influence in Caroline's life was Uncle Teddy, a flesh-and-blood reminder of both her father and her cherished uncle Bobby. In Hyannis Port, Ted took Caroline and John sailing on their father's boat, *Victura*. "It all fell to Ted — he picked up where his brothers left off," said one Hyannis Port neighbor. "You could see him with Caroline, and they'd be walking along the beach skipping stones on the water. It was really very touching."

But both Walsh and Uncle Teddy would soon be in for some hard times. As the head of the kids' Secret Service detail, Walsh took the brunt of Jackie's anger whenever she grew tired or frustrated over not being able to lead a "normal" life. As Christmas approached, Jackie became upset over the fact that Caroline and John were subject to "the stares and pointing, and the stories . . . the strangest stories that haven't a word of truth in them. . . . I guess they have to make a living, but what's left of a person's privacy or a child's right to privacy?"

In late December 1968, she wrote a six-page letter to Secret Service Director James J. Rowley complaining that "there are too many agents, and the new ones are not sensitive to the needs of little children."

Caroline and her brother, the letter went on, "must think that they lead normal lives, and not be conscious of a large number of men protecting them from further violence.

They must not be made conspicuous among their friends by the presence of numerous agents, or have the households in which they live thrown into turmoil by the intrusion of agents who do not care about them or understand their problems."

Jackie went on to say that she wanted the detail cut from eight to four agents, and that they "should be with the children from the time they leave the house in the morning until they return at 5:30 for supper. I would like to request that the afternoon and night shift of extra agents be terminated. These are the men who are unnecessary and cause confusion. The children are secure in the apartment in New York at night." She added that in New Jersey and Hyannis Port, the local police provided sufficient protection at night.

Weekends at the farmhouse in Bernardsville were most problematic, Jackie felt. "Agents tramp outside the children's windows all night, talking into their walkie-talkies," she pointed out. "Cars of each agent pile up in the driveway so that our little country house looks like a used-car lot." Jackie pointed to one embarrassing incident when an agent "either went to sleep or was listening to the radio so loudly in his car with the windows steamed up that he did not hear a neighbor's child locked in the car next to him who had been crying hysterically for an hour, and was finally found by her parents. Another time an agent went in and forcibly dragged my children home for supper though I had told his superior that they might stay, etc., etc." Then there was the incident, she reminded Rowley, when the agents followed the wrong car out of the driveway and lost them for two hours.

There was no question, Jackie informed the Secret Service director, that, while in Greece, Caroline and John were more than adequately protected by Ari's private army. But her overriding message was clear: "The children are growing up. They must see new things and travel as their father would have wished them to do. They must be as free as possible, not encumbered by a group of men who will be lost in foreign countries, so that one ends up protecting them rather than vice-versa. . . . As the person in the world who is the most interested in their security, and who realizes most what threats are in the outside world, I promise you that I have considered and tried every way, and that what I ask you for is what I know is best for the children of President Kennedy and what he would wish for them. . . . Thank you so much, dear Mr. Rowley. I hope you have a happy Christmas. Most sincerely, Jacqueline."

Slashing the Secret Service detail in half placed a greater burden on Walsh and his men, but one thing did not change — he continued to be an emotional anchor in Caroline's otherwise turbulent life. Whenever a new pet was added to the menagerie at 1040 Fifth, Caroline proudly showed it to the man they would always know as "Mr. Walsh." By 1969, there were two dogs, three guinea pigs, two birdcages (one pink and one blue) filled with finches and canaries, and a rabbit. Soon there would be an addition — a black-and-yellow garter snake that Caroline would hold in her hand while Walsh looked on in mock horror.

The year would turn out to be one of the most difficult in the life of Uncle Ted, now in the midst of his own quest for the White House. On July 18, Ted drove his 1967 Oldsmobile off the Dyke Bridge at Chappaquiddick, drowning the young campaign worker who was riding with him, Mary Jo Kopechne. The tragic accident and Ted's bungled efforts to cover it up put an abrupt end to his presidential aspirations.

Caroline watched as her mother stood by Uncle Ted (Teddy White described it as "another lesson in solidarity"), but once again her confidence was badly shaken. "Her last Kennedy uncle almost drowns in this horrible accident," Chuck Spalding said, "and then the papers practically accuse him of murder. After all that had happened, it must have seemed to her that the world was a very uncertain, very frightening place."

Still, Jackie wanted Ted to continue to be a

surrogate dad to her kids — and she went out of her way to make that clear to him even as the Chappaquiddick scandal raged around them. During a visit to Hyannis Port, Jackie asked Ted if he would take the place of Bobby as Caroline's godfather. "It was a special trust," he later said. "It meant a great deal, and so did the support she gave me at the time."

For all its repercussions, Chappaquiddick did not spoil Jackie's fortieth-birthday celebration. While Caroline and John nibbled on cake, Ari presented their mother with more than $2 million worth of diamonds and rubies. It did not amount, however, to what Jackie had already spent on herself during their first year of marriage. Jackie's spendthrift ways had pushed Jack to the brink, and it would not be long before Caroline watched her mother and Ari argue bitterly over her compulsive spending.

For the time being, at least, there would be unity on one issue: how best to stop the press from intruding on their privacy. There were times when she courted photographers, instructing Nancy Tuckerman to inform certain newspaper editors where she would be lunching, even what she would be wearing. Such access had to be on her terms, however, and never allowed for photographs of the children.

The paparazzi, of course, obeyed no such

rules. The most aggressive of these was New York photographer Ron Galella, who stalked Jackie everywhere, crouching behind parked cars and lunging from doorways as he snapped away. Even on holidays, she had to be on the lookout for the ubiquitous Galella. One Mother's Day, he confronted Jackie as she walked toward 1040 Fifth holding a bouquet Caroline and John had proudly presented to her at lunch. At the last minute, she held the flowers up to her face, foiling Galella. Another time, Galella intercepted Ari and Jackie as they were leaving P. J. Clarke's bar on Third Avenue, forcing them to duck into a nearby record store.

One Christmas, Jackie outran a man Galella had hired to pose next to her wearing a Santa suit. And when Galella materialized from nowhere to shoot Caroline sledding with her mother and brother, a bodyguard plowed into the photographer, artfully depositing him in a snowdrift.

Jackie was not the only target, however. Caroline was in the middle of her tennis lesson in Central Park one afternoon when Galella jumped onto the court and began taking pictures. A grim-faced Secret Service agent, unable to prevent photos from being taken in a public place, stood nearby. "I'm not making you nervous, am I, honey?" Galella asked as he kept snapping.

"Yes, you are," Caroline answered, trembling with frustration as she turned toward her mother.

With that, Mom sprang into action, sprinting across the park with Galella in hot pursuit. "There was no way he was ever going to catch up with her," Caroline remembered years later. "My mother can run awfully fast — especially when she's mad."

That fall, Jackie had transferred Caroline from Sacred Heart to Brearley, an exclusive Upper East Side girls' school with a more progressive — and academically rigorous — atmosphere. Like Jackie's alma mater, Chapin, Brearley also catered to the wealthiest and most socially prominent Manhattan families. But at a Brearley School carnival, Galella dashed up to Caroline and began running around her, furiously taking snapshots and humiliating her in front of her new friends. "You got the idea," one of her classmates later recalled, "of what it was like to be singled out from everyone else like some freak. It was very hurtful for Caroline, and you could see the tears of frustration well up in her eyes."

Not long after, Galella showed up in Central Park again, this time jumping out from behind a tree and surprising John as he pedaled his bicycle. A Secret Service agent arrested Galella for harassment, but when the charges were dropped, Galella sued Jackie for $1.3 million, charging Jackie with false arrest, malicious prosecution, assault, and "interference with my livelihood." She countersued for $6 million, charging that Galella's actions caused her mental anguish. She also asked for an injunction that would keep the photographer at least 300 feet away from 1040 Fifth and 150 feet away from her and the children at all times. The case would languish in the courts for years, but Jackie would get an even more sweeping injunction — one that kept Galella 150 feet from Jackie but a full 225 feet from Caroline and John. On appeal, the photographer would get those distances reduced significantly — to a privacy zone of 25 feet for her and 30 feet for the children. In the end, the case, which Ari had advised his wife not to pursue, would wind up costing him nearly $300,000 in legal fees.

Grandpa Joe's death on November 18, 1969, at age eighty-one closed another chapter in the Kennedy family saga. For Caroline, it also meant the loss of another link to her Camelot past. Three days later, she and John were among the seventy mourners at Hyannis's St. Francis Xavier Church. Caroline wore a new set of braces and a large white bandage on her forehead — a result of a spill she took while riding in New Jersey.

Jackie took the children to spend that Christmas of 1969 with Aunt Lee and Uncle

Stas at the Radziwills' Queen Anne mansion in England's Berkshire Hills. They foraged the grounds of the estate for boughs to festoon the house, drank eggnog while they decorated the tree, dined on goose, and opened presents — all without Ari.

It was not long before the papers were full of speculation that Jackie's marriage was doomed — the victim of her out-of-control spending and his continuing affair with Maria Callas. Moreover, several highly personal letters Jackie had written to her former beau Ros Gilpatric — including one she dashed off while honeymooning with Onassis — somehow surfaced on the open market. Ari, feeling betrayed and humiliated, would never forgive her for this particular indiscretion.

Jackie was determined to fight the perception that her marriage was falling apart. When Ari was photographed dining with Maria Callas at Maxim's, Jackie flew to Paris the next day and insisted on being photographed with her husband at the exact same table. Callas, apparently incapable of sharing the love of her life with another woman, tried to commit suicide seventy-two hours later with an overdose of barbiturates.

At an early age, Caroline had a full appreciation of what appearances meant to her mother. In 1970, Jackie selected New York portraitist Aaron Shikler to paint both her and her husband's official White House portraits — a direct result of the wonderful job Shikler had done painting her children two years earlier. Back then, when Caroline was eleven and John was eight, she told Shikler, "They look just right to me now. I would like to remember them at this age, as they are, just now."

Once the portraits of Jack and Jackie were ready for an unveiling at the White House, First Lady Pat Nixon invited Mrs. Onassis and her children to attend. Fearing that a public ceremony would create a circus atmosphere that might upset Caroline and John, Jackie declined. Jackie explained that she really didn't "have the courage to . . . bring the children back to the only home they both knew with their father under such traumatic conditions."

Now that Ron Galella was legally required to keep his distance, Caroline's daily life in New York was relatively hassle-free. But there was the occasional unscripted encounter with the press. One October afternoon, Caroline, dressed in her Brearley uniform — blue-green plaid miniskirt, white pullover, wide belt, blue knee socks, and shiny black loafers — was eating lunch with a girlfriend at the counter of an Upper East Side coffee shop when Associated Press reporter Jurate Kazickas sidled up to her and began asking questions.

Instead of running, Caroline put down her

half-eaten cheeseburger, took a sip of her Coke, and cheerfully answered Kazickas's questions — pausing periodically to trade knowing glances with her friend and start giggling. What impressed Kazickas most was Caroline's poise. Just five weeks away from turning thirteen, she "was nonchalant, completely at ease," the writer recalled, "and very pretty." As she spoke, Caroline looked at the reporter "with a direct, steady gaze from wide, cornflower blue eyes."

Her answers were straightforward: No, she did not want to be a debutante. Yes, she had taken piano lessons but dropped them "because I don't play very well." Her favorite books: historical fiction, particularly a biography of Dolley Madison she had just finished reading.

"She's a real brain," Caroline's friend chimed in.

"Oh, yeah," Caroline replied with a laugh, elbowing her friend good-naturedly. "But I'm not very good at math. My favorite subject last year was history. I don't know what it will be this year. . . . I'd like to learn more about Africa, though."

Caroline thought Greece was "very beautiful," though she could not decide whether she preferred it to Hyannis Port. As for the pressures of celebrity: "I don't think of myself as famous," Caroline said with a shrug. "I'm not really bothered by too many reporters or photographers. It seems they're only around when I'm with my mother. I just don't think of what it'll be like when I'm older." What were her plans for the future? "I don't know," Caroline said. "I haven't thought about it too much. Yes, I've thought about the Peace Corps, but I don't know if it will still be going by the time I could join."

As for her social life, Caroline had stopped spending time with a group of friends from Sacred Heart because, according to Caroline's friend at the lunch counter, "they got all sophisticated. They like boys, and they wear makeup. Ugh."

Unlike her mother, one of the greatest fashion influences of the twentieth century, Caroline claimed not to be the least bit interested in clothes. "I don't pick them out myself," she said, "and I only get something when I need it."

Caroline's tight circle of friends swore that the prevailing image of JFK's daughter as solemn and aloof could not have been further from the truth. "Oh, she's really wild," said one. "She's just so much fun." But not even her closest pals at school were privy to facts concerning her family. "She hardly ever mentions Greece or her father — or her stepfather."

Indeed, adult visitors to 1040 Fifth were so wary of somehow upsetting Caroline that they avoided any topic of conversation that might remotely be considered intrusive. As Caroline teetered on the brink of puberty, one family friend told Kazickas, "she is most at ease talking about subjects that are not too personal. It's an unspoken thing that you only bring up light, amusing subjects when you are together. There is a real openness and naturalness about her when the subject is a general one. She also asks amazingly intelligent questions."

Everyone agreed that if Caroline appeared to be growing into a well-adjusted young woman despite all the tragedies that had touched her life, the credit went to Jackie. Despite the controversy surrounding her marriage to Onassis — or perhaps because of it — Jackie seemed to be spending more time than ever with her daughter. "I think her mother has tried to raise her just as if she were an ordinary child," a frequent guest to 1040 Fifth observed, "so that she is not to feel any different from anybody else. That's why Jackie guards her so frantically from publicity. And I think she has done a wonderful job of bringing her up."

It was precisely because of that sensitivity to her daughter's fragile feelings that she had declined First Lady Pat Nixon's invitation to attend the unveiling of the Kennedy portraits at the White House. But when Mrs. Nixon tendered an invitation for a private visit followed by dinner with the current First

Family, Jackie agreed. On February 3, 1971, President Nixon, who still harbored warm feelings toward his old friend in the Senate, dispatched Air Force One to pick up Jack's family and fly them to Washington.

On the flight down from New York, Caroline made a bet with her accident-prone little brother. "First," Caroline said, "I'll bet you that you won't get through the visit without your shirttail coming untucked, and *second*, I'll bet that at dinner you're going to spill your milk."

As their limousine pulled up to the White House, memories began to flood back for Caroline. She remembered the walkways where her father, despite his bad back, would hoist her in the air or play leapfrog. The sound of his clapping echoed in her ears. Jackie studied her daughter's face and was pleased to see Caroline smiling from the moment they arrived at their old home.

Pat Nixon greeted the family at the door, and Jackie was surprised to discover that the wife of her husband's presidential foe was warm, engaging, and especially at ease with Caroline and John. President Nixon showed the children around the Oval Office, where Caroline pointed out how she and her brother both used to hide beneath the massive desk.

Nixon's daughters, Tricia and Julie, had asked to show their counterparts around the upstairs quarters — the "High Chair Room" where Miss Shaw watched over them as they ate, the solarium where Caroline had once attended Jackie's special White House school, and their old bedrooms. Although both rooms had since been redecorated, Jackie noted that Caroline's face "just lit up" when she walked into her bedroom for the first time in seven years.

At dinner that night, John could proudly boast that his shirttail was still tucked in. And his milk stayed right where it was supposed to — until dessert arrived and, as John would later remember, "something caught my attention." Not only did John knock over his glass of milk, but he somehow managed to propel the contents into the President's lap. Nixon, John said, "just didn't even blink and kind of wiped it up." From across the table, meanwhile, Caroline threw her brother a smugly self-satisfied look. Later, as they headed for the airport, Caroline chanted, "I told you so," until her mother ordered her to stop. On the flight home aboard Air Force One, Caroline excitedly shared her memories of their time at the White House — the good times with Daddy that until now had been buried under a mountain of fear, guilt, anxiety, and grief.

Not long after returning to New York, Jackie wrote to Pat, "Thank you with all my heart. A day I always dreaded turned out to be one of the most precious ones I have spent with my children."

The White House visit, in fact, brought Caroline and her mother closer together than ever. In June 1971, while cruising the Mediterranean aboard the *Christina*, Jackie made a point of heading out on sight-seeing excursions with her thirteen-year-old daughter to places like Monaco and Portofino. Caroline and Jackie were, said a cousin of Caroline's, "terribly close. Watching the two of them together, talking, gossiping, with their heads together discussing some problem, it's more like watching two sisters. . . . It's not at all the same with John. John can be irritating, and Jackie gets irked with him. But not with Caroline. They're like one soul." At times, mother and daughter created an even more conspiratorial atmosphere by conversing in French.

On the domestic front, however, things were not going so smoothly. First, Ari exploded with rage when he was informed that Christina, now twenty, had eloped to Las Vegas with Joseph Bolker, a twice-divorced real-estate developer twenty-seven years her senior. The marriage, buckling under pressure from Ari, would last scarcely six months.

At around the same time, Onassis was dealt another blow when his ex-wife, Tina, secretly married his archenemy and business rival, Stavros Niarchos. Niarchos's previous wife, Tina's sister Eugenie, had died under mysterious circumstances, and Ari feared for Tina's safety. Ari and Christina reacted to the news with unbridled hysteria. "Ari was," said his longtime aide Johnny Meyer, "positively apoplectic."

Up to this point, Caroline and her family had not really been exposed to the Levantine aspects of the Onassis family temperament — window-rattling tirades, dark moods that lasted for months — and the anxiety was beginning to mount. Jackie, now smoking and biting her fingernails more than ever, began losing weight at an alarming rate — twenty-four pounds in ten days.

RIDDLE OF JACKIE'S ILLNESS, blared the front-page headline in Britain's *The People*. "Jackie is ill," read an editorial in *France Dimanche*. "Her eyes give the impression of deep suffering." HAS JACKIE GOT CANCER? asked the headline in *Ta Nea*, Athens's afternoon newspaper.

No one was more confounded — or concerned — than Jackie. Using an alias, she underwent three days of tests at Paris's Villejuif cancer clinic. The results came back negative. What Jackie did suffer from was an eating disorder. Doctors were amazed when she informed them that her daily diet consisted of two and a half ounces of meat, yogurt, three and a half ounces of green vegetables, one apple, and half a grapefruit.

There would eventually be words to describe Jackie's disease, but "anorexia" and "bulimia" were not part of the standard medical lexicon at the time. For a while Jackie apparently suffered from both. Onassis told his friend, the notoriously ruthless lawyer Roy Cohn, that Jackie "starved herself to stay thin. Sometimes she would go on a binge and eat everything in sight — then throw it all up."

Caroline evidently knew nothing about her mother's binging and purging, although she was old enough at thirteen to realize that Ari's black moods were putting undue strain on the marriage. That summer on Skorpios, Ari bristled at the arrival of Jackie's friend Peter Beard, the handsome wildlife conservationist, photographer, and ladykiller. While Onassis sulked, Jackie and Lee clearly delighted in Beard's company.

The dashing adventurer made an impression on Caroline as well. The next spring, Beard brought her and John along on a snake-hunting expedition in the Florida Everglades. Caroline tried to overlook the fact that a swarm of reporters and photographers were dogging their every step.

Now that she was entering adolescence, Caroline discovered that the tone of the articles being written about her was beginning to change. Newspapers and magazines in the

United States and abroad began speculating about her boyfriends — she did not have any as of yet — the nature of her relationship with her mother and her stepfather, and her taste in everything from clothes to music. One of the zanier stories appeared on the cover of the October 1971 *Photo Screen* magazine, along with a file photo of Caroline in church wearing a white lace mantilla. RE-PORT ROCKS EUROPE! WEDDING PLANNED FOR 13-YEAR-OLD CAROLINE KENNEDY! read the headline, and beneath it: THE TEARFUL BRIDE'S ATTEMPT TO RUN AWAY! JACKIE SHOCKED! ARI DEMANDS: "SHE MUST OBEY ME."

Such outrageous stories were a source of acute embarrassment for Caroline. But her brother, who was also the object of countless tabloid stories, kept her from taking it all too seriously. John was, after all, the family's resident loose cannon, and as he grew older and even more rambunctious, Caroline took big-sisterly pride in his antics. Her affection for him was evident in the poem about John she gave grandmother Rose for Christmas that year: "He comes spitting in my room, jabbing left and right," it began, "Shouting, OK, Caroline, ready for a fight?"

By May 1972, there was no way Caroline could ignore the escalating tensions between her mother and her stepfather. Jackie no longer invited him to her dinner parties, even when he was staying at his Pierre Hotel suite. And he made clear his resentment of the woman he now called "coldhearted and shallow." Roy Cohn said Onassis "was fed up with Jackie's spending. She was completely out of control, and yet she felt she owed him nothing. He kept saying he didn't like being taken for a sucker, that she was taking him for all he was worth."

It wasn't just the money — Jackie doled out $60,000 for shoes in a single day — that rankled Ari. Out-of-control spending, smoking, and extreme dieting were only a few of Mommy's compulsions. She had gone back to her old habit of capriciously hiring and firing servants — nearly one hundred over a four-year period. She went through nineteen chefs alone. A crew member on the *Christina* was fired for singing in Greek while he swabbed down the decks. Jackie discharged a maid because she had "a sad face. She depresses me." (Caroline's mother had more reason to be wary when she attended catered events. One waiter who happened to serve her at several formal parties pilfered used dessertspoons and framed them. Another stuffed a tiny camera down the front of his trousers to snap pictures of Jackie through his fly.)

That June, Caroline, eager to escape the bickering, set out for Europe for the first time without her mother. An avid student of photography — she had been given pointers on how to operate a Leica by Peter Beard during his summer on Skorpios — Caroline was secretly compiling a portfolio of her own. Now she embarked on her first trip abroad sans Jackie with three cameras slung around her neck. Caroline, said one observer, "looked just like a Japanese tourist."

As Jackie had done several years before, Caroline journeyed to Spain, where she immersed herself in the ritual and lore of bullfighting. After attending a corrida in Madrid, Caroline accepted an invitation from one of Spain's top matadors, Palomo Linares, to visit his ranch. There he taught her how to use a bullfighter's cape as he charged at her with horns mounted on a wheel.

When photos of Caroline's bullfighting lesson hit the papers, Jackie was livid. But Caroline remained in Spain with her chaperone, Dorothy Arias, visiting the Domecq winery to see how sherry is made, dancing the flamenco, and even taking time out of her schedule to visit the U.S.–Spanish nuclear-submarine base at Rota. Her favorite part of the trip, Caroline would later tell friends, was visiting the Andalusian ranches where horses and bulls are bred for the ring. But when Prince Alfonso De Hohenlohe actually invited Caroline to be a *rejoneador*, or bullfighter on horseback, at a benefit corrida in Marbella's Plaza de Toros, Jackie finally summoned her home. Agreeing with Jackie's decision, one of Caroline's hosts asked, "What was the girl going to do with all those old people in Marbella? Enough is enough."

In September 1972, Caroline left Brearley and started eighth grade at Concord Academy, located in the historic Massachusetts town of the same name some twenty miles west of Boston. It was here where Minutemen had picked off British soldiers in the first encounter of the Revolutionary War, and where such literary figures as Nathaniel Hawthorne, Henry David Thoreau, Ralph Waldo Emerson, and Louisa May Alcott had lived at one time or another.

With three hundred students, mostly female, Concord Academy was known as a liberal-minded prep school with a progressive curriculum that included Japanese literature, silversmithing, and the "study of utopias." Uniforms were not required, day trips to nearby Boston were encouraged, and students were permitted to sleep through breakfast if they so chose — a teacher (there was one for every four students) would wake them so they would not miss their first class.

This marked the first time Caroline was out from under her mother's protective wing — and out of the crossfire between Ari and Jackie. The effect was immediate. Caroline grew out her light brown hair in pre-

Raphaelite curls, socialized more with her schoolmates, played practical jokes and pranks on a few chosen boys, and even relaxed enough to let her grades slip — if only a little. "For the first time, she could be herself," a former Concord classmate recalled. "Her mother wasn't this larger-than-life *thing* looming over her and, frankly, over the rest of us. She obviously adored her mother — whenever Mrs. Onassis visited, they would go out and get an ice-cream cone and be jabbering away like two girlfriends. But I think she was also happy to see her mother leave, so she could go back to just being Caroline."

Of course, there were moments when there was no escaping Mom. In November 1972, Caroline cringed with embarrassment when nude photos of her mother sunbathing on Skorpios were splashed across the Italian men's magazine *Playmen* under the headline THE BILLION DOLLAR BUSH. *Screw* published the photos in black and white, but it was Larry Flynt's new magazine, called *Hustler*, that benefited most from the color shots of Caroline's totally naked mother; based on the Jackie layout alone, *Hustler* sales rocketed from several thousand to over 2 million copies.

Ari, it later turned out, was actually behind the pictures. He was tired of her constant complaints about the press, and he reasoned that once the rather graphic photos were published, there was really nothing left the press could do to upset her.

The idea backfired. Badly. Not because Jackie was mortified, but because her children — Caroline in particular — would be humiliated to have these photos of her seen by their friends. Jackie demanded that Ari sue the photographers and every publication that ran the pictures. He refused.

Caroline's new friends at Concord Academy shielded her from the inevitable snickers and snide remarks. But not all the comments were negative; in fact, much was made of Jackie's sleek figure, the result of her unhealthy eating habits, that belied her forty-three years. "Can you imagine what it's like," said Truman Capote, "to be Jackie's daughter and have the world expecting you to be this goddess-in-waiting? Well, Caroline is no stick figure. The girl has a healthy appetite and seems to be a perfectly normal weight, which must drive her mother around the bend."

At Miss Porter's School a generation before, Jackie had been berated by her mother for not being as fashionably emaciated as some of her classmates. It was now Caroline's turn to be routinely criticized for not exercising a little self-discipline when it came to food.

Caroline shared Jackie's love of chocolate — not to mention hamburgers and french fries — and had soared in weight. The change had not gone unnoticed in the press. Caroline was now being variously described as "plump," "stocky," and "sturdy" — adjectives that horrified lean-to-the-bone Jackie.

Mom had several suggestions — taking ballet lessons as a form of exercise, for instance. "But," Jackie sighed, "she just wasn't interested." A friend of Jackie's echoed Truman Capote's observation: "It must have been hard to be the daughter of a svelte, beautiful, stylish woman like Jackie, to be compared to that incredible standard Jackie set."

Undeterred, Jackie went to her New York physician, Dr. Henry Lax, for advice on how to bring Caroline's weight under control. At one point, according to Lax's assistant, Jackie got on the doctor's phone, called Caroline, and began scolding her for being at least twenty pounds overweight. The conversation quickly turned ugly, with Jackie "screaming" at her daughter for not taking the matter more seriously.

True to form, Jackie took control of the situation. She persuaded Dr. Lax to prescribe diet pills for Caroline — a four-month supply in all. "Back then nobody thought twice about the side effects, or the possibility of getting hooked on these pills," said Chuck Spalding, another of Max Jacobson's patients. "If you wanted to drop a few pounds quickly, you took them. If you felt tired, no problem!"

Caroline was not the only Concord Academy student being pressured to take diet pills. "My mother got our doctor to write a prescription for me, and I was happy to take them," a classmate of Caroline's said. "But once you start, it's awfully hard to stop. I don't think 'addiction' is too strong a word to describe the situation I was in — and a lot of other girls whose mothers wanted them to be fashionably thin." Jackie did not play favorites when it came to weight loss: She also pestered her stepdaughter, Christina, to slim down.

Notwithstanding the diet pills, Caroline took advantage of her newfound freedom at prep school to pursue a lifelong dream. While everyone in the family was well aware of her brother's near obsession with planes — helicopters, in particular — few appreciated that Caroline had shown a similar interest in aviation. Even before John was born, after all, it was Caroline who toddled out to greet candidate Jack Kennedy as he stepped off the plane named for her. With a less-than-enthusiastic nod from Mom, Caroline signed up for flying lessons at nearby Hanscomb Field.

That December, Ari secretly met with Roy Cohn and set in motion plans to end his marriage. Under Greek Orthodox law, simple grounds of incompatibility would suffice. But what worried Ari, said Cohn, was that

"Jackie would try and hold him up for a huge amount — $100 million or more."

Before he could work out a strategy, however, tragedy struck. On January 22, 1973, Alexander Onassis was taxiing into position at Athens Airport in the family's Piaggio amphibious plane. A new pilot was at the controls, and Alexander, who had flown the plane countless times, was on board to check him out. The plane took off, veered to the right, and slammed into the ground.

Ari and Jackie, who were in New York at the time, were told that both men had been injured. Only Alexander's injuries were critical, however; he was unconscious, suffering from what doctors determined to be irreversible brain damage. They boarded an Olympic Airways jet for Greece, but not before Jackie phoned Caroline at the Concord Academy and called a halt to her flying lessons.

After lingering for hours on life support, Alexander died. Ari would never recover. From this point on, Jackie confided to her cousin Edie Beale, "everything went wrong." Ari "lost his mind" after Alexander died. He was "no longer interested in life" and, said Jackie, became "a perfect horror to live with." Observed Yusha Auchincloss: "Ari was angry at life, and he took that anger out on Jackie."

On those occasions when Caroline or John watched Onassis lash out at their mother, Jackie took them aside and patiently explained that Alexander's death had undone Ari, that he was not really responsible for his behavior. "They were two very sensitive, compassionate kids," Pierre Salinger said. "If Jackie told them he was just too overcome with grief over the death of his only son, they'd understand that — to a point."

In truth, Ari was careful not to take his anger out on Jackie's children. Yet it was also painfully evident that he had lost interest in them. He no longer asked Caroline about her schoolwork and her pets, and the long walks, long talks, and extravagant gifts were a thing of the past. Caroline now sarcastically referred to him as "my Turkish stepfather," a reference to the fact that the "Golden Greek" had actually been born in Turkey — a fact he preferred to downplay.

Nevertheless, Jackie tried to lift her husband's spirits. Four days after Alexander's funeral, Caroline and John were on an Olympic Airways jet bound for Dakar, Senegal. There they joined their mother and their stepfather aboard the *Christina* for a ten-day cruise that would, Jackie hoped, somehow ease Ari's pain. Jackie also invited Pierre Salinger and his wife, Nicole. Both men loved cigars, and they loved to argue about American history and politics. "Pierre and Ari are two of a kind," Jackie said. "They're never happier than when they're bellowing at each other over a snifter of brandy."

Salinger was on board for another purpose as well. Jackie worried that JFK was just becoming a faded memory for Caroline and John, and she asked Pierre to tell Jack's children about their father. Salinger stressed JFK's "wonderful sense of humor and his love of life — and especially of them," he recalled. Of that first tutorial aboard the *Christina*, Salinger admits to having "few memories . . . except for a clear picture of those two innocent, beguiling faces turned up to me and listening with rapt attention."

Later, on Skorpios, Salinger told Caroline and John about their father's love of history and his passion for reading. "You know," he told Caroline, "at the White House it wasn't safe to leave anything interesting lying around on your desk because your dad would just stroll by and abscond with it."

"I know," Caroline laughed. "Mommy told us that he used to do that to her *all the time*."

Fifteen-year-old Caroline was eager to learn all she could about her father, and she interrupted Salinger frequently with questions — about what JFK was like to work with, what he loved about the job, what he was proudest of, and what he most wanted to accomplish. "Caroline was already a keen student of American history," Salinger said, "and she asked some surprising questions about the Cold War and the Cuban Missile Crisis, among other things."

Overhearing these conversations, Ari was anything but pleased. He had grown tired of Jackie's constantly bringing up her first husband. "Ari and I got along marvelously," Salinger said, "but his mood changed whenever Jackie started talking about Jack. Nerves were frayed, and you wondered how much of an impact this tense atmosphere was having on the kids."

Caroline was relieved when it came time to return to her life at Concord Academy — and out from under the ominous cloud that hung over the heads of Mr. and Mrs. Onassis. In the course of the next few months, Jackie made a valiant effort to keep Ari from dwelling on Alexander's death. When she wasn't throwing elaborate parties in his honor, Jackie kept him moving — from Spain to the Caribbean to Mexico to Egypt. When none of this worked, Jackie begged him to see a psychiatrist. Ari refused.

Not surprisingly, Onassis continued to deteriorate mentally — and physically. He was rapidly losing weight, and he complained of fatigue, blinding headaches, and dizzy spells. His right eyelid drooped. Checking into New York's Lenox Hill Hospital that December under the name of Philips, Onassis underwent a series of tests. The verdict: Ari suffered from myasthenia gravis, a relatively rare, incurable muscular disease.

At first, Onassis told no one — not even his wife, who by now was so fed up with his behavior that she did not even bother to visit him in the hospital. Caroline was surprised to learn that her stepsister, Christina, had now taken up residence in New York, monitoring her father's health and learning the ropes of the family business. In Greece, Christina had gone out of her way to be kind to Caroline and John despite her deep-seated hatred of their mother.

No sooner was Ari released from the hospital than photos of his drooping eyelid were published in newspapers around the world, leading to speculation that he had suffered a stroke. Christina's solution was to take white adhesive strips and tape her father's eyelid to his forehead — an even more bizarre image that sent reporters everywhere scurrying for medical dictionaries.

From her leafy outpost in Massachusetts, Caroline squirmed with embarrassment when Maria Callas appeared on the *Today* show in April 1974 to declare that Ari had been "the big love of my life" and to strongly imply that the relationship was still going on. "It was fairly easy for Caroline to ignore all the talk about her mother's marriage," a former classmate recalled. "No one was going to bring it up in her presence. But did the rest of us talk about it when Caroline wasn't around? Of course we did, and I suppose

Caroline must have known it."

Another old friend of Jackie's, social commentator and animal-rights activist Cleveland Amory, thought the "incessant buzz" about their mother's private life "could not have been the most terribly healthy thing" to happen to either Caroline or John. "He dealt with it, I suppose, by just being this whirlwind of activity. John was a terribly hyperactive kid, constantly in motion, getting into mischief — a good kid, but also a real handful for the teachers and his mother. Poor Caroline was the one who was taken for granted. She was always in control, never a problem. So I think she just developed this ability to act as if nothing was happening and move on. Denial is a wonderful way of coping in the short run, but of course there comes a time when you either explode — or implode."

For Caroline, life with two Secret Service agents lurking nearby had been the norm for as long as she could remember. Because of the controlled environment at Concord Academy, Caroline's bodyguards found it easier to "hide in plain sight," as Jackie had demanded. "I'm sure it must have bothered her occasionally that she didn't have total privacy," said one of her teachers. "But she also seemed to like these two gentlemen, and if they were around, you certainly couldn't see them most of the time. They protected her, but they also respected her need to breathe a little."

It was not so easy for John in New York, however, where at any time one of 10 million anonymous people could leap out of nowhere and harm JFK's son. One afternoon in April 1974, John and two friends ditched his Secret Service detail for two hours. Eventually they tracked him down just as he left the Trans-Lux Theater on Broadway, where he and his friends had caught a showing of Mel Brooks's hot new comedy *Blazing Saddles*.

The most startling incident would occur a few weeks later, around 5:00 p.m. on May 15, when thirteen-year-old John headed off on his expensive Italian ten-speed toward Central Park's tennis courts. Suddenly a strung-out drug addict named Robert Lopez jumped out of the bushes, swung a stick at him, and yelled, "Get the hell off the bike or I'll kill you! Get off the bike!" Lopez shoved John to the ground, grabbed the boy's tennis racket, and took off. After he was arrested for another robbery later that year, Lopez also confessed to robbing John.

Caroline was more surprised by her mother's reaction to John's mugging than she was to the mugging itself. Jackie, John Walsh wrote in a memo to his Secret Service superiors, was "pleased that this had happened to John, in that he must be allowed to experience life."

Jackie made it clear that she did not want

the agents "on his heels. . . . I want him followed but don't want him to feel he's constantly being guarded. It's not healthy."

Tellingly, Jackie did not mention Caroline or her safety at all. "Presumably she felt that the threat to her daughter at prep school was insubstantial," one agent observed. "Or maybe it was just that Caroline had always been reliable, and John was this loose cannon. Either way, the focus always seemed to be on John at Caroline's expense."

That spring, while Jackie remained behind in New York to party conspicuously without her husband, Ari and his daughter cruised the Mediterranean aboard the *Christina*. On a stopover in Monaco, they entertained Prince Rainier and his wife, Princess Grace. "It was very sad," Rainier said of Ari's rapidly deteriorating condition, "to have come so far just to end up heartbroken and ill on board this vast yacht with only your daughter for company." Toward the end of the cruise, Jackie joined Ari in Spain. To the astonishment of the other guests at a Madrid nightclub, she pulled her frail husband out onto the dance floor while she played the castanets.

La dolce vita notwithstanding, Jackie, who had once been the *Washington Times-Herald*'s intrepid "Inquiring Camera Girl," had been toying for years with the idea of returning to work. When NBC producer Lucy Jarvis asked her to work on an NBC documentary on

Angkor Wat, Ari protested on the grounds that it was unseemly to "turn a princess into a working girl." But Jackie overrode his objections when Peter Beard asked her to write the afterword to his Isak Dinesen–inspired book *Longing for Darkness: Kamante's Tales from "Out of Africa."* Dinesen, Jackie wrote, was "one of the first white people to feel that 'black is beautiful.' "

Not long after, Jackie joined the Municipal Art Society in its fight to prevent Grand Central Station from being torn down and replaced by a skyscraper. (Credited with saving Grand Central, Jackie would be memorialized by a large plaque inside the landmark station.) The *New Yorker* also published Jackie's first piece in twenty-two years, an article on the International Center of Photography and its colorful founder, Cornell Capa.

With no one to stop her from working the way Ari had stopped Jackie, Caroline seized the opportunity to work on a documentary about east Tennessee coal miners for PBS in the summer of 1974. Caroline spent more than six weeks interviewing miners — many suffering from black lung disease — as well as their wives, widows, and children.

The Kennedys — and for that matter the entire American viewing public — were not prepared for the graphic images ABC aired on March 6, 1975. For the first time anywhere, Geraldo Rivera showed an unedited copy of JFK assassination footage taken by Abraham Zapruder on November 22, 1963. Ever since that day a dozen years earlier, Americans had thought they were intimately familiar with the film, blissfully unaware that several frames showing the impact of the fatal bullet had been carefully deleted. Now they witnessed the bullet striking Kennedy, and his head literally exploding in an orange ball, spewing blood and gore in every direction. Caroline made a futile attempt to avoid the images, looking away from the television whenever they flashed unexpectedly on the screen. But the gruesome pictures were not confined to television; as the controversy raged, they appeared in newspapers and magazines. "It was terrible, just awful," Jackie's friend Cleveland Amory said. "There was no way to avoid those awful few frames of film. A lot of us felt the horror of that day all over again. It was as if we never knew what *really* happened in Dallas, all that Jackie had to endure. Can you imagine how Caroline felt? This was her father. . . ."

As it happened, there were other, more pressing events to deal with. It was mid-afternoon on March 15, 1975, when Jackie called Caroline from New York to tell her Ari had died at the American Hospital in Paris with Christina at his side. He was seventy-five. Caroline was not surprised at the news; for three days his doctors had been urging

Jackie to fly to Paris because they felt that Onassis, in a coma following gallbladder surgery, would expire at any minute. One of the reasons Jackie had remained in New York was that she wanted to catch Caroline's documentary on miners when it aired on PBS.

If her mother's matter-of-fact tone did not strike her as inappropriate, then Ari's aide Johnny Meyer was taken aback by it. She was, he remembered, "almost cheerful" on hearing news of her husband's death. Christina, whose mother, Tina, had died under mysterious circumstances just four months earlier, did not handle the loss quite so well. Hours after her father died, Christina slashed her wrists in only the latest of several failed suicide attempts. She, like the rest of Ari's inner circle, would blame the "Black Widow" Jacqueline for all their many misfortunes.

Neither Caroline nor John could pretend to be grief-stricken over Ari's death. The grandfatherly figure who showered them with gifts and attention had long since vanished, replaced by a bitter old man who had grown to hate their mother. While Jackie went straight to Paris to see Ari's body lying in state in the hospital chapel, Caroline, John, their grandmother Janet Auchincloss, and their uncles Ted and Jamie flew on ahead to Skorpios.

On the day of the funeral, it quickly became evident that Ari's American family was not welcome. Instead of being permitted to walk directly behind the coffin as protocol would normally dictate, the widow was shoved to the rear by the burly Christina and her equally formidable aunts.

Jackie, dressed in black leather and smiling broadly behind oversize sunglasses, clung tightly to John. Of all the Kennedys present, Caroline, for whom such occasions were already standard fare, seemed the saddest. "Of all of them," said one of the Greek photographers covering the funeral, "Caroline seemed the most somber — not emotional, like the Greeks, but very sad, yes."

Three days later, Caroline and John were at the Élysée Palace in Paris, standing in for their grieving mother at a lunch given by French President Valéry Giscard d'Estaing. Jackie, meanwhile, had already begun the eighteen-month-long process that would end with Christina paying her an extra $26 million to settle any future claims on Ari's billion-dollar estate. It would be, Christina would later say of Caroline's mother, "a small price to pay to be rid of her forever."

In the seven years since her father had wed the widow of John F. Kennedy, Christina had lost her brother, mother, and father. A quarter century before Caroline became the last of her family left to carry on, Christina quickly proved herself to be up to the task of running her father's global business empire. Her personal life was another matter. On November 19, 1988, after four failed marriages, countless suicide attempts and breakdowns, and a long history of prescription-drug abuse, Christina was found dead in a half-filled bathtub at the age of thirty-seven. Her only child, three-year-old Athina, was sole heir to the entire Onassis fortune.

Christina's unhappiness stemmed, those close to the family believed, from the fact that Ari and Tina Onassis were absentee parents. Christina and Alexander saw little of their mother and father, and were essentially raised by a succession of nannies and governesses who spoiled them shamelessly.

It was the lack of discipline, Jackie would say, that doomed Christina from the start. She wasn't about to let the same thing happen to her children. John presented a formidable challenge early on. By the time he was twelve, he had already developed a taste for Ari's favorite scotch — Johnnie Walker Black Label — red wine, and strong Greek cigarettes. At Collegiate, he began smoking pot and was disciplined several times for being stoned in class. To make matters worse, his grades were mediocre. Jackie, fearing that her son's misbehavior might be rooted in some psychological problem, sent him to a psychiatrist.

At times like these, Jackie had always taken solace in the fact that she never had to worry about Caroline. Her pranks at Concord

Academy had been innocent, even endearing. Once she'd poured bubble bath into a school fountain, another time she'd paid back a dare at a local coffee shop by doing a belly dance down the aisle and then kissing a strange boy. Caroline cursed every once in a while, and even developed a fondness for randy jokes. She'd had a romance or two, but thankfully nothing serious. Caroline also smoked now — a habit Jackie had only herself to blame for — and drank socially, though no one ever saw her drunk. Like her brother, Caroline smoked marijuana on occasion. Unlike him, she never got caught.

Even more than most kids, Caroline had looked forward to her sixteenth birthday — and not just because she was old enough to obtain a driver's license. When she turned sixteen, her Secret Service protection would officially end. No longer would she be spied upon by well-meaning men trying to look unobtrusive in dark suits and sunglasses. Or so she thought. When Caroline discovered that her mother had hired two private detectives to watch over her, she was, in the words of a friend, "livid."

Caroline angrily demanded that her mother drop the bodyguards immediately. "How can I live my own life with strange men always watching me?" she asked, choking back tears. "You cannot do this to me!"

There was nothing Caroline could do to

change her mother's mind; Jackie still feared for her children's safety, and she was not about to leave Jack's daughter unprotected. Yet, for the first time, Caroline had stood up to her mother. Shaken by Caroline's uncharacteristically defiant attitude, Jackie turned to her Hyannis Port neighbor Larry Newman for advice. "Larry, do you have the same problems with your girls as I have with Caroline?" Jackie asked. "She knows everything, and I don't know anything. I can't do anything with her."

"Jackie, you know it isn't going to be any different; it isn't going to get better," Newman replied. "What you've got to do is let her grow up alone. Keep your distance. I'll tell you what I do with my girls — we have wonderful conversations."

"I can't talk to her," Jackie said, shaking her head.

"Maybe," Newman suggested, "you don't talk about the things *she* wants to talk about."

To be sure, Caroline's mom had very precise ideas about what was right for Jack's children, and she tolerated little in the way of adolescent backtalk. One friend, John Loring, remembered an oft-repeated line of Jackie's: "Well, I wouldn't want Caroline to do a thing like that." For the most part, Caroline simply went along.

In Caroline's senior year at Concord, however, mother-daughter relations suddenly became strained. Ever since Peter Beard had lent her his Leica four years earlier, Caroline had been perfecting her own style as a photographer. When word got out that Caroline had assembled a portfolio of her own photographs, agents clamored to represent her. Excited at the prospect and encouraged by Andy Warhol, among others, Caroline went ahead with plans to hold her first exhibition at Manhattan's Lexington Labs Gallery. She was even more excited when she was told that the Associated Press would pay $10,000 just for the rights to publish several of her photos.

As the date of the exhibit's gala grand opening approached, the switchboard at Concord Academy was flooded with calls from newspapers and magazines wanting to talk to Caroline. School officials, unable to cope with the number of requests — not to mention the horde of reporters who descended on the campus — asked Jackie to intervene.

Over Caroline's fevered protests, Jackie canceled the exhibit. "Your name is being exploited, Caroline," she told her daughter. "Do you honestly think your photographs by themselves — without the Kennedy name being attached — are worth ten thousand dollars? They may be someday, but you've only just gotten started as a photographer. I won't have your name — your father's name — used that way."

Six months later, the exhibit of Caroline's photos would open at the Lexington Labs Gallery with Jackie's less-than-enthusiastic approval — but this time without an opening reception and without publicity. "Mrs. Onassis," gallery owner Philip Passoni said at the time, "wanted to keep the whole thing low-key." Most of the eighty black-and-white photographs were portraits of Tennessee mine workers and their families — studies Caroline had made while working on the documentary for PBS. There were also photos of a bull-fight from her trip to Spain, as well as some animal studies and landscapes. There were only a handful of family photos, but two in particular spoke volumes. One was of John holding his nose as he fearlessly jumped off the upper deck of the *Christina* into the Mediterranean. The other was a self-portrait of Caroline, dressed in a Gypsy costume with a cigarette in her hand, a ring in her nose, and a seductive expression on her face.

Exploitation of the Kennedy name was one thing, but nothing irked Jackie more than her daughter's refusal to go on a diet. At five feet seven and about 145 pounds, Caroline was still too chubby for Mom's taste. One weekend, Jackie and *Grand-mère* Rose Kennedy picked Caroline up and took her to lunch at Boston's venerable Ritz-Carlton Hotel. At the end of the meal, Caroline asked to see the dessert menu.

"You're not having dessert," Jackie insisted. "You'll be so fat nobody will marry you." The remark was overheard by other diners despite the speaker's famously breathless voice.

Then Rose, who had always taken great care to remain stylishly bony, offered some advice of her own. She told Caroline to always stand with her arms away from her sides so she would "always look thin."

John, who would never have to worry about being overweight, kidded his sister — not about her own eating habits but about how much pressure the image-conscious Jackie was bringing to bear on Caroline to lose weight. "Caroline and John had this marvelous banter going from the beginning," said their uncle Jamie Auchincloss. "They loved to tease each other, just loved it. When they were teenagers, 'gross' was the word of the day. Caroline was always talking about the 'gross' things her brother would do, and he would just dissolve with laughter."

Caroline was not the only one suffering from the Kennedy women's obsessive body consciousness; the pressure to be thin was also felt by one of Caroline's favorite cousins, Maria Shriver. But only Caroline was routinely compared to her famously svelte mother, and as a result her self-esteem plummeted. In a fit of pique that bordered on the bizarre, she shaved off one eyebrow. "My face," she offered by way of explanation, "is too symmetrical."

At Concord Academy's June 5 graduation ceremonies, Caroline seemed anything but anxious as she waited to join the processional. When newspapers across the country ran a photograph next day showing JFK's gum-chewing daughter blowing a large bubble, Jackie showed it to Caroline. "Charming," Jackie said disapprovingly, "just charming." Caroline knew that her mother really had nothing substantive to complain about. A stellar student athlete, Caroline had already been accepted to Radcliffe, the women's college associated with her father's alma mater, Harvard.

Even though she was already pinning the Kennedys' hopes of recapturing the White House on her son, Jackie also had big plans for Caroline. Mom may have worked for a brief time as a photojournalist in Washington, but it was not something she wanted for Jack Kennedy's daughter. She wanted Caroline to spend these formative years in what she considered to be "serious" pursuits. Toward that end, Jackie made sure that Caroline was kept busy that first summer after graduation. Part of her vacation would be spent at NBC, helping in the production of documentaries on Scandinavia and the Middle East. The biggest chunk of the summer would be spent interning in Uncle Ted's Washington office.

Jackie insisted that her children learn not only about their political legacy but also something about how government works. Caroline was an eager pupil, said Ted Kennedy's aide at the time, Richard E. Burke. The interns' jobs were rotated week to week, and whether she was working in the mailroom or helping research legislative issues, Caroline approached each assignment with, as her father would have said, vigor.

Because of its proximity to the capital, Caroline spent part of her time at Hickory Hill that summer. But according to Burke, "she didn't seem fazed by the pressures and craziness that beset some of the others." Caroline was, he observed, "rather shy, a bit reserved," but she also "fit in easily with others, and played an impressive shortstop on our softball team."

Burke noticed that she almost never mentioned her father, and whenever people said how much they admired him she thanked them politely and quickly changed the subject. One afternoon Burke was driving Caroline to a softball game when suddenly she said, "Oh, Rick, can we turn here?" They were on N Street in Georgetown, and as they passed the old redbrick town house at 3307, he slowed to a crawl. "I remember this," she said softly, "from when I was here with my father."

As easy as it was to get along with her Uncle Ted's staff in Washington, there were many times when Caroline felt, as she once told a friend at school, "like I don't really fit in anywhere." Caroline's natural reserve did, in fact, often led others to believe that she was aloof. "Everyone hates me!" she said to a friend. "They all think I'm a snob." Quite the contrary. No one was more society-conscious than Jackie, who first made a splash as Debutante of the Year in 1947. But despite repeated demands from her mother that she plan a formal coming-out party for her eighteenth birthday, Caroline steadfastly refused.

Instead Caroline preferred to go to Greenwich Village bars, rock concerts, and clubs — the usual hangouts for the college-bound offspring of wealthy New Yorkers. The absence of glowering bodyguards gave her a certain measure of freedom, but at times that seemed more than offset by the omnipresent press. "There are times when I feel like just any other person enjoying my life, and then wham — there's a photographer and I go back to being this thing called 'Caroline Kennedy,' " she said. "I hate it."

One evening during the summer of 1975, Caroline went with several friends to hear a band perform at a Greenwich Village club. Clad in black jeans, a white shirt, and a black sweater tied around her neck, Caroline stood unnoticed in the middle of the crowd, swigging beer from the bottle. Rightly sensing that she was being photographed, she let her long hair fall around her face to block any shots, put her head down, and slipped out a side entrance.

Similarly, when she attended the Robert F. Kennedy Pro-Celebrity Tournament in Forest Hills, New York, that year, photographers pursued her to the buffet tent. Surrounded by the working press and the merely curious as she tried to eat lunch with a small group of friends, Caroline suddenly shoved her plate aside, leaped to her feet, and stormed past startled celebrities waiting in the buffet line. "Is my life always going to be like this?" she exploded. "It's like living in a goldfish bowl!" As she left, Caroline turned to one of her friends and said, "Look, I know why people are interested in me, and I hate to appear rude. But sometimes I just can't stand it!"

Caroline and her mother did agree on one thing — that before she enrolled at Radcliffe, she might benefit from a so-called gap year abroad. Caroline had always shared her mother's interest in art — in addition to photography, she'd dabbled in painting at Concord Academy — and signed up for a ten-month work-study program at Sotheby's auction house in London.

For Jackie, Caroline's year abroad would serve another vital purpose: It kept her away from their troublemaking Kennedy cousins. Without a father to keep them in line, Ethel's sons had long since spun out of control. As children, they'd terrorized Hyannis Port, vandalizing boats tied up at the pier, firing BB guns at passing cars, throwing lit firecrackers into neighbors' homes — even pulling out a knife and robbing a young girl of presents at her own birthday party.

Things only got worse as they grew older. Bobby's oldest son, Joe Kennedy II, dabbled in drugs as he hopscotched from one college campus to the next, getting by not on grades or test scores but solely on the strength of the Kennedy name. On Nantucket one weekend, Joe was speeding along one of the island's narrow dirt roads in a Jeep while his brother David and David's girlfriend, Pam Kelley, hung on for dear life. To avoid an oncoming car, Joe swerved off the road and into a ditch, sending all three people in the Jeep flying. Neither Joe nor David was badly injured, but Kelley was left a paraplegic, paralyzed from the waist down. None of which got in the way of Joe Jr.'s being elected to Congress and, for a time, considering a run for governor of Massachusetts.

Bobby Kennedy Jr. and cousin Bobby Shriver were still in prep school when they were arrested for marijuana possession. Shriver cleaned up his act, but Bobby Jr., along with David and their cousin Chris

Lawford, graduated to heroin.

When it came to marijuana use, Jackie was fighting a losing battle. John, who somehow never picked up Jackie's nicotine habit, smoked pot in the bathroom at 1040 Fifth, as well as in the building's stairwell and on the roof — taking care to always bring along a can of Lysol to mask the odor. After John enrolled at Phillips Academy in Andover in 1976, he made no effort to deny that he smoked pot when campus security caught him in the act. Secret Service agents, who were still guarding him at the time, made no effort to stop him. Nor did they inform Jackie, determining that, in the words of one agent, experimenting with marijuana was "a rite of passage." It was more than that, however; though he would go on to only experiment with cocaine, John would continue to smoke pot on a more or less regular basis for the remainder of his life.

While she would never become dependent on any illegal drugs, Caroline was no less adventurous during this period. She reportedly went so far as to grow marijuana plants among the cabbages and tomatoes in her mother's vegetable garden at Hyannis Port. Together, John and Caroline sampled their homegrown stash without Jackie's ever knowing.

Much of this time, Jackie was too busy wrestling with Christina's legal team over the size of her settlement to be aware of the extent to which her children — John in particular — were dabbling in controlled substances. Had she known, she would almost certainly have blamed it all on Ethel's reckless brood.

Not surprisingly, when Ethel called to invite Caroline and her brother to Hickory Hill, Jackie was far from eager to see them go. According to Ted Kennedy's aide Richard Burke, Jackie said, " 'No way.' With all that stuff going on at Hickory Hill — especially with the problems the boys were having — Jackie just didn't want Caroline and John there."

When it came to the frenzied, macho world of the Kennedys, Jackie did not want Caroline and her brother "sucked in, and they weren't," said one friend, David Halberstam. Agreed another confidant of Jackie's, Peter Duchin, "One of the big decisions Jackie made in her life was to get the children the hell out of Hyannis Port and away from the Kennedys."

Jackie wanted Caroline and John to share in the Kennedy legacy, but also to develop the sort of self-discipline that many of their Kennedy peers lacked. "Jackie accomplished this very, very shrewdly," Halberstam said, "bringing them up in New York but letting them show the flag at Kennedy functions."

"Jackie likes her distance," Ted Kennedy

remarked, "but I can see why." Indeed, Caroline was not the only Kennedy girl barred from Hickory Hill by her mother. Burke overheard Caroline and her cousins Maria Shriver and Sydney Lawford talking about "what a mess [Bobby's kids] all were and how their mothers would not let them go near Hickory Hill. There was definitely a hands-off attitude on the part of those three mothers — Eunice, Jackie, and Pat."

Caroline stood out from the rest of the Kennedy pack for other reasons. She was athletic, but nowhere near as competitive as her cousins. "She could lose and did lose — often," said a schoolmate. "But she didn't let it get to her." Caroline shrugged when asked about her tennis game. "I'm not," she said, "very good at it."

Decorum was not a top priority at Hyannis Port. At the Kennedy dinner table, for example, "manners pretty much went out the window," recalled family friend Chuck Spalding. Conversely, Tish Baldrige pointed out, Caroline and John were "sophisticated far beyond their years — very much their mother's children." In stark contrast to the rest of the tribe, Caroline and John were keenly aware of other people's feelings. If there was one slice of cake left at a picnic, their Uncle Jamie said, Caroline would never take it. Neither would John. If asked, they would reply, "No, thanks. You have it."

By virtue of their good manners and their singular lack of the Kennedy killer instinct — neither John nor Caroline adhered to the family's win-at-all-costs credo — Jackie's children were to a certain degree shunned by their Hyannis Port cousins. It did not help that, as Aristotle Onassis's stepdaughter, Caroline was now often reputed to be one of the world's richest teenagers — a bit of tabloid speculation that was not remotely true.

Her cousins would taunt Caroline about her Bouvier and Onassis ties, claiming she was "not even a real Kennedy." But like it or not, Caroline and John were, along with their mother, the undisputed stars of the entire family. "Everyone knew the pressure on John to become a great man was tremendous," said a former classmate at Andover. "But he used to say he felt sorry for Caroline because to a certain extent people expected him to screw up along the way, while she was expected to be perfect — all the time." Rose Kennedy's secretary, Barbara Gibson, said it all: "Caroline was the most trustworthy. I would lend her my car."

When Caroline left for her stint at Sotheby's London headquarters in October 1975, Jackie breathed a sigh of relief. Once again, she had cleverly managed to get one of Jack's children away from the Kennedys for an extended period of time — and presumably out of harm's way.

While she looked for an apartment of her own, Caroline stayed as a guest in the home of Conservative Member of Parliament Sir Hugh Fraser, a longtime friend of JFK and until recently the husband of the celebrated British biographer Lady Antonia Fraser. Himself the father of teenage girls who happened to be away at school, Sir Hugh told Jackie that he would be delighted to look after Jack Kennedy's daughter. Although Jackie provided her with a monthly allowance of around $250, Caroline lived rent-free in Fraser's four-story town house on tree-lined Camden Hill Square, a quiet neighborhood of two-hundred-year-old homes in London's fashionable Kensington district.

Each weekday between 8:15 and 8:30 a.m., the fifty-seven-year-old Sir Hugh would drive Caroline to Sotheby's in his red Jaguar sedan. That was the plan on Thursday, October 23. Caroline had just finished her breakfast and was about to head out with Fraser when the phone rang — an important call from fellow MP Jonathan Aitken. Now that it appeared their departure would be delayed, Caroline went back to her bedroom to fetch something.

Meantime, Fraser's next-door neighbor, the eminent cancer-research specialist Gordon Hamilton Fairley, was out front, taking his dog for a walk. The married father of four had a lot on his mind. As head of the tumor-research unit at St. Bartholomew's Hospital, Dr. Fairley had already overseen the development of several drugs to battle acute myeloid leukemia and was on the verge of yet another breakthrough.

Fairley and his dog were standing next to Fraser's Jaguar at 8:53 a.m. when it happened. The blast from the bomb, which had been planted under the front wheel, hurled the car up into the air and flipped it onto its roof before it burst into flames. Dr. Fairley and his dog were killed instantly; the doctor's legs were blown off and his body hurled across the sidewalk and into Fraser's front garden. Fraser was thrown out of his chair by the blast, his forehead cut by flying glass as windows throughout the neighborhood shattered. Caroline, still upstairs in her room, was knocked to the floor but otherwise remained miraculously untouched. Seven others suffered minor injuries, including Fraser's cook, who was in the kitchen when the blast sent plates and glassware flying out of the cupboards and crashing to the floor. "It was a terrific explosion," said a receptionist at a car-rental agency a quarter mile away. "I thought it was an earthquake."

Caroline was "very shaken," Fraser said at the time, though she had the presence of mind to realize that her mother would be panic-stricken when she heard the news. Fraser's overturned car was still burning in the middle of the street when Caroline phoned the U.S. embassy and asked that her mother be contacted immediately and told that her daughter was all right.

Initial speculation that Caroline might have been the target evaporated when Fraser, an outspoken foe of the IRA, admitted that he had received several death threats in recent weeks. Trembling and barely able to speak, Caroline was taken to the nearby home of Sir Hugh's sister, Lady Maclean. Described by Lady Maclean as "far too shocked to talk," Caroline holed up in her room until the next day, when she mustered enough courage to return to Sotheby's. "I am fine," she told reporters. "I am sure this has nothing to do with me." Scotland Yard agreed. "We are convinced," said Deputy Assistant Commissioner Ernest Bond, "that Mr. Fraser was the target, not Caroline Kennedy."

No one appreciated more than Fraser just how close a call it had been. "Normally I would have been in the car when this happened, but I was on the telephone," he said. "That call saved my life — and Caroline's. Thank God for the telephone. Had it not been for that call, we would all have died."

To those in the field of cancer research — specifically those aware of his success at harnessing the body's immune system to battle tumors — Fairley's senseless death was a devastating blow with far-reaching repercussions. "I can think of no greater catastrophe for clinical research than his loss," said Fairley's colleague, Dr. Peter Alexander. Another top researcher, Dr. Nigel Kemp, agreed. "I honestly don't think there's another person in this country at the moment with his knowledge and experience in this particular sphere. I don't think we can actually replace him — that's part of the tragedy."

In an emotional speech in the House of Commons, Fraser urged the public "not to be intimidated by the viciousness of terrorism." Then he paid tribute to Dr. Fairley. "It might be borne in mind by the public," Fraser said, struggling to maintain his composure, "that this innocent victim in this case was a most distinguished man and has contributed perhaps more to the saving of human life than perhaps anyone in this House, or in the whole medical profession."

Indeed, Dr. Fairley was also considered to be a leading pioneer in the treatment of Hodgkin's disease and non-Hodgkins lymphoma. "In a sense," said one of his colleagues, "the bomb that killed Dr. Fairley also took the lives of all those people suffering from cancer now and in the future who might have been cured — especially people with non-Hodgkin's lymphoma." People, as it would come to pass two decades later, like Jackie.

For now, Caroline had her hands full fending off demands from her mother that she return to the United States. Jackie did not wish to alarm her daughter, but she was convinced that Caroline was the target of the attack. If the IRA were strictly out to blow up Fraser, why hadn't they done it months or even years earlier? Sir Hugh had long been one of the IRA's most vocal critics. Why did they wait until now, just days after Caroline's arrival in London, and why did they choose the one time of day they knew that Caroline and Sir Hugh would both be in the car? Even though the Kennedys had always been seen as sympathetic to the IRA's cause, any terrorist act that happened to take the life of a famous American would have that much more impact.

Perhaps it wasn't the IRA at all. Jackie was well aware that there were lone would-be assassins roaming the planet, and she still believed that her children were prime targets. Either way, Jackie did not want her daughter to remain in England one minute longer than she had to.

"You're just being paranoid, Mother," Caroline told Jackie. "The bomb had nothing to do with me. I'll be fine."

"I don't care, Caroline," Jackie insisted. "It's not safe in London right now," Jackie told her over the phone. "I'll get your plane ticket —"

"I said no, Mother," Caroline said. "I will be *fine*. I am going back to Sotheby's tomorrow, and that's the end of it."

But Jackie was not alone. Uncle Ted called to say that he agreed with Caroline's mother — "It's just too dangerous for you there, Caroline" — and John phoned to let her know he was also concerned for her safety.

In each case, Caroline stood her ground. She would never admit it to either John or their mother, but she had been severely traumatized by the bombing. She had witnessed the gruesome scene moments after the blast — the burning car, shards of glass and bits of blood and gore everywhere. She also saw what remained of the cancer researcher and his dog strewn about Sir Hugh's garden. The horror of that morning would stay with Caroline, though — as with so many other tragedies she had stoically endured — she rarely spoke of it again. "I know she had nightmares about it for months," said another young American enrolled in the Sotheby's program. "But she never let on. I guess when you've been through so much, when you have so many horrible memories, you have to learn to shelve them away somewhere. It's sad to say, but for Caroline I guess the bombing was just one more horrific thing."

At least Jackie could find some small comfort in the fact that Caroline was moving out of the Fraser house. It would take months to repair the damage done by the blast, but, more important, Caroline could not bring herself to remain there.

For the first time in her life, Caroline began hunting for a place of her own. Christina Onassis, who became emotional when she learned that her former stepsister had almost been killed by a bomb, offered Caroline the use of her flat in Mayfair. But Caroline, still upset at the way the Onassis women had treated her mother at Ari's funeral, politely declined. While she looked around for an apartment, Caroline stayed for a time with her parents' old friend Lord Harlech. Then, at Jackie's urging, she moved into the London home of Stas Radziwill. Aunt Lee had divorced her prince the year before, but Jackie had always been particularly fond of Radziwill. It was a comfortable arrangement for Caroline, who remained close to her Radziwill cousins and still viewed Stas as her uncle.

No sooner had Caroline moved in than another IRA bomb exploded, this time destroying an Italian restaurant near the Radziwill home. Again Jackie was on the phone, begging her daughter to come home. Caroline, still certain that these bomb blasts were mere coincidences, was more determined than ever to stay. After another heated exchange over the phone, an exasperated

Caroline blurted to a friend, "Mom can be so thick!"

Officially, Scotland Yard continued to insist that Caroline had never been the intended victim of the bombers. But investigators were never able to tie the IRA to the explosive device. Years later, one of the investigators on the case conceded that Scotland Yard was convinced Caroline had, in fact, been targeted for death along with Hugh Fraser. "These people were terrorists," the investigator said, "and their intention was always to create havoc and fear in Great Britain. But here was a chance to create an international incident, dragging America into the whole mess by killing someone they loved. The daughter of Jack and Jackie killed by an act of terrorism. Can you imagine it?"

Not even a reign of terror could prevent Caroline from savoring this first taste of unfettered independence. "For the first time in my life," she said, "I am far enough away to make all my own decisions. I can go where I want, wear what I want, do what I want. And I intend to."

Back in New York, Jackie lit up another cigarette, poured a glass of wine, and called Stas Radziwill. "Every mother has the right to worry about her child — that's only natural," she said. "But when your daughter is named Kennedy . . . I have more reason than most, don't you think, Stas? Don't you think?"

1

2

With her proud parents, her godfather Robert
Kennedy, and uncle Stephen Smith looking on,
Caroline is cradled by her aunt Lee during chris-
tening ceremonies at St. Patrick's Cathedral in
New York City on December 13, 1957. She is fif-
teen days old.

Two-year-old
Caroline enjoys
some quality time
with Mom and
Dad in Hyannis
Port.

3

4

The day Jackie gave birth to Caroline's baby brother, John, the President-elect and Caroline left their Georgetown home for a stroll.

5

Caroline was straining for another peek at her infant brother as the new First Family arrived at the White House on February 4, 1961. Jackie, though beaming for the cameras, was still suffering the aftereffects from John Jr.'s difficult delivery.

In the White House nursery, Caroline found baby John's toes irresistible. Caroline, who turned three just two days after his arrival, was told John was her birthday present.

6

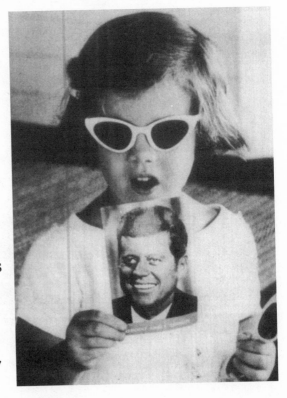

Caroline proudly displays a photo of her dad the President. Well into adulthood, Caroline collected anything bearing the image of her father, from stamps and posters to buttons and coffee mugs.

7

8

Before her
brother was
old enough to
walk, "Buttons"
entertained her
father by
hiding beneath
his desk and
doing hand-
stands in the
Oval Office.

9

December 25, 1962. At Joe Kennedy's estate in Palm Beach, Caroline and Clipper the German shepherd shared the bedlam of Christmas morning with the Kennedys, the Radziwills, and assorted kids.

10

11

While John spies from a doorway, Dad indulges in some presidential horseplay with Buttons. At times, the horseplay turned literal — as when JFK led Caroline and her pony, Macaroni, up a White House walkway.

12

Caroline had the best seat in the house during a family get-together in Palm Beach in April 1963. Jackie, rarely seen smoking, lights up in the background.

13

14

While her playmates eagerly anticipated their turn on the small trampoline Jackie had installed at the White House playground, a gleeful Caroline went airborne.

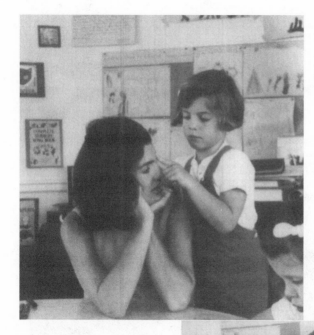

15

16

At the special school Jackie set up inside the White House, Caroline takes a break from her coloring to confer with Mom.

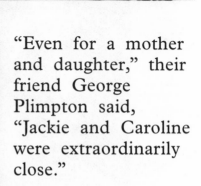

"Even for a mother and daughter," their friend George Plimpton said, "Jackie and Caroline were extraordinarily close."

17

19

Headed for the hospital at Otis Air Base, where Jackie was recovering after the death of her infant son, Patrick, Buttons has a private word with Dad. Arriving home, Jackie was greeted by Caroline, John, and Dad cavorting with the family's canine menagerie.

20

While her favorite Kennedy cousin, Maria Shriver, looks on, Caroline mugs aboard the presidential yacht *Sequoia* on July 28, 1963.

18

21

The President was delighted when his two favorite goblins surprised him in the Oval Office on Halloween, 1963.

22

Just nine days before JFK's assassination, Caroline put her arm around her father and listened to the bagpipes of the legendary Black Watch Regiment. It was the last time the family was photographed together.

23

24

"We're going to say good-bye to Daddy now," Jackie whispered to her daughter as they knelt beside his flag-draped coffin in the Capitol rotunda. Caroline slid her hand beneath the flag, then kissed it. Followed by Uncle Bobby and the rest of the Kennedys, Caroline and John held on tight to their mother's hands as they left the Capitol.

The end of an era. Caroline, Jackie, and John leave the White House for their new home in Georgetown on December 6, 1963.

25

On February 1, 1964, Caroline's aunt Janet Auchincloss (Jackie's half sister) takes a stroll through Georgetown with Caroline, Jackie, and cocker spaniel Shannon.

26

Bobby Kennedy's funeral at St. Patrick's Cathedral in New York City, June 1968. Again, a shattered Caroline (*second from right*) said good-bye to someone she loved.

A less-than-enthused Caroline after the Greek wedding of her mother to Aristotle Onassis on October 20, 1968.

Caroline, Jackie, and John were given a government escort when they toured Greece in early 1970. Later that year, twelve-year-old Caroline boarded one of her stepfather's Olympic Airways planes bound for Skorpios.

33

34

35

As her mother had years before, Caroline sampled Spain's bullfighting scene in 1972. Here, she gets a few tips from one of Spain's top matadors, Palomo Linares.

36

Caroline, sixteen, takes a tumble on the ice while skating at a Rockefeller Center benefit for underprivileged New York City schoolchildren in 1974.

37

Surrounded by her family — John, Jackie, Uncle Ted, and grandmothers Rose Kennedy and Janet Auchincloss — Caroline graduates from Concord Academy on June 5, 1975.

38

Caroline and John — here applauding the action at the Robert F. Kennedy Pro-Celebrity Tennis Tournament in 1977 — spoke to each other "nearly every day of their lives," said their former governess, Marta Sgubin.

Caroline was, in the words of one friend, "destroyed" when the man everyone had expected her to marry, writer Tom Carney, abruptly wed someone else in 1980.

Following in her father's footsteps — and to the obvious delight of Jackie — Caroline graduated from Harvard's Radcliffe College on June 5, 1980.

The aspiring journalist stops to review her notes after interviewing mourners at Elvis Presley's funeral in Memphis, Tennessee. Her first-person account ran in Rolling Stone.

41

42

An affectionate moment for Caroline and boyfriend Ed Schlossberg during a contemporary art auction at Christie's in New York City. Several of Schlossberg's prints were among the works being auctioned.

43

44

A Camelot wedding: July 19, 1986. Uncle Ted looked on approvingly as brides-maids helped the bride with her train. After the ceremony, Mr. and Mrs. Ed Schlossberg posed on the steps of Our Lady of Victory Church near Hyannis Port.

Caroline and Ed take a stroll around their Park Avenue neighborhood with infant daughter Rose Kennedy Schlossberg in 1988.

45

46

47

Caroline and John made their was through the crowd that gathered at 1040 Fifth Avenue following their mother's death from cancer on May 19, 1994. Days later, following Jackie's funeral in New York, Jackie's children clung to each other as her body was carried out of the church — bound for burial alongside JFK at Arlington National Cemetery.

48

Mom made some last-minute adjustments on the dress of flower girl Rose Kennedy Schlossberg at the 1994 wedding of her cousin Tony Radziwill.

Street scenes: Tatiana, Caroline, and Uncle John drew a crowd when they left St. Thomas More Church following ceremonies commemorating the thirty-first anniversary of JFK's death. Months later, Mom clasped Rose's hand and kept a watchfull eye on Tatiana while Dad pushed Jack along in his stroller.

49

50

334

51

At a White House function in June 1996, Caroline and Ed breeze past JFK's haunting official portrait.

52

In August 1997, then-President Bill Clinton and his family sailed with Caroline off Martha's Vineyard. Clinton idolized JFK, and Caroline found a kindred spirit in the Clintons' daughter, Chelsea.

Bundled up against the cold, Tatiana and Rose look like any other New York City school kids as they walk up Madison Avenue headed for home in February 1998.

53

"We're obviously very close," John said of Caroline, who shared the stage at the Profile in Courage Awards ceremony on May 29 — their dad's birthday. "And as a young brother you look up to your sister."

54

Near their summer home on Long Island, Caroline dealt with the disappearance of her brother's plane by hitting the open road with Ed.

55

With her husband and son, Jack, Caroline leaves the Schlossbergs' Park Avenue apartment for her brother's memorial service at St. Thomas More Church. Understandably shattered, Caroline tried to hold herself together for the sake of her kids.

56

57

A hands-on mother like Jackie, Caroline shared her thoughts with Jack as she walked him home from school in October 1999. At a horse show in Bridgehampton, New York, the following year, Mom and Tatiana spotted a friend in the bleachers.

58

In what was touted as "Kennedy Night" at the 2000 Democratic National Convention in Los Angeles — forty years after JFK's nomination in that city — Caroline, Uncle Ted, and other family members paid tribute to Camelot.

59

Exhibiting more than just a touch of her mother's legendary sense of style, Caroline headed for the April 23, 2001, gala opening of "Jacqueline Kennedy: The White House Years" at New York's Metropolitan Museum.

60

61

Lending their mother a hand, thirteen-year-old
Tatiana and Jackie look-alike Rose, fourteen,
showed up at the Kennedy Library for the
Profile in Courage Awards in May 2003.

62

People remember Caroline
as the cute little girl in the blue coat
at her father's funeral.
And in some ways she still is.

— *Tom Carney, Caroline's first love*

Jackie deserves credit for the way she
brought up Caroline and John Jr. She
did it by herself, and she did it
against all odds.

— *Betty McMahon, neighbor and friend*

Why? I haven't written a book, I haven't sung a song. I haven't acted a part. I haven't done anything. I'm just famous for my name, and they won't leave me alone!

— *Caroline, to her friend Andy Karsch*

REPORTER: What name will you go by after you marry Ed Schlossberg?

CAROLINE: Caroline.

7

"They look so beautiful together," Andy Warhol whispered to his friend Bob Colacello as the young couple waltzed across the room. It was 5:00 a.m., and Warhol was the guest of honor at a party being thrown by Lord and Lady Lambton. For much of the evening, Warhol had been perched on a sofa observing the good-looking art dealer and the pretty American art student while they behaved "as if they were the only two people in the room."

Warhol may indeed have thought Caroline and twenty-four-year-old Mark Shand made a handsome pair. "But," Andy added, "if this gets in the papers, I just know that Jackie's going to blame it all on me."

The next morning a photograph of Caroline and her shaggy-maned date ducking out of the Lambton bash at 6:00 a.m. was splashed across the front page of several London tabloids. By the time Warhol arrived back in New York, the picture had been carried in hundreds of newspapers across the country. No sooner had Warhol stepped into his East Sixty-sixth Street town house than the phone rang. It was Jackie.

"Andy, have you seen the pictures in the papers of Mark Shand and Caroline leaving the Lambtons'?" she asked. "What the hell is going on, Andy? You should never have invited Caroline to a party like that."

"But, Jackie, I didn't invite anybody," Warhol protested. His hosts, he pointed out, had been in charge of the guest list.

The Lambton affair was only the latest in a nonstop round of parties Caroline attended; just a few days following the bomb blast that nearly killed her, Caroline had danced into the predawn hours with Shand at a wedding reception. Caroline had actually known Shand for three years; Aunt Lee introduced them when Caroline was vacationing at the Radziwills' retreat in Barbados. It was Shand, himself a graduate of the Sotheby's art-study course, who — with Jackie's full approval at the time — had talked Caroline into enrolling in the program.

Until now, Caroline's romantic experiences had been limited to childhood crushes (on cousin Stephen Smith as a toddler, and at five on playmate Robert "Scubbie" Bartlett) and a few dates at Concord Academy. Urbane, athletically handsome Shand represented something new and exciting. Jackie told Warhol, "I'm afraid he may have simply swept Caroline off her feet."

Shand denied that there was anything at all in the way of romance between them. Caroline was "lovely, but too young," he said. Besides, Shand already had a girlfriend closer to his age — actress Barbara Trentham, who had appeared in the film *Rollerball* and was, at twenty-eight, fully a decade Caroline's senior.

No matter. Caroline was determined to explore her newfound freedom to the hilt, drinking in pubs and dancing until dawn on weeknights, then heading out for rowdy weekends in the country. Whenever Shand's work took him abroad in search of paintings to sell, there were plenty of other young aristocrats eager to take his place. Among those Caroline dated during this period: Nicholas Soames, a grandson of Winston Churchill and a close friend of Prince Charles; soccer player John Boswith; Jonathan Guinness of Ireland's brewery dynasty; Prince Rupert of Prussia; playboy Adam Carr; portly grand prix racing-team owner Lord Hesketh, and his bearded younger brother, Bobby Fermor Hesketh. A daredevil with a fondness for ballooning and skydiving, Bobby Hesketh threw a small dinner party for Caroline shortly after her arrival in London and then took her to a pub to celebrate her eighteenth birthday.

Even more than Shand, it was twenty-five-year-old Sebastian Taylor whose involvement with Caroline upset Jackie the most. Taylor had once been involved with Princess Elizabeth of Yugoslavia, who was thirteen years his senior. Princess Elizabeth made headlines of her own by leaving her family for Richard Burton after the breakup of Burton's second marriage to Elizabeth Taylor.

"She's a girl who enjoys a cocktail or a glass of champagne," said another of Caroline's escorts, Adam Carr. "She'll brighten up when she's had a drink." Once she'd "brightened up," Caroline spoke openly about her reasons for not returning to the United States. "Caroline made it pretty clear to me," said Carr, "that she came to London to get away from the Kennedy clan."

"I'm afraid Caroline is in way over her head," Jackie confided to a friend. At least one observer of the London social scene agreed. "Many people in Mark Shand's in crowd are heavy drinkers, drug users, and prone to strange, erotic experiments," he said. "A young, impressionable girl surely can't travel with that fast crowd for long without being adversely affected." Andy Warhol, for one, was impressed with the decadent scene — appreciating full well that Caroline was merely an observer. Leaving the Lambton party just ahead of Caroline and just behind rockers Mick Jagger and Keith

Moon, Andy proclaimed, "I haven't seen so many freaks for years!"

For months, the headlines continued unabated. SHE'S QUEEN OF THE HOP, proclaimed one. CAROLINE'S ALL-KNIGHT PARTIES, quipped another. More convinced than ever that London was not the place for Caroline, her mother called her every day and pleaded with her to pack up and come home. But to no avail. "She is staying put," said Mark Shand's friend, *Daily Mail* columnist Nigel Dempster. The reason, Dempster guessed, was that "Caroline has her sights set firmly on Mark. He's the object of her affections, if she is not exactly the object of his."

By May 1976, the London high life had taken its toll on Caroline. Suffering from acute gastritis, she flew home to the United States and checked into New England Baptist Hospital. Kennedy family physician Dr. Russell S. Boles chalked Caroline's stomach pains up to diet. In addition to champagne and beer, Caroline had been subsisting largely on a diet of hamburgers, "bangers" (sausages), and chili. As soon as she was released from the hospital, Caroline flew back to England.

Almost as much as the persistent threat to her daughter's health and safety, Jackie fretted over the amount of press coverage Caroline's London escapade was generating. Most of the tabloid stories were anything but flattering, and, like any parent, Jackie did not want to see her child's feelings hurt. "She's very immature and knows little about the ways of the world," one new "friend" observed. "At her age, British girls are far more advanced and sexually experienced." Caroline's fashion sense — her wardrobe consisted largely of ankle-length skirts, capes, and bulky sweaters — came in for plenty of criticism. "She seems to like to look scruffy," one Sotheby's coworker was quoted as saying. "Perhaps it's a reaction to all those clothes her mother buys." Chimed in Dempster, "She's not the most attractive seventeen-year-old girl — she's overweight, and certainly not sophisticated."

Jackie knew that her daughter would be hurt by such comments. "I never intended to let John and Caroline be subject to the glare of publicity," she said. "I want them to lead the life of normal youngsters. After all, those poor children have been through so much over the past few years. I just want," Jackie went on, "to be like any other mother with two children and lead an uncomplicated life."

Ironically, even as Caroline was testing her wings in London, Jackie was fashioning a new life for herself — a life as a single working woman. In September 1975 she had taken Tish Baldrige's advice and gone back to work, as a "consulting editor" at Viking Press. She insisted that all her coworkers call

350

her "Jackie," attended staff meetings and layout sessions, even stood in line at the Xerox machine.

The result was a total transformation. "She's become more independent," Baldrige said. "Now she realizes she doesn't need a dominating man to lean on. Jackie is looking radiant." To George Plimpton, Jackie was suddenly "like the girl I first knew who had a great sense of fun and enthusiasm. It must have been an extraordinary thing for her to be on her own."

Just as Caroline neared the end of her stay in London, tragedy struck again. On June 27, 1976, after a night of cards at a friend's country house, Stas Radziwill collapsed and died of a heart attack while undressing for bed. He was sixty-one years old.

Jackie flew to England to attend the funeral with Caroline. Accompanying Mrs. Onassis was Maurice Tempelsman, a wealthy diamond merchant who with his wife, Lily, had been a frequent guest at the Kennedy White House. One month younger than Jackie, Tempelsman was born into an Orthodox Jewish family in Antwerp, Belgium. In 1940, the Yiddish-speaking Tempelsmans fled the Nazis for New York, where he skipped college to join his father's diamond-importing firm. With the help of his attorney, Adlai Stevenson, Tempelsman forged important links with the powerful Oppenheimer diamond-mining family. It was not long before he became a "sightholder" — one of only 160 people in the world allowed to purchase diamonds directly from the DeBeers cartel.

Caroline knew that Maurice was still very much married, not to mention the father of three children. She would also soon learn that the devoutly Orthodox Lily Tempelsman had no intention of giving her husband a divorce.

The balding, pudgy, self-effacing Jewish diamond merchant may have seemed an unlikely choice for Jackie. But Caroline was impressed by the way he doted on her mother, and by the simple fact that he did not leave Jackie's side the entire time she was in England. "Maurice was totally, utterly devoted to Jackie," said Jackie's friend Aileen Mehle. "He'd move heaven and earth to make her happy — and he had the money to do it!"

At Stas Radziwill's funeral, it seemed to other mourners that Mrs. Onassis, her face etched with grief, was visibly more upset than the deceased's ex-wife. "Jackie loved Stas," said his niece Isabelle, Countess d'Ornano. "He counted in her life."

Since Caroline had been staying at Stas's house, his unexpected death also hit her hard. Even here, thousands of miles from home, she found herself in the all-too-familiar position of wearing black and listening to the muffled sobs of her relatives.

Caroline's London adventure ended in August, and she returned to New York. Although it had been only six weeks since the funeral, she scarcely recognized her mother. Alfred Eisenstaedt, the legendary *Life* magazine photographer who had shot both JFK and Jackie on many occasions, saw a remarkable physical change in Caroline's mom. "She was forty-seven but might as well have been twenty-two," Eisenstaedt observed. "Hard work — and I think she took her job more seriously than people realized — had made her look younger."

Caroline enrolled at Radcliffe in September 1976 and moved into Winthrop House, the same dormitory that her father, her Uncles Bobby and Teddy, and her cousin Kathleen lived in when they attended Harvard. Indeed, wherever Caroline looked, there were reminders of what the Kennedy name meant to the Harvard community, and vice versa. Her family had only recently opened the university's John F. Kennedy School of Government, and it often seemed that everywhere — in local shops, on the walls of taverns, in classrooms and lecture halls — hung portraits of JFK.

"Sometimes," she confided to a friend, "I wish I could just wake up and not be 'Caroline Kennedy.' Just for one day, I'd like to be somebody else."

Toward that end, Caroline tried desperately to blend in with the rest of the student body. She parked her one luxury — her red BMW sports car — on campus but nearly always preferred to get around Cambridge on her bike or riding the bus. Still eschewing the elegant fashions for which her mother was famous, Caroline preferred faded jeans, pullovers, and scuffed clogs. "She shops in the same places all of us shop," said a fellow student, "and that's why we all end up looking the same. Some people cultivate that carefully casual look and spend a lot of time and money on it. Caroline couldn't care less."

In stark contrast to her spendaholic mom, Caroline was, like the rest of the Kennedy clan, something of a tightwad. Caroline's father, as well as her Kennedy uncles and aunts, was nearly always short on cash, forcing others to pay for meals and carfare. On those occasions when she did pick up the tab, Caroline, again like her notoriously stingy Kennedy relatives, proved to be a poor tipper. "Waitresses," said one acquaintance, "hate her."

Still, Caroline was also prone to unsung acts of generosity. Even as a freshman in college, she began writing large checks for charitable causes. When a classmate told her about a young man who had dropped out of school and now was begging for handouts in

Harvard Square, she walked up to the stunned stranger and slipped him several hundred dollars in cash.

Following her ten months at Sotheby's, Caroline decided to major in fine arts. The syllabus included courses in classical architecture, art history, anthropology, humanities, language history, Afro-American studies, and philosophy.

Not unexpectedly, Caroline also brought with her a strong social conscience — and a powerful need to learn all she could about her father's role in history. The little girl who'd covered the walls of her bedroom with photos of her dad and collected the more than three hundred commemorative stamps that had been issued around the world bearing his likeness now read everything about him she could find. She devoured scores of books about his administration and his political career, taking care to skip over the lurid accounts of his personal life.

By the time she reached Radcliffe, Caroline had already campaigned for Uncle Teddy, attended rallies for 1972 Democratic nominee George McGovern, and rung doorbells for antiwar congressional (and later Senate and presidential) candidate John Kerry. As an undergraduate, she frequently attended campus meetings and lectures on pressing social issues, hoping to go unnoticed. That was especially true the day newspapers were full of details concerning the $26 million settlement Jackie received from the estate of Aristotle Onassis. That same week, Caroline went ahead with plans to attend John Kenneth Galbraith's lecture "The Nature of Poverty."

On another occasion, Caroline was among thirty-five hundred students protesting Harvard's ownership of stock in U.S. companies doing business with South Africa. "One, two, three, four, throw apartheid out the door," she shouted, holding a candle aloft. "Five, six, seven, eight, don't support the racist state."

Jackie, meantime, was busy deciding what would be the best way for Caroline to spend her summer vacation. During a lull in her relationship with Tempelsman, Jackie had become briefly involved with *New York Daily News* columnist Pete Hamill — a highly publicized fling that came as quite a shock to the woman he had been living with for seven years, actress Shirley MacLaine.

With Hamill's help, Jackie arranged for Caroline to spend the summer earning $156 a week as a copy girl at the *Daily News*. Arriving each morning in a chauffeur-driven limousine and carrying a bag lunch, Caroline followed her bodyguard to the elevator, went straight to the seventh floor, and started work — fetching coffee for harried editors and reporters, changing typewriter ribbons, and delivering messages. At one point, a veteran staffer went on a tirade about privileges for the rich that was "obviously aimed at her," said another reporter. "But she was not particularly embarrassed. She just gave him a cold stare."

Caroline kept to herself at the paper, sitting on a wooden bench reading until her name was called. "We can tell she's coming," said a reporter, "by the clomp of her clogs."

To celebrate the end of her first week on the job, Caroline went with law student Allan Talbott to see the hot movie of the summer, *Star Wars*. Afterward they ducked into nearby Willie's Bar for burgers and a beer. Willie's had become a favorite hangout for Caroline, and what few dates she had often wound up there.

This time, however, a reporter did spot them — and Caroline did not seem to mind at all. "I expect this will get written up as my first romance," she said with a smile. "I don't mind, because I will be seeing him again. We've had a lovely, casual evening — the type I prefer." As for the informal nature of her surroundings: "I didn't think we would get spotted if we stayed in just the regular places in the neighborhood. Everybody thinks they'll find me at fancy restaurants and discotheques — but I'm much happier just having a normal date."

But for Caroline, a "normal date" was at best elusive. While Caroline was still working at the *Daily News*, a young man took her to see a Broadway show. As the cab neared the theater, she became anxious. "I really hate to be indoors," she explained. "You don't know what will happen to you, and you have so little control. I don't know who'll sit next to me or who will recognize me, and the feeling is confining."

To battle those feelings, they exited the cab a few blocks before they reached the theater, then timed their entrance just as the houselights dimmed. Before the intermission lights could go up, she bolted from her seat. "I'm going to hide in the bathroom until later," she explained to her date.

At the *Daily News*, Caroline got her first break when Elvis Presley's death at age forty-two shocked the nation. Pete Hamill took her along with him to Memphis to cover the story. Tape recorder in hand, Caroline interviewed mourners at Graceland — including Presley's ex-wife, Priscilla, and his father, Vernon — and was allowed to spend time beside Elvis's open casket. But soon Caroline became the story, and the crowds made it difficult for her to function as just another working journalist. When *Daily News* editors canceled the piece because Caroline failed to phone it in to the news desk on time, she did something her peers in the newsroom would almost certainly never have been permitted to do — she sold it to *Rolling Stone*.

"At the far end of the room was the gleaming copper coffin that contained the body of Elvis Presley," Caroline wrote. "His face seemed swollen and his sideburns reached his chin. 'He doesn't look anything like himself,' the woman beside me said softly. 'He just doesn't look anything like himself.'"

Back at Radcliffe, Caroline still had a hard time fitting in. She dated little, confiding to a handful of people that she felt like an outcast. "I don't know if people really like me for myself, or if it's just my name they want as a friend," she confided to Rick Licata, a cub reporter at the *New York Daily News* she was also dating at the time. "Who can I believe?" Mark Director, who worked with Caroline on the *Harvard Crimson*, sympathized. "Caroline," he said, "just wants to be accepted for herself."

The press had, for whatever reason, left both Caroline and John alone at their respective schools. But Caroline always lived in fear of being too conspicuous, of attracting the kind of attention that would have New York paparazzi packing their bags and catching the next plane up to Boston. "They're like sharks," she told a friend. "They can smell blood in the water."

Nevertheless, Licata was impressed with how she handled the unexpected. One day they were out for a walk when a man spotted

Caroline and raced up to them. "They should have shot your whole family!" the man shouted at her.

Licata was horrified, but Caroline just shrugged it off. "Oh, I get that all the time," she said. "There are just as many people who tell me how wonderful my father was, and that makes up for it."

Unfortunately, few of Caroline's three hundred fellow Winthrop House residents would ever get the opportunity to meet her, much less get to know her. "She's the resident celebrity nobody knows," said fellow student Alyssa Karger. "Caroline keeps very much to herself, and very few of us even see her around." Another student who happened to be enrolled in several classes with Caroline said, "I've often seen her eating breakfast alone in the corner of the house dining room. If she was somebody else, you'd probably go over and say hello or something. But everybody is hesitant to introduce themselves to her — more so than if she was somebody else."

Ken Getz, who also lived in Caroline's dormitory, agreed. "All heads turn when she walks into a room," Getz said, "and it's obvious she feels uncomfortable about it. She seems to be scared of talking to us, and a lot of us are scared to talk to her. She is always with the same two or three people."

"For all her life she's had to live with the

Kennedy mystique," Licata explained. "It is very difficult for her to screen people — to find out who are her real friends and who are hangers-on. There are very few people she can trust."

Yet many on campus viewed Caroline as remote and aloof. It did not help when, after accepting an invitation to a big campus party, she failed to show. "Everybody was pretty angry about it," said Pete Rasine, an economics student. "I think everyone got the impression Caroline was a bit of a snob. They were counting on her being at the party — it would have made it kind of special. The impression of her around Harvard seems to be that she's spoiled and she doesn't do anything she doesn't want to do."

Whatever their differences — Caroline still chafed at Jackie's need to control her life down to the last detail — mother and daughter were closer than ever. Jackie visited Winthrop House on several occasions, and — much to her delight — was never recognized. Or so she thought. One student who watched them from a distance as they sat on a bench talking was impressed by how happy they both were in each other's company. "I know when my mother came up to see me, we were both kind of tense," said the student. "But there was this easy banter between Caroline and her mother. Obviously lots of kidding, lots of laughter. It was a surprise, because Jackie Onassis always seemed like this intimidating figure to me. In this context, at least, she was very warm, very . . . well, motherly."

One sticking point continued to be Caroline's weight. Still resisting pressure from her mother to go on a strict diet, Caroline indulged her love of junk food. After a party at the home of a mutual friend, Andy Warhol wrote in his diary that Caroline's face was "so beautiful, but she really got fat, her behind is so big." He also pointed out that, because Jackie was angry when her daughter recently returned home from a party at 4:00 a.m., this time Caroline was the "first person to leave. I think Jackie has her on a schedule. Now she has to be home before midnight."

Just as she had with Caroline, Jackie was also carefully stage-managing John's life. As part of her ongoing effort to "toughen up" JFK's son while at the same time keeping him away from the Hickory Hill bunch during the summers, Jackie sent John to help rebuild an earthquake-ravaged Guatemalan village in 1976 and the next year to an island off the rugged Maine coast for survivalist training.

When they did manage to get together in New York, John and Caroline clearly delighted in each other's company. They attended several high-profile events together —

the opening-night bash for the Al Pacino film *Bobby Deerfield*, for example, and several private parties at Studio 54. But they seemed happiest strolling down the streets of Manhattan trading stories about their mother. Caroline and John "always smiled," said a friend, "when they spoke to each other."

Brother and sister also shared the Kennedy passion for speed. At 8:35 p.m. on July 4, 1977, Caroline's BMW was clocked going eighty-six miles per hour — thirty-one miles per hour over the speed limit — as she raced to the Hamptons with an unidentified bearded male in the passenger seat. The police, red lights flashing and sirens blaring, pursued Caroline for four miles before she finally pulled over. "She was very polite to me," said Suffolk County Highway Patrolman Edward Dietler, who recognized Caroline as he handed her a speeding ticket. "She didn't push her importance or whatever."

Six months later, a warrant was issued for Caroline's arrest when she failed to show up in court to answer the speeding summons. Three Kennedy family attorneys rushed to the Suffolk County Courthouse to explain that Caroline had accompanied her Uncle Ted on a fact-finding mission to Asia and "completely forgotten" about the ticket. Judge Paul Creditor withdrew the warrant and rescheduled Caroline's court date, but not before commenting, "For a twenty-five-dollar fine, she brings in three thousand dollars' worth of attorneys."

Arrest warrants aside, Jackie still had the upper hand with her children. But, try as she might, Caroline's mom could not control everything and everyone in her life. Without advance notice to Jackie, Viking had agreed to publish Jeffrey Archer's *Shall We Tell the President?*, a suspense novel about an imaginary plot to assassinate Ted Kennedy after he took office in 1981. The book was published to scathing reviews in 1977, and Jackie, feeling betrayed, switched to Doubleday.

Jackie's romantic life in the late 1970s was also less than stable, as she ricocheted from Frank Sinatra to Pete Hamill to documentary-film producer Peter Davis to Warren Beatty and back to Maurice Tempelsman. Like Jackie, who pored over every word written about herself and her family in the tabloids, Caroline followed her mother's personal life in the daily press.

Yet there was always time for Jackie to play matchmaker for her own daughter. In the spring of 1978, Jackie invited one of her Doubleday coworkers, Yale-educated Tom Carney, to 1040 Fifth for dinner. An aspiring novelist and screenwriter, Carney was the son of veteran Hollywood writer–turned–cattle rancher Otis Carney. Tom's parents divided their time between the old Beverly Hills estate of Humphrey Bogart and Lauren Bacall and the Carneys' cattle ranches in Wyoming and Arizona.

From the start, Jackie saw Carney as Kennedy marriage material. He was not only an Ivy Leaguer and Irish Catholic (Carney was Jesuit schooled and had even been an altar boy), but he was a full decade older than twenty-year-old Caroline — just the right age difference, Jackie firmly believed, between a prospective bride and groom. Carney also looked the part — tall, lanky, and athletic, he would have easily blended into any Hyannis Port gathering in his jeans, Bass Weejuns, and rumpled sportcoat.

Caroline and Carney clicked instantly, and they were soon seen everywhere around Manhattan — roller-skating in Central Park, discoing at Studio 54 and Xenon, swimming in the surf at Hyannis Port, strolling hand in hand down Fifth Avenue. Carney was, said those closest to her at the time, Caroline's first serious relationship. "I don't believe she had ever really been intimate with anyone before Tom," said one. "He was so much like the rest of her family — Tom even *looked* like a Kennedy — that she felt comfortable around him. He was the first man she ever allowed to get really close to her. She totally fell in love with him and wanted to marry him."

The feeling was mutual. "I love Caroline," Carney said after he took her to Wyoming to meet his parents. "And I'm sure not going to marry anyone else." Carney's parents were just as smitten with Caroline. Miss Kennedy was, said Fredrika Carney, "like a soft drink — bubbly, refreshing, and full of life."

That August, Carney went along with Jackie and Caroline when they vacationed on St. Martin. Although no formal engagement announcement was planned, he guessed that they would have an elaborate church wedding as soon as Caroline graduated from Radcliffe.

In the meantime, Carney did express concern over the difference in their ages and complained that it was "a drag" to have to visit her at college. "She's still a schoolgirl," he said. "I feel so old having to go there to visit my girlfriend. She's the youngest girl I ever went out with." But, he insisted, "We have a lot in common. We never run out of things to talk about. We enjoy doing the same things. . . . I'm ready to get married. I want to settle down."

Carney was eager to start a family ("I would certainly raise my children as Catholics") and claimed that he had thought "long and hard" about the prospect of living the rest of his life in the spotlight. "Hopefully it will all work out for the best, since we are a very low-key couple. I do love her."

However awkward she may have been at Radcliffe, Caroline blossomed in Carney's presence. "She was just beaming whenever he came around," said another Winthrop House resident. Being in love was the catalyst for other changes as well. Although Jackie had been unrelenting in her efforts to get Caroline to lose weight, it wasn't until she met Carney that Caroline suddenly became a diet-and-fitness fanatic. Within a four-month period, Caroline lost over thirty pounds and dropped several dress sizes.

"Caroline is a pretty straight sort of gal," said Harvard classmate Michael DeLure. "In a way she's a bit prudish, sort of straitlaced. She's not the type who would just jump into bed with any guy. I wouldn't be surprised if she married Carney."

On October 20, 1979, Jackie, Caroline, and John journeyed to the Boston suburb of Dorchester for the dedication of the John F. Kennedy Library. I. M. Pei's stark white futuristic structure with its high glass walls looking out over the sparkling waters of Dorchester Bay reflected JFK's eternally youthful, forward-looking appeal.

Twenty-six of Caroline's cousins were present at the dedication ceremonies, along with Uncle Ted and aunts Ethel, Eunice, Pat, and Jean. Caroline, now twenty-two, sat next to her brother. When she stood up, the results of her new diet-and-exercise regimen were plainly evident. The assembled crowd, which included then–President Jimmy Carter and many famous faces from the New Frontier era, was surprised to see that Jack's daughter had turned into, in Andy Warhol's words, "a raving beauty" — all cheekbones and gleaming white teeth and flowing chestnut tresses.

Despite her glamorous new look, Caroline was still painfully shy. It was all she could do now to muster the courage to stand in front of that crowd of dignitaries and introduce her younger brother, now a freshman at Brown University. Not yet nineteen and already a strikingly handsome cross between the Bouviers and the Kennedys, John stepped up to the podium and recited Stephen Spender's poem "I Think Continually of Those Who Were Truly Great."

In reality, Caroline had for years played a significant behind-the-scenes role at the JFK Library. When Caroline was sixteen, Jackie brought her to see the museum while it was temporarily housed at a federal archives center in Waltham, Massachusetts. "I was afraid at first that the impact of all the memorabilia, the paintings of her father and other material would be upsetting," said Jack's old friend and aide Dave Powers, now the museum's curator. "But she was far less upset than she was inspired, and she immediately became devoted to the project." Caroline's first idea, Powers recalled, "was to donate the fifty-one dolls she had received as gifts from the different heads of state." Since then, Caroline, whom Powers described as "a very bright and creative girl," had become a major force behind the museum, coming up with new ideas for exhibits and attending virtually every meeting of the board of trustees.

At the dawn of the 1980s, Jackie and Caroline carefully nurtured their memories of JFK. Like her mother, Caroline, who gradually came to see herself as a principal protector of her father's legacy, still collected JFK memorabilia: stamps, coins, statues, plaques, banners, flags, books — knick-knacks and mementos of every conceivable variety. She also occasionally cut pictures of her father out of newspapers and magazines, just as she had done when she was a little girl back in Sister Joanne Frey's religion class.

Caroline could look at the famous photographs of herself and John crawling beneath Daddy's desk or waving good-bye as he took off from the White House lawn in his helicopter, and the memories flooded back. These were sensations she could not share with John, who was not certain he really remembered any of it. Caroline would often prod her brother to recall one incident or another. "Oh, you know, it was the time he . . ." she would say. Or "What about that day when we all . . ."

But too often John would shake his head.

"You know," he confessed, "I don't even remember him. Sometimes I think I might, but I don't."

Caroline and Tom Carney, meanwhile, still appeared to be steering a course toward matrimony. They spent Christmas together in Barbados. Wherever they went in New York, they were invariably intercepted by paparazzi — leaping from behind parked cars as they exited a movie theater, lying in wait outside Tom's three-room apartment on the Upper East Side. Unlike her brother, Caroline had never really grown accustomed to being stared at and pursued. "I can deal with it, I guess," she said, "but there are times when I just want to scream." Once, in a coffee shop, she suddenly felt too self-conscious to eat, convinced — and rightly so — that all eyes were on her. "Tell me," she said anxiously, "when nobody is looking at me."

On June 5, 1980, Jackie looked on with pride from behind her trademark dark glasses as Caroline received her bachelor's degree in fine arts from Radcliffe. But the euphoria was short-lived. In August, around the time she expected to be marching down the aisle with Carney, he abruptly called off their relationship. "What ended it was the publicity," said Carney. "I couldn't see spending the rest of my life with cameras hovering around my head." Nor could his ego, he admitted, survive his being labeled "Mr. Caroline Kennedy."

"Caroline was shattered, just destroyed," recalled one of the few people she could confide in. "She had no warning. It just took her completely by surprise." To make matters worse, weeks later she learned that Carney had become engaged to someone else, a striking forty-one-year-old brunette named Maureen Lambray. Coincidentally, Lambray had worked on Bobby Kennedy's staff as a photographer covering his 1968 presidential campaign.

As the holidays approached, Caroline sat with friends in a popular Manhattan rib joint, Wylie's, and poured out her heart to friends. According to Wylie's owner, Jerry Shaw, Caroline wiped tears from her eyes as she confessed that she was "trying to get over this . . . but it's really terribly tough.

"What am I going to do without him?" she asked, pointing out that it was not only the first time she had ever been dumped but that Carney was "the very first man I ever dated that my mom really liked. Now what do I do? Thanksgiving, Christmas, and New Year's are all coming up. I have a million guys I can date, but, frankly, who cares?"

Caroline decided to lose herself in work, joining the Metropolitan Museum of Art's Film and Television Department as a production assistant. The job would prove serendipitous, for in seeking to lose herself in work, she would find her future husband.

Although her mother's massive apartment was located across the street from the museum — only steps from her office — Caroline preferred to set up housekeeping on the other side of Central Park. With two male friends, she moved into a $2,000-a-month, three-bedroom apartment on the Upper West Side and each morning took a crosstown bus to work.

Caroline still saw her mother two or three times a week and spoke to her brother on the phone every day. For the moment, Big Sister was refereeing the battles that raged between John and Jackie over his dream of becoming an actor. As an undergraduate at Brown, John would have major roles in plays ranging from *The Tempest* and David Rabe's *In the Boom Boom Room* to J. M. Synge's classic *Playboy of the Western World* to Miguel Piñero's *Short Eyes*, in which John played a child molester.

When *Saturday Night Fever* producer Robert Stigwood offered him the chance to play his father in a feature film based on JFK's early years, John pleaded with his mother to let him take the role. But Jackie, said a Brown classmate, "told John in no uncertain terms that acting was beneath him, that he was his father's son, and that he had a tradition of public service to uphold. They really had terrible fights over this. . . . What he wanted from her was respect, and for a while there he just didn't feel as if he had it."

Caroline recognized that her brother had talent as an actor and sympathized with his desire to break free from their mother's control. But she also shared Jackie's concern that Hollywood was merely out to exploit the Kennedy name. After Brown, John and his then-girlfriend, Christina Haag, played doomed lovers in Brian Friel's *Winners* at Manhattan's Irish Arts Center. Caroline and Jackie both pointedly refused to attend.

Caroline, meanwhile, had a new man in her life. At work, she met six-foot-two-inch-tall, prematurely graying Edwin Arthur Schlossberg, a self-styled cultural historian/ artist/author, an acolyte of Buckminster Fuller and founder of a small company that produced multimedia video projects for museums and businesses. Son of a wealthy Manhattan-based textile manufacturer, Schlossberg was also Jewish and thirteen years older than Caroline — a difference that closely mirrored the twelve-year age gap between Jack and Jackie.

Schlossberg was raised on New York's Upper West Side and attended Birch Wathen, one of the city's most exclusive private schools. He was described in his school yearbook as "a serious, self-fashioned poet philosopher" and was willed "a brace for his knee and ego."

Like Caroline, Schlossberg was the product of an Ivy League education. While still at Columbia in the mid-1960s, Ed was, as he later put it, "invited into the process" of creating art in New York. He hung out with painters Jasper Johns and Robert Rauschenberg and became a close friend of avant-garde composer John Cage.

After a brief stint writing novelty books and doggerel, he tried designing T-shirts before trying his hand as a conceptual artist. Schlossberg's own first creations were bits of what he called "concrete poetry" — scraps of letters on Plexiglas panels that could be maneuvered to create bits of verse. Schlossberg also stenciled poetry onto rice-paper scrolls held together by bamboo poles.

In 1968, "Bucky" Fuller hired Schlossberg to be his teaching assistant at Southern Illinois University. "I learned a lot from Bucky — both negative and positive," Ed said of the visionary responsible for the futuristic Dymaxion car and the geodesic dome. "He was fantastic at writing menus. But he wasn't interested in cooking dinner. . . . I just thought he has had this life of ideas: fantastic, amazing, poetic, beautiful ideas. Then he moves on. It is often harder," Schlossberg came to realize, "to slog through it and make sure the thing gets done."

Schlossberg went on to earn a Ph.D. from Columbia in science and literature in 1971; his doctoral thesis consisted of an imaginary chat between Samuel Beckett and Albert Einstein. A stretch, to say the least, it nonetheless impressed some of Schlossberg's admirers on the faculty as academically daring.

Schlossberg's veneer of erudition masked the fact that he was still not quite earning a living. "My father worried that I would starve pursuing the poet's life," he cracked. That changed when, at a White House conference on children and youth, he met the director of the Brooklyn Children's Museum and was offered a job on the spot. Schlossberg consulted with MIT's leading experts on artificial intelligence and set out to create a hands-on interactive experience for museum-goers.

Using the money he made writing books on computer games, Schlossberg started ESI — Edwin Schlossberg Incorporated — a multimedia design company, in 1977. The firm was soon hired to design exhibitions at Sesame Place, an "interactive play" park outside Dallas, and an "educational animal farm" for the ASPCA in Framingham, Massachusetts.

Still, Ed's firm was struggling to get off the ground when he met Caroline. With the Schlossberg family fortune as a cushion, it scarcely mattered; Ed would never have to worry about making his rent. Caroline was instantly captivated by Schlossberg's offbeat charm. "He has a Kennedy quality to him," explained Ed's friend Mark Rosenman. "He has ambitious ideas, a vision for society." There were other similarities. "He and Caroline are both sort of loners," Rosenman observed. Whether it was at Ed's SoHo apartment or his weekend house in the Berkshires, "they like to camp out by themselves."

When she told Andy Warhol that she had fallen for Ed, the pop-art icon was not surprised. "Caroline likes funny people," Warhol posited. "He probably was babbling intellectually, and she got fascinated. He was probably saying strange, peculiar quotations or something."

Unfortunately, Schlossberg was not the only babbler in Caroline's life. In August 1981, she was eating lunch alone at a restaurant near the museum when a clean-cut man pulled up a chair and sat down.

"Are you Caroline Kennedy?" Kevin King asked.

"Yes," she said tentatively.

"I'm Kevin King," he said, "and I'm sure that we've met before in San Francisco."

"Hmmm. I've never been in San Francisco," she replied.

King persisted. "I know that I've met you,"

he said. "There are all these forces. People pushing me around. Forces manipulating me." Then he pulled out a map of the museum, and in the margins was scrawled her home address.

That night, Caroline was too upset to go home to her West Side apartment. She slept at her mother's instead. Caroline had reason to be alarmed. The year before, Mark David Chapman had gunned down John Lennon just a few blocks away, outside Lennon's apartment at the Dakota. Earlier in 1981, John Hinckley Jr., who was obsessed with Jodie Foster, shot President Ronald Reagan in a bizarre attempt to impress the actress.

The day after that first encounter with Kevin King, Caroline phoned a Secret Service agent who used to guard her, and together they took a cab to her apartment. King was sitting on her doorstep. Too frightened to get out of the cab — even with the Secret Service agent — she returned to 1040 Fifth.

King, police would later learn, was a delusional thirty-five-year-old law school graduate from Palo Alto, California, who harbored the belief that he and Caroline Kennedy were destined to wed. King lived at the YMCA but spent his days and nights lurking in the shadows outside Caroline's apartment building. Late one night, King rang the doorbell of Caroline's neighbor, William Morris, yelling, "I must see Caroline Kennedy! I'm in love with her, and I'm going to marry her." Another night, he brought his luggage and slept in the hallway.

Jackie hired three additional bodyguards to tail her daughter, but that did not deter King from showing up at concerts Caroline attended and restaurants she frequented. Then King began sending notes and letters to Caroline at her office. "Why don't you marry me?" he asked in one. "You can borrow some rice from your mother's wedding." Another note concluded, "Next time I'll fuck all your relatives if you don't marry me."

Caroline did not want to press charges at first, but Jackie finally convinced her to file a complaint. When police showed up at the YMCA to arrest King on harassment charges, they reportedly found, among other things, a detailed account of Caroline's movements, a list of the aliases she and her mother used to make reservations, an issue of *New York* magazine containing a story about John Lennon's murder, and a note that read, "Sirhan was right. It should have been Ethel."

"We had all the makings of a Hinckley and a Chapman," said John Venetucci, one of the three arresting officers, "but we nipped it in the bud. We felt like we defused a potential bomb." Agreed Sergeant Jay Kosack, "We could have prevented a homicide."

It was not the last Caroline would see of

King. At his one-day trial before Manhattan Criminal Court Judge John Bradley, King acted as his own counsel — and at one point subjected Caroline to a grueling cross-examination. But it was under the gentle prodding of Assistant District Attorney Alan Buonpastore that Caroline became emotional.

"Tell me," he asked, holding up one of the notes King had sent her, "did this letter frighten you?"

"Yes," Caroline replied, fighting back tears. "Knowing the things that have happened in the past . . . it made me a little nervous. . . ."

King seemed unfazed even after Judge Bradley found him guilty on all eight misdemeanor counts. "If she has any interest in me," he told the judge, "I'd still like to marry her." Sent to Rikers Island, King then began calling her office from jail. "My heart won't rest until I win her," he told a reporter from his jail cell. "I feel she is a person I can give my care to. Caroline could be a great wife. I would like to support her and protect her from all." Later, in a letter to Caroline, King wrote, "You must give me the chance to give you the love you deserve. . . . Please do me the favor of appearing at the court sentencing — then I can propose to you in person."

At his sentencing hearing two weeks later, King screamed as he was dragged kicking from the courtroom, "I don't intend to change my mind! I have a right to love the person I am attracted to!"

King would not be the last stalker Caroline would have to contend with. Two years later, Herbert Randall Gefvert would begin a similar pattern of harassment, culminating in his arrest in 1984 for threatening to kill Caroline by blowing up the Metropolitan Museum. In one of his many incoherent calls to Caroline, Gefvert, a manic-depressive who drifted in and out of mental hospitals, also claimed that "twenty hit men" were lying in wait to murder her.

For the time being, at least, Caroline breathed a sigh of relief that Kevin King was finally in custody. She now felt free to pursue a relationship with the man she had really fallen for. After a party in Aspen in December 1981, Warhol noted in his diary, "Saw Caroline and the Schlossberg boy. They're madly in love."

It was not long before Caroline was spending most nights at Schlossberg's million-dollar loft in SoHo. Ed had even taken to redesigning Caroline's look. She surprised the guests at her twenty-seventh-birthday party by showing up in uncharacteristically slinky yellow-and-black silk pajamas. "Ed picked that out for her," a friend said. "He buys most of her clothes."

As their romance heated up, Caroline and

Ed spent time together at Red Gate Farm, Jackie's newly completed retreat on Martha's Vineyard. In 1978 she had quietly paid the island's Hornblower family $1.1 million for 356 acres (later expanded to 474 acres) along Squibnocket Pond in the Vineyard's Gay Head section. Dotted with scrub oaks, Scotch pines, marshes and ponds, the undeveloped tract included 4,620 feet of beachfront.

Caroline's mom had spent another $3 million building what she called "my wonderful little house" — nineteen rooms, eight fireplaces, a separate guesthouse, and, of course, breathtaking views of the Atlantic. Jackie's daughter and the tall, middle-aged man with the unruly gray hair became a familiar sight strolling on the sand, just yards from the stretch of beach adjacent to Mom's property where scores of sun-worshippers were legally permitted to frolic in the nude.

It was not far from her mother's estate on Labor Day, 1981, that Caroline had an unexpected — and unwelcome — encounter with a figure from her past. She was bicycling along one of the Vineyard's narrow, winding roads with her friend David Michaelis when a car pulled up alongside her, edging her onto the sandy shoulder. Several photographers were leaning out the car window, snapping away.

"Hi, Caroline!" shouted Ron Galella, his

face just eighteen inches from hers. "How are you? It's me!"

Then the cars raced ahead, pulled into a clearing, and the photographers scrambled out. Caroline and Michaelis turned their bikes around, but the car pursued them again, this time swerving in front of the couple to block their path.

To get away, Caroline then pulled into the opposite lane, risking a head-on collision with oncoming cars just to escape being photographed. Later, Caroline broke down while relating the incident to Ed. "I was in an absolute panic," she told him.

Jackie had been having similar run-ins with their old nemesis. A few weeks before, Galella ambushed her when she came out of a movie theater in the middle of the afternoon. Then, on that same Labor Day weekend, Jackie and Maurice were trying to board Jackie's powerboat when, Jackie recalled, Galella "came zooming by, making a wake, frightening us. The engine of our boat stalled. We couldn't start it." Three weeks later, the indefatigable Galella struck again — this time as Jackie and Maurice left a performance of Twyla Tharp's dance company at the Wintergarden Theater in New York.

That night, Tempelsman drove Jackie to a police station, where they filed a criminal complaint against Galella. They charged that Galella had repeatedly violated the 1972 court order that prohibited him from coming close to Jackie and her children. Under cross-examination by Marvin Mitchelson during the subsequent trial, Caroline described her feelings that day on the Vineyard. "I was frightened," she said, "and noticed that my heart was beating very fast. I've been frightened by Mr. Galella before. I didn't know what he was going to do."

"Doesn't your heart often beat fast when you're riding a bicycle?" Mitchelson asked.

"Only when I'm trying to get away," she snapped back.

"Why were you so fearful?"

"I didn't want to fall," she said. "I felt I was being edged over to the sandy side of the road."

"You were angry, weren't you?" Mitchelson smirked.

Caroline leaned forward. "I was *frightened,*" she answered, eyes flashing.

Finding in the women's favor, the judge ordered Galella to pay Jackie $10,000 in damages and to never take another picture of her or Caroline again.

Throughout the ordeal, Ed stood by Caroline. But that did not keep Caroline's maternal grandmother, among a few others, from being mortified by Caroline's choice of beaus. Three years after Uncle Hughdie's death, Janet Auchincloss had married her childhood friend Bingham Morris, a suitably rich and inordinately well-bred investment banker. Now the devoutly Catholic Mrs. Janet Lee Bouvier Auchincloss Morris was being told that, as her daughter became increasingly enamored of Maurice Tempelsman, her granddaughter was involved with Ed Schlossberg — both men from Orthodox Jewish families.

Indeed, a streak of anti-Semitism ran through both sides of Caroline's family. Scottish-American Hugh Auchincloss, according to his stepson Gore Vidal, "was an anti-Semite of the reflex variety. He told stories about Jews the same way he told stories about blacks and so on." Joe Kennedy was another matter. Even as he served as U.S. ambassador to the Court of St. James's prior to World War II, the Kennedy patriarch was openly sympathetic to Hitler — a position that forced an enraged Franklin Roosevelt to recall him.

Bobby had been Caroline's surrogate father and Jackie's soul mate after Dallas. But RFK, a champion of civil rights in the 1968 presidential race, had nonetheless also inherited his father's anti-Semitic streak. On more than one occasion, he had been heard to scream such slurs as "Jew bastard!" at someone he felt had crossed him or his family.

Between riding to the hounds with Virginia bluebloods and the "restricted" country clubs of the Northeast, Caroline's mother existed in a world that was even more gentile than it was genteel. Yet no one ever recalled hearing her protest. "Of course Jackie heard the jokes and the nasty remarks all the time," Cleveland Amory said. "She might on some level have been slightly sickened by them, but those were the rules of high society, and she was more than willing to play by them."

It took her marriage to Onassis to free Jackie from such narrow-minded thinking, or so she told her friend Vivian Crespi. But Caroline had also grown up in an Ivy League world that, even as the twentieth century was beginning to wind down, remained thick with anti-Semitism. From Sacred Heart and Concord Academy to Harvard and the bastions of exclusion on Park and Fifth Avenues, Caroline had lived a decidedly gentile life.

Swarthy, earthy Onassis gave his Irish-American stepdaughter a new perspective. So did Tempelsman, a kind man Caroline had grown genuinely fond of. At her Christmas party in 1981, Jackie welcomed Ed warmly and led him around the room. "I want to introduce you to somebody," she said in her little-girl whisper. "I want you all to meet my daughter's new friend, Ed Schlossberg."

Jackie, as it so happened, was also intrigued by Schlossberg's peculiarly elusive brand of brilliance. And Ed was not particularly athletic — a trait she found refreshing, given the Kennedys' passion for head-to-head combat on the playing field. Most important, said Jackie's friend Slim Keith, "Ed made Caroline happy — just like Maurice was making her happy."

By the end of 1983, speculation was rampant that Caroline and Ed were on the verge of matrimony. They were, in fact, unofficially engaged. But until both Caroline and Ed were ready to start a family, neither felt there was any rush to set a date. Caroline had been content working in the Metropolitan Museum's Office of Film and Television, but she now expressed interest in going to law school. Ed, meanwhile, had finally managed to get his design firm off the ground; several major projects were on the drawing boards, and he now employed a full-time staff of thirty-five designers. "Things are happening for Ed, and their living arrangement is working out great," John told a friend. "They have a quiet life together — the kind of life Caroline has always wanted — so why spoil it by getting married?"

Jackie, however, was not so pleased with the permanent live-in arrangement. Despite the fact that the still-married Maurice Tempelsman was living with Jackie at 1040 Fifth, she urged her daughter to wed Schlossberg and consider starting a family. While the tabloid press spun tales about raging battles over a prenuptial agreement (wealthy in his own right, Schlossberg volunteered to renounce any claim on Caroline's estate) and Schlossberg's seeing other women, Caroline had her own reasons for holding off on marriage plans. "She knew it would become a huge circus," recalled a former coworker at the museum. "She's really a very private person, and I got the impression she just wasn't ready for the whole Charles-and-Di wedding scene."

Then there was Mom. "Caroline and Jackie were incredibly close," Jamie Auchincloss said. "But as a rule, women in their twenties really don't like to be told what to do by their moms. That was probably even more true in Caroline's case, because Jackie always insisted on running the show." Complained Caroline, "Mom's always on my case about the doctor or the dentist or my clothes."

Jackie, meantime, still had her hands full with John. She was screening his calls to sort out the girls she deemed unsuitable, and she continued to dampen any hopes he may have had of having an acting career.

There was no way for Jackie to know that, while she kept her son on a tight leash, dependable, responsible Caroline would come closest to getting caught up in the reckless antics of Bobby's tribe. Caroline had always been close to Bobby's son David, who as a little boy had witnessed his father's murder on television and never fully recovered from the trauma. By the 1980s, he was hopelessly hooked on heroin and making regular trips to Harlem to feed his addiction.

On April 25, 1984, David's body was found in Palm Beach's Brazilian Court Hotel. He had died after injecting himself with the painkiller Demerol, the tranquilizer Mellaril, and cocaine. Yet only a small amount of cocaine was found in the room, as well as traces of the drug in the toilet, leading police to speculate that someone must have tried to dispose of the drugs before police arrived.

The night before, Caroline and Sydney Lawford were at the Kennedys' Palm Beach mansion with their aunts Eunice Shriver and Jean Smith. David had gone on a binge, and everyone was concerned that he might overdose.

That fatal morning, Caroline and Sydney went to the Brazilian Court looking for David. They checked out the lobby and the dining room, then called his room. No answer. Caroline then left a note at the front desk asking David to call her. Once back at the Kennedy mansion, Caroline got a call from David's girlfriend, Paula Scully. She told Caroline that paramedics were at the hotel. Caroline went back and spotted a policeman. "We pulled up," Caroline later recalled. "We went up to him, and he said, 'That's all right, girls, he's dead.'"

Both Caroline and Sydney reeled back in disbelief. While Sydney dissolved in tears,

Caroline remained preternaturally calm. ("I'm so proud of Caroline," Jackie had once observed. "In times of crisis, she always manages to stay in control.") After quizzing the police about what had happened — David had been found facedown on the floor between two beds, his neck twisted against the nightstand — Caroline phoned her aunts Jean and Eunice with the horrible news. Later, she took on the wrenching task of driving to the morgue and identifying David's body. He was just twenty-nine years old.

The Palm Beach police, however, were not entirely satisfied with Caroline's version of what transpired at the Brazilian Court the day David was found. Her recollections seemed inconsistent with those of the concierge who had discovered the body. In depositions, he was asked if anyone could have gone into the room before he did that morning. "Could have been Caroline Kennedy," he answered. "She called the room; there was no answer. She walked back toward the room, knocked on the door; this is what I heard. This is when I saw her coming out of the south wing area."

Caroline denied being anywhere near the room, and the police eventually dropped the matter — but not before a Florida judge blasted prosecutors for not making her sworn statements public. Authorities, said Judge John Born, were "being governed by what the

Kennedys want." It was the only time Caroline had come close to being dragged into a Kennedy scandal.

Whether she was giving depositions in Florida or testifying in a New York courtroom about incursions on her privacy, Caroline had already been exposed to more courtroom action than most people see in a lifetime. Even more significantly, she had lived a life in which issues like the right to privacy and personal safety were never taken for granted. Always an avid student of politics and public-policy issues, she now decided to go back to college to learn more about the U.S. Constitution and its guarantees. When Caroline enrolled at Columbia University Law School in the fall of 1985, Jackie told one Doubleday colleague she "could not have been more thrilled."

With the exception, perhaps, of March 2, 1986 — the day she officially announced the engagement of her daughter to Ed Schlossberg. Rose, not Jackie, was one of the reasons for Caroline's decision to finally take the plunge. Caroline's beloved grandmother, about to turn ninety-six and bedridden, still managed to express delight that her favorite granddaughter was marrying. What about the rumors that she did not approve of Caroline's marrying outside the Catholic faith? "Nonsense," said Rose's former secretary,

Barbara Gibson. "Caroline's happiness is the most important thing. She is devoted to Caroline."

There was also strength in numbers. Caroline's fears that her wedding would be the sole focus of media attention were allayed somewhat by the fact that three Kennedy weddings would take place within months of each other — television newswoman Maria Shriver's to Arnold Schwarzenegger in April, Timothy Shriver's to lawyer Linda Potter in June, and Caroline's in July. There would even be a royal wedding to steal some Kennedy thunder — Prince Andrew and Sarah Ferguson were scheduled to tie the knot at Westminster Abbey just one week after the Kennedy-Schlossberg nuptials.

Caroline got a taste of what a sideshow a Kennedy wedding could become on April 26, 1986, when she was maid of honor at her cousin Maria's wedding. Looking bemused, Caroline was paired up with musclebound best man Franco Columbu, a former Mr. Universe and two-time Mr. Olympia. "Don't look at him as a Republican," Maria told Uncle Teddy when family members complained that the groom was not one of them politically. "Look at him as the man I love. And if that doesn't work, look at him as someone who can squash you."

Caroline's wedding date — July 19, 1986 — happened to be Ed Schlossberg's forty-first birthday. It was also, much to the shock of those who were less than fond of the Kennedys, the seventeenth anniversary of Chappaquiddick. Nevertheless, the show went on as scheduled, with more than two thousand spectators — hundreds of them members of the press — jamming the streets of Hyannis Port and nearby Centerville, where the ceremony was conducted at the Church of Our Lady of Victory.

The mother of the bride had been laboring feverishly behind the scenes, overseeing the menu — cold pea soup, shrimp, chicken with lemon-mustard sauce, sirloin, and ice cream — selecting the arrangements of Cape Cod summer flowers, approving the design of the billowing white reception tent aflutter with multicolored flags, sending out the invitations. (Although hundreds of non–family members were invited, Jackie pointedly excluded her own Bouvier relatives from the wedding. After her first cousin John Davis wrote books about the Bouviers and the Kennedys, Jackie severed all ties with him and Black Jack's devoted twin sisters, Michelle and Maud.)

Jackie wisely chose to leave the dress entirely up to Caroline. "Unlike most mothers," said the designer, Caroline Herrera, "Mrs. Onassis did not interfere with Caroline's wedding-dress design." Jackie had told Herrera, "I am not going to get involved, because Caroline is the one who will wear it. I want her to be the happiest girl in the world."

Ed asked John to be the best man. It would be the fourth time that summer John had served in that capacity. "And I get better each time," he said with a wink. Caroline returned the favor to the new Mrs. Schwarzenegger, asking her to be matron of honor.

Emotions ran high at the bridal dinner the night before the ceremony. John, who had just been named "America's Most Eligible Bachelor" by *People* magazine, stood to deliver a toast. "All our lives, it's just been the three of us — my mother, Caroline, and me. Now," he said, turning to Ed, "there are four."

The event was, said guest John Kenneth Galbraith, "quite an eyeful" — from Caroline's size-four (she was now a size smaller than Jackie) white silk-organza gown with its tulle petticoat, shamrock appliqués, lace veil, and twenty-five-foot train to the wedding party's lavender-and-white outfits by Ed's favorite designer Willi Smith. Inside the church, guests were crammed in "like sardines," said JFK's longtime aide Dave Powers.

"The New Frontier!" Powers shouted as he entered the church and saw the faces of such familiar Kennedy-era figures as Ted

Sorensen, Arthur Schlesinger Jr., Pierre Salinger, and McGeorge Bundy. "This was one of the happy get-togethers," Powers said later. "There's been enough unhappiness for the family. But this time we were together, happy, recalling the good days. And there really was a strong feeling of Jack's presence."

The mother of the bride, wearing a size-six Herrera-designed pistachio crepe suit, clutched her handbag and waved to the onlookers with a gloved hand as she entered the church alone. The somewhat sheepish groom gave the crowd two high fives. Emerging from a rented white stretch limousine with her Uncle Teddy (a fresh white sheet concealed a cigar burn in the upholstery left by George Burns the week before), Caroline beamed as she waved to the well-wishers. Ted helped her with her train and patted her back reassuringly as she walked up the church steps. As they reached the door, Caroline and her uncle turned with their fingers to their lips and signaled to the crowd outside to quiet down. They did.

The ceremony was conducted by two priests; Schlossberg had already agreed to have a Catholic wedding and to raise whatever children they might have as Catholics. The groom's mother, though genuinely fond of both Caroline and her mother, seemed less than enthusiastic about the arrangement.

Sighed Mae Schlossberg, "We're Jewish, you know."

The occasion turned out to be anything but solemn, as the giddy bride and her equally giddy matron of honor tried in vain to stifle their giggles. Tellingly, Caroline omitted the word "obey" from their otherwise traditional vows. "She was really having fun up there," said longtime family friend Art Buchwald. "I've been to a lot of weddings, and Caroline is the happiest bride at the altar I've ever seen."

The mother of the bride, so famous for maintaining a stoic facade at all costs, broke down crying during the ceremony. Afterward, as Mr. and Mrs. Ed Schlossberg exited to the cheers of the waiting crowd, Jackie stood on the church steps, eyes red and swollen, tears streaming down her cheeks. Still smiling, she bit her lip and rested her head on Ted's shoulder. Then, unexpectedly, Ed's mother tripped and tumbled down the stairs, twisting her ankle.

Things would only get more emotional at the reception. Under the tent that had been set up on the emerald green lawns at Hyannis Port, Uncle Ted raised his glass in the first toast of the evening. "I'm filling in for my brother Jack," he told the 425 guests who were dining by the light from Japanese lanterns hung inside the tent. "To the mother of us all," he said, first paying tribute to

Rose before welcoming the parents of the groom into the family. Then, his voice cracking, Ted turned to the bride and groom. "We've all thought of Jack today, and how much he loved Caroline and how much he loved Jackie. . . . Caroline, he loved you so much." Ted, still struggling to maintain his composure, then raised a glass to the mother of the bride — "that extraordinary woman, Jack's only love. He would have been so proud of you today."

Caroline and Jackie were in tears — along with, it seemed, everybody else. "Nobody had a dry eye when the senator spoke," said Carolina Herrera. "It was a very emotional day. Very moving."

After they cut the four-tier white wedding cake topped with tiny bride-and-groom Godzillas, Caroline and Ed danced as Jackie's friend (and fellow Vineyard resident) Carly Simon sang "Chapel of Love" and "Loving You's the Right Thing to Do." But even on her special day, Caroline was upstaged by two other guests. When Jackie danced with her son, Aileen Mehle observed, "everything just stopped. We just sat transfixed. And when they stopped dancing, everyone burst into applause."

The grand finale was to be a fireworks display orchestrated by Caroline's old friend George Plimpton. Plimpton had wanted to beat a fog that was rolling in, and he asked

Simon's manager if she couldn't sing after the fireworks. "Carly Simon doesn't *follow* fireworks," the manager replied.

"So she sang," Plimpton recalled, "and by the time she was finished, this huge fog bank that looked like the white cliffs of Dover was almost there." They nonetheless managed to fire off fifteen displays in honor of the guests that were there — a rose for Rose Kennedy, a bow tie for Arthur Schlesinger — with Plimpton narrating each display.

The fog bank eventually did roll in over the compound, so that guests heard the fireworks booming but saw nothing. "And this," Plimpton announced, "is what Ed Schlossberg does for a living."

Schlossberg's new mother-in-law doubled over with laughter at the remark. "Jackie *loved* it," Plimpton recalled. "She got a huge kick out of it, because it was totally appropriate. We were all in the dark when it came to what Schlossberg actually *does*."

Not that anyone who knew them was seriously questioning Caroline's choice. "Caroline is very happy with this man," Salinger observed. Ed's friend Ronald Feldman, the owner of a New York art gallery, was convinced Caroline and Schlossberg were "a perfect match. They want to live their life quietly together. He's not interested in being a prince, nor Caroline a princess."

Nor was she interested in taking on any

projects that would seriously compromise her privacy or that of her husband. Not long after the wedding, Caroline was asked to serve as chairwoman of the 1988 Democratic National Convention. To the astonishment of her Kennedy relatives, she declined. "The Kennedys were devastated," Ted's aide Richard Burke said. "They could not understand how anyone could refuse such a political plum and the power it would have involved, but Caroline found their lack of comprehension a good example of everything that was wrong with the Kennedys."

The new Mrs. Schlossberg was, however, interested in being more than a housewife. After the newlyweds honeymooned on Maui and in Japan and then settled into an Upper East Side apartment, Caroline returned to her law studies.

With Caroline launched on a marriage and a career, Jackie's main worry now was that JFK's only son would flounder. "Caroline is focused and dedicated," she told a friend when comparing her two children. "John is . . . spread out." Much to her relief, John started classes at New York University Law School six weeks after Caroline's wedding.

There was another bit of happy news Jackie had hoped to hear from Caroline, and it came one day in late 1987. "Guess what?" Caroline asked her fifty-nine-year-old mom over the phone. "I'm *pregnant!*"

Jackie was first on Caroline's list of more than fifty people — aunts, uncles, cousins, friends — she would call over the next few hours. She had a special message for the man who'd replaced JFK and then Uncle Bobby as her surrogate dad. "Uncle Teddy," she said, "you're going to be a grandfather!"

While Ted Kennedy was simply elated at the news, Jackie was also apprehensive; her own history of difficult pregnancies — not to mention miscarriages, a stillbirth, and the death of Caroline's infant brother Patrick — led her to worry that the same difficult path might lie ahead for her daughter.

As it turned out, his wife's pregnancy would be, in Ed Schlossberg's words, "just perfect. She wasn't sick a day, not one day. She felt great all the time, and she didn't miss a single day from school" — not even in January and February, when New York was hit by several severe winter storms. "Caroline attended every class, every lecture, every seminar," confirmed a classmate. "She came to school at nine each morning and didn't leave until five."

Several guests at the wedding had noted with alarm that Caroline, who traded her cigarette habit for an addiction to diet and exercise, was thinner than anyone had ever seen her. "Even skinnier than Jackie," Larry Newman observed. "And that's saying something." Now she scarcely looked as if she was bearing a child.

"She had been rail thin at her wedding," said *Cape Cod Times* reporter Anne Brennan, but by her seventh month had "added the poundage that transformed her into a beautiful young woman. Her face had rounded out but did not have the coarseness and pudginess that often occurs in pregnancy. She looked fabulous!"

"She was so thin all through the winter," one Columbia classmate noted, "that even when she wore large, loose clothing, you wouldn't have known. Actually, the only sign even as late as April was that her face filled out, which made her look prettier."

On May 17, 1988, Ed, Jackie, John, Uncle Ted, Nancy Tuckerman, and Caroline's former governess Marta Sgubin were on hand for Caroline's law-school graduation. As rain pelted the canvas tents that had been set up on the Columbia campus, Caroline's name was called, and the Kennedys and Schlossbergs cheered. Maurice Tempelsman was also there for this important moment in Caroline's life, seated apart from the family so that he would not be photographed with Jackie.

Between Lamaze classes with her husband, Caroline wasted no time boning up for the bar exams, which were to take place in late July. Although she was thirty, five years under the age at which most women would consider amniocentesis, she opted to have the procedure done because of the family's medical history. (Caroline's mentally retarded aunt, Jack's sister Rosemary, had been institutionalized most of her life. Grandpa Joe made the unilateral decision to have her lobotomized after she presumably became difficult to control. Rosemary's condition inspired the family to start the Special Olympics.)

The test yielded what sex Caroline's baby would be, but both she and Ed asked not to be told. "We want to be surprised," she explained. On June 24, Caroline calmly told her husband she was feeling "funny." Her obstetrician, Dr. Frederick W. Martens Jr., suggested she start timing her contractions and start the breathing exercises she and Ed had been practicing for weeks. Caroline was on the phone to a friend that night when a "ding" went off in the background. "That's my egg timer," she explained. "I have to time my contractions, and I can't find my watch."

Late that afternoon, Jackie dispatched her limousine to pick Caroline up and take her to New York Hospital–Cornell Medical Center. There, she registered under an alias frequently used by the Kennedys — "Mrs. Sylva" — and checked into a $720-a-day private room protected by two security guards.

Jackie ("Can you believe it? I'm going to be a *grandmother!*") paced in the waiting room, chewing gum — and her nails — in lieu of cigarettes. John, who was also on hand for the baby's birth and had arrived at the hospital with a stash of bubble-gum cigars to hand out, tried in vain to calm his mother. "I know, I'm sure everything will be fine," Jackie said, wringing her hands anxiously. "It's just . . ."

"Mom," John said, putting his arm around the grandmother-to-be, "do me a favor: Chill."

Compared with Ed Schlossberg, Jackie was composure itself. In the delivery room, Caroline was calm, and, said a hospital employee, "her husband was a total wreck. She wound up comforting *him* most of the time."

At 3:30 a.m. June 25, Caroline gave birth to a seven-pound, twelve-ounce girl they named Rose Kennedy Schlossberg. Unlike her mother, Caroline did not require a cesarean — although she was given an epidural — and the delivery went smoothly, with Daddy standing bedside in his green hospital gown. Caroline, as usual, remained calm and composed during her entire labor. But when the nurse handed baby Rose to Daddy, he fought back tears. "She's perfect," he said. "She's absolutely beautiful."

Jackie breathed a sigh of relief, and John started passing out his bubble-gum cigars on behalf of his dazed brother-in-law. At Caroline's urging, Ed called Uncle Teddy who was, he later said, "speechless with joy" at the news. It then fell to Teddy to spread the word among the aunts, uncles, twenty-six cousins — and Rose. Now ninety-eight and being cared for by a full-time nurse, the Kennedy matriarch was suffering from senile dementia and often forgot that Jack and Bobby were dead. But when she was told that Caroline's newborn baby had been named after her, Grandma's face "lit up," said one of her caregivers. "All of a sudden she seemed to know exactly what was going on. 'Wonderful, wonderful,' she kept saying in that crackly voice of hers." Incredibly, the curtain of secrecy around Caroline's pregnancy was drawn so tight that it would be another three days before the world would learn that Caroline had given birth to Jack and Jackie Kennedy's first grandchild.

Home for Rose and her parents would be a sprawling eleventh-floor, twelve-room co-op at Park Avenue and Seventy-eighth Street that the Schlossbergs purchased four months earlier for $2.65 million. The apartment where she grew up and where Jackie still lived was ten blocks to the northwest, and even closer were the apartments of Eunice Shriver and Jean Kennedy Smith. And just two blocks away was the Carlyle Hotel, home away from home to JFK and, for a brief time after the assassination, to the family he left behind.

Rose's nursery at the Schlossbergs' Park Avenue apartment — painted pink after the baby's arrival — was located next door to Mommy and Daddy's bedroom, so both parents would be available to help out with the odd midnight feeding and diaper change. The nursery brimmed with the usual stuffed animals and toys, and Ed designed a glow-in-the-dark mobile of the solar system to hang over Rose's crib. As if to include her own father in Rose's life, Caroline installed pieces from her extensive Kennedyana collection in the nursery — buttons, photos, posters, mugs, all bearing the likeness of JFK.

Unlike Jackie, Caroline chose to breast-feed her baby. Indeed, Caroline would be much more of a hands-on mother than Jackie had been, though she, too, would have the help of live-in nannies and governesses.

The squalling newborn forced Caroline to postpone her bar exams, but she would take them the following February and pass with flying colors on the first try. Her brother, just finishing up his second year at NYU Law School, would not be quite so lucky. In the meantime, he exploded on the national scene in a way that surprised everyone — including his big sister.

Now attractive in a way that exceeded even Hollywood's exacting standards, John stepped to the podium at the 1988 Democratic National Convention in Atlanta to introduce his

Uncle Ted. Walter Isaacson of *Time* worried that the roof of the Omni Auditorium might collapse "from the sudden drop in air pressure caused by the simultaneous sharp intake of so many thousands of breaths."

"Over a quarter of a century ago," John began, "my father stood before you to accept the nomination for the presidency of the United States. So many of you came into public service because of him and in a very real sense it is because of you that he is with us today."

Caroline, who watched John's speech on television, was startled by his flawless performance. Their mother, who had waged a war of attrition to force John to abandon his dreams of becoming an actor, was nothing less than overjoyed. For the first time, it looked as if her son, who was spending the summer clerking at the L.A. law firm of Manatt, Phelps, Rothenberg, and Phillips, might indeed be cut out for the family business — politics.

Then things took an unexpected turn, when on the cover of its September 12, 1988, issue *People* proclaimed John "The Sexiest Man Alive." The story began: "Okay, ladies, this one's for you, but first some ground rules. GET YOUR EYES OFF THAT MAN'S CHEST! He's a serious fellow. . . . Scion of the most charismatic family in American politics and heir to its most famous name."

John was flattered at the attention. "Listen," he told Barbara Walters, "people can say a lot worse things about you than you are attractive and you look good in a bathing suit." Jackie, however, was not amused. "She wanted people to take John seriously," Jamie Auchincloss said. "She thought the whole sex-symbol thing was just demeaning."

Predictably, John came in for some merciless ribbing from his friends. Caroline joined in the fun, teasing John about his helmet of dark hair and his sculpted physique. If this law-school thing didn't work out, she suggested, he could always go into modeling.

Rose was just three months old when Caroline brought her to meet her namesake in Hyannis Port. Rose the elder was in her wheelchair on the front porch waiting for them when the Schlossbergs drove up. "Rose greeted them with a big, big smile," recalled Betty Gargan, who was married to Kennedy cousin Joe Gargan. "All the great-grandchildren come up all the time to visit her. It's the high point of her days."

One of the low points for all Kennedys — Jackie, Caroline, and John in particular — was the anniversary of JFK's assassination. The nation observed the twenty-fifth anniversary with all manner of ceremonies, essays, and retrospectives. Jackie avoided every one of them, joining Caroline and John for a private morning mass at St. Thomas More, the modest one-hundred-year-old stone church on East Eighty-ninth Street that the trio had over the years come to regard as theirs.

Three weeks later, everyone was back at St. Thomas More for the christening of Rose Kennedy Schlossberg. They were joined by Uncle Ted and the usual assortment of Kennedy aunts, uncles, and cousins. Not long after, Rose suffered a bout of hiccups, which inspired her father to write a children's story. "Hiccup's Tale" was all about the Bloboreneo family, and the "smartest, most observant and littlest" Bloboreneo, who narrated the story of the Skebleens and their "awful, ugly" enemies, the Grossstttuffferrrsss. As the story went, the Grossstttuffferrrsss absconded with all the Christmas trees in the world, and it was the clever little Hicccup who managed to get them all back.

By the time Rose reached her first birthday, Dad joked that she could "walk, talk, and program a computer. She can do all sorts of things. She's a wonderful, amazing, brilliant baby," he gushed, "and I love her." Was she being brought up the way Caroline was raised? someone asked. "I wasn't there," Ed shrugged, "so I can't make comparisons. But I can tell you this: Caroline and I are bringing her up with everything that's good."

Caroline, meantime, had begun to rethink

the direction her own life was taking. She had originally intended to practice family law, but since Rose's arrival, the notion of traipsing into an office every day hardly seemed appealing. Caroline preferred to push Rose around the neighborhood in her blue stroller, zipping the two blocks over to Central Park, where she could push her on the swings and help her down the slide. Then there were the trips to Martha's Vineyard and Hyannis Port and Ed's rustic getaway in the Berkshires — not to mention visits to the Kennedy estate in Palm Beach, where for the first time baby Rose was taken to dip her feet in the Atlantic. "I always knew I'd like being a mom," Caroline told one neighborhood mother. "I just never realized it could be so much fun."

Nevertheless, Caroline was still her father's daughter; as much as any other Kennedy of her generation, she devoutly believed she had an obligation to serve the public. "There was never any question that Caroline would want to make a difference," said Jackie's friend Daniel Patrick Moynihan. "She has a profound sense of what it means to be a Kennedy. It's in her blood."

Make a difference, yes, but how? Caroline and John had more or less divided up responsibilities when it came to those projects that bore the Kennedy name — she was an active member of the Kennedy Library board, and he was the family point person at the John F. Kennedy School of Government at Harvard. Caroline had also played a major role in commissioning the statue of her father that stood outside the Boston Statehouse, and she'd proposed that the Kennedy Foundation bestow an annual award that would recognize the qualities of leadership and selflessness exemplified in JFK's 1956 Pulitzer Prize–winning book *Profiles in Courage.*

As she pondered her options, Caroline joined her mother and brother at the funeral of Jackie's mother, who died on July 22, 1989. Aunt Lee wept quietly, but neither Jackie nor her children registered any emotion during the brief service at Newport's Trinity Church. *Grand-mère* Janet Auchincloss had been diagnosed with Alzheimer's disease in 1983; for at least the last two years, she scarcely recognized her own children, much less Caroline and John.

Two weeks later, Jackie was in Paris to mark the centennial of the French Revolution. She celebrated by stopping in at Porthault (purveyors of "the linen of queens") to buy scallop-edged white cotton sheets festooned with pink bunnies for baby Rose.

Caroline was already pregnant for a second time when, in the fall of 1989, she talked to her mother about writing a book. Dad had, after all, published another bestselling book before *Profiles* — *Why England Slept* — and toyed with a career in journalism prior to embarking on his remarkable political odyssey. And while Jackie vowed that she would never write her memoirs ("I want to live my life, not record it"), she had already proven her editorial skills at Doubleday.

Plimpton proclaimed Jackie one of the best editors in publishing. Theodore White agreed. "She does the work of ten editors," White said, "and she has such a fertile imagination." Gita Mehta, another of Jackie's authors, described her as "an extraordinary, nineteenth-century sort of editor." Novelist Louis Auchincloss, one of Jackie's cousins by marriage, said she was nothing less than "a writer's dream."

Caroline knew exactly what she wanted to write about. She and a law school friend, Ellen Alderman, had been so deeply moved by the stories of people whose civil rights had been violated that at first they considered doing a documentary film on the document that spells out those freedoms, the Bill of Rights. But eventually they determined that they could better tell the story on the printed page. Aimed to coincide with the Bill of Rights' bicentennial, their book would be an anthology not unlike Profiles in Courage.

Over the next year, Caroline and Alderman crisscrossed the country researching cases that illustrated the workings of the Bill of

Rights. They spoke to a magazine editor in Wisconsin who revealed the secrets of the hydrogen bomb (freedom of the press), a Ku Klux Klan member with a cable-TV program in Missouri (freedom of speech), a group of Native Americans blocking the construction of a road through their sacred burial grounds (freedom of religion), and a Baltimore mother suspected of child abuse who refused under oath to divulge her son's whereabouts (the right against self-incrimination). Caroline was most moved by the case of two brothers sitting on death row in an Arizona prison (protection against cruel and unusual punishment). The brothers were convicted of murder after their father, who had escaped from prison with their help, murdered several members of an Arizona family before being apprehended.

By the time Caroline gave birth to Tatiana Celia Kennedy Schlossberg (named for the artist Tatiana Grossman, a favorite of Ed's) on May 5, 1990, she and Alderman had already finished writing *In Our Defense: The Bill of Rights in Action*. Less than a year later, William Morrow and Company would publish the book to critical praise and brisk sales. Largely on the strength of the Kennedy name — she made the calculated decision not to add the name "Schlossberg" — *In Our Defense* landed on the *New York Times* bestseller list.

No one was happier for Caroline than John, and he phoned to congratulate his sister the instant he learned her book was a bona fide bestseller. "He was always so proud of her," Sgubin said. "As a boy, he used to complain that she could get away with things that he couldn't get away with, but John really adored his sister his whole life."

Caroline's triumphs, however, were counterpoint to John's highly publicized shortcomings. Unlike Caroline, he failed the bar twice — forcing him to endure such humiliating (and unforgettable) headlines as THE HUNK FLUNKS and THE HUNK FLUNKS — AGAIN. For the third attempt, Jackie and Caroline suggested it might be a good idea for John to hire a tutor for $1,075 to help him pass.

There would, in the meantime, be family obligations to attend to. Caroline and her brother joined their cousins in celebrating Rose Kennedy's hundredth birthday on July 22, 1990. Two days later, John took the bar exam again — and passed. After he was told the results several months later, the second person he called was "Old Married Lady" — his new nickname for Caroline. The first person he called was Mom.

Throughout his embarrassing bar exam ordeal, John continued to put in his time working as one of sixty-four rookie assistant prosecutors in the Manhattan DA's office.

"Oh, it stinks," he replied when someone asked him how he liked it there. "I'm just doing this for a while to meet my family's expectations, and then I'm going to do something else."

Notwithstanding such career pressures, Caroline worried about the emotional toll John's tempestuous affair with actress Daryl Hannah was taking on her brother. Hannah, in the throes of her own stormy relationship with mercurial rocker Jackson Browne, ricocheted between the two men, leaving John confused and at times heartbroken. Still, when Hannah was hospitalized with a mysterious fever on the Brazilian set of *At Play in the Fields of the Lord*, John burned up the phone lines to her doctors. She was delirious for nearly a week, and when she came to, she awoke to find her room filled with a thousand long-stemmed American Beauty roses — with love from a worried John.

At about the same time, family loyalty was again tested when medical student William Kennedy Smith, who among the Kennedy cousins was closest to John and a special favorite of Caroline's, was charged with raping twenty-nine-year-old Patricia Bowman on the lawn of the Kennedy estate in Palm Beach. The incident followed a night of drunken revelry with Uncle Ted and Ted's son Patrick.

Willie's mother, Jean, had always been the

closest to Jackie of all the Kennedy sisters. Out of loyalty to her, Caroline and John joined the rest of the clan for the annual Labor Day picnic at Hyannis Port. The all-important photo op that resulted at least conveyed the notion that all the Kennedys — Jackie's kids included — were standing behind Willie. (In a bizarre and largely unnoticed incident a few days later, Caroline and a hundred other guests at a wedding were cleared out of East Hampton's exclusive Maidstone Club when someone on a bus overheard the words "bomb," "Hamptons," and "Caroline" in the same sentence. No bomb was found.)

In December 1991, most of the Kennedy family — Ethel, Pat, Eunice, and their respective offspring — showed up at Willie's trial to declare their unwavering belief in his innocence. John spent five full days in the courtroom, huddled with Willie's defense team, and told reporters that he was standing by his cousin because "we grew up together." But Caroline, who also grew up with Willie, did not feel so obliged. Following their mother's lead, she resisted efforts to get her to attend the trial. "Caroline," said one of her mother's closest friends, "feels loyalty to the family but only up to a point. She's her mother's daughter in that sense — you cannot pressure Caroline to do anything she doesn't want to do. And Caroline did not want to get involved in that whole sordid mess." Smith was eventually acquitted of the charges and later went on to practice medicine.

There were other times when, against their will, Caroline and her family were thrust onto center stage. With the release of Oliver Stone's controversial film *JFK*, Americans were once again embroiled in a national debate over who killed Kennedy. Caroline and John both adamantly refused to see the movie, but there was no way they could avoid the media frenzy it triggered. "Maybe I'll just have to leave town," John told one journalist. Caroline, meantime, comforted their mother — and made plans for the arrival of the third little Kennedy-Schlossberg.

Caroline was already pregnant with her third child when she journeyed to Boston in May 1992 with her brother for what would become an annual ritual: the presentation of the Profile in Courage Award. Six weeks later, Caroline was a face in the crowd at Madison Square Garden when delegates at the Democratic National Convention paid tribute to her Uncle Bobby. Later, she and Ed waved Clinton placards and cheered as the convention nominated the Arkansas governor for president. Caroline was won over by film of a starry-eyed sixteen-year-old Clinton shaking hands with JFK in the White House Rose Garden her mother had created.

Uncle Ted conceded that the image established "an emotional link" for Jackie as well.

The "link" was so strong, in fact, that Jackie invited Hillary Clinton to lunch at 1040 Fifth. The main topic of conversation between the two mothers: how Bill and Hillary might best protect their daughter, Chelsea, from the voracious Washington press corps.

Of course, now that her own son was grown and involved with a Hollywood actress, there was no way Jackie could shield him from the media horde. In September 1992, Daryl Hannah was hospitalized in Los Angeles. John rushed to her side, brought her to New York, and nursed her back to health. IT'S LOVE, proclaimed the cover of *People* magazine, which described the glamorous pair as having "fame, fortune, fabulous bone structure — and each other."

Caroline and Jackie were not happy with the headlines, nor with the fact that they seemed to be accurate. "Caroline tweaked John about the stories in the press," said a friend of John's. "She has this wicked sense of humor, and she couldn't resist teasing him whenever the opportunity arose. But this time she also got serious and told him that she didn't like the position he was being put in. Caroline was no pushover, but she knew that her brother was a complete softie. She was always telling him to watch out for him-

416

self and not be taken advantage of. John didn't always listen to his mother, but most of the time he took Caroline's advice. Most of the time, not all of the time."

Even before the birth of Caroline's third child, John Bouvier Kennedy Schlossberg, on January 19, 1993, Jackie was a doting grandmother — or "Grand Jackie," as Rose and Tatiana had taken to calling her. It was clearly the role Mrs. Onassis savored most. Frequently, Caroline's mom would make the ten-minute stroll down to the Schlossbergs' building, pick up the kids, and strike out for Central Park. Like any other parent or grandparent in Manhattan, she became expert at maneuvering strollers through crowds and revolving doors (all the while keeping a watchful eye on suspicious-looking characters as well as mean-looking dogs) and at hailing cabs while never letting go of tiny hands.

Several times a week, Grand Jackie was sighted buying cotton candy for Rose, sharing an ice-cream cone on a park bench with Tatiana, or pushing both girls on the swings at the Seventy-sixth Street playground. Usually with a little extra help from one of the nannies, Caroline also brought the kids by 1040 Fifth at least once a week. Jackie's friend Rose Styron remembered that she was "so wonderful with them. She got such a kick out of watching them tumble and play together."

"With her flagrant imagination," Nancy Tuckerman said of Grand Jackie, "she was able to hold their attention for hours on end. There was this enormous red wooden chest in which she kept all sorts of hidden treasures for them: pirate loot, Gypsy trinkets, beaded necklaces, rings with colored stones."

Tuckerman recalled that "as soon as they arrived, everything from the chest was dumped out on the bedroom floor, and the children would dig in. They'd deck themselves out with jewelry and put on costumes they'd made from old scarves and odd bits of material. Jackie would then take them on a so-called fantasy adventure. She'd weave a spellbinding tale while leading them through the darkened apartment, opening closet doors in search of ghosts and mysterious creatures. Once they were finished playing, they have their traditional afternoon tea party sitting on the living-room floor."

Caroline also loved to bring her children to Red Gate Farm on Martha's Vineyard, where Grand Jackie spent entire days fishing, boating, and swimming with them. While Caroline cradled infant Jack, Jackie worked in the garden with Rose and Tatiana, planting tomatoes and zucchini. The grandchildren were given the run of the house, where Jackie would sit on the floor for hours coloring and playing with them. Caroline recoiled in horror when Rose and Tatiana spilled paint on one of the antique rugs Jackie had brought back from India. "It doesn't matter," Jackie told Marta Sgubin, who now worked as Jackie's cook and housekeeper. "It's only an old rug."

Jackie was a little less indulgent of John, who left Red Gate Farm a shambles after throwing a party for his friends there on Memorial Day, 1993. When the maid reported that empty liquor bottles and half-smoked joints littered her pristine island sanctuary, Jackie gave John a stern lecture. "Your friends may not have been brought up properly," she told him, "but you should know better."

By contrast, even with three small children in tow, Caroline was a model guest. "Caroline is not as compulsively neat as her mother," the maid said. "But she made sure her children learned to pick up after themselves and not leave a mess behind for their grandmother to deal with. They really loved her, you know."

In August 1993, Caroline was along when her mother invited President Clinton and his wife to Martha's Vineyard for a cruise aboard Maurice's seventy-foot yacht *Relemar* (named for his children, Rena, Leon, and Marcy). Caroline was waiting on the upper deck with the rest of the family when the Clintons arrived, but when she started down to greet them, Jackie held her back. "No, we're not going down," Mom said. "Teddy, you go down and greet the President." When Caroline's uncle pointed out that Maurice was already downstairs to welcome the Clintons, Jackie cocked her head. "Teddy, you do it," she said. "Maurice isn't running for reelection." Caroline laughed.

Later, *Relemar* dropped anchor off a tiny deserted island, and everyone went for a swim. Caroline was by no means the daredevil her brother was, but she had extensive experience diving off the high decks of the *Christina*. So she and Chelsea, holding their noses, gamely jumped off *Relemar*'s thirty-foot-high diving platform. Goaded by her husband into following them, Hillary was terrified when she looked down. But her husband and the others — Caroline and Chelsea included — egged her on. "Don't be a chicken, Hillary," the President taunted his wife. "Jump! JUMP!"

Suddenly Hillary heard Jackie's voice above the others. "Don't do it, Hillary!" Jackie yelled from down in the water. "Don't do it! Just because they're daring you, you don't have to." Grateful for Jackie's words, Hillary descended to a less terrifying height before leaping into the frigid water.

Caroline and Jackie ended their summer idyll on Martha's Vineyard with their annual Labor Day beach picnic for family and friends — an affair they tried to schedule a day or two before the annual Hyannis Port blowout. With Caroline looking on, their friend Carly Simon and a decidedly tone-deaf Grand Jackie sat on the beach teaching Jack Schlossberg how to sing "The Itsy Bitsy Spider."

For Caroline, such moments were transporting. "I have never seen my mother so happy," she said, "as when she's around the kids." Jackie did not hesitate to let Caroline know how much these newest additions to their family meant to her. "They make my spirits soar!" she said of Caroline's children.

Time with the grandchildren also provided a welcome respite from having to worry about her son. Earlier that summer, John had called Caroline from California to say that he and Daryl Hannah had taken out a marriage license and were planning on getting married in Santa Monica. Those plans fell through, but a few months later, Caroline received another call from her brother. The day after tomorrow, John told her, he and Daryl were getting married in a top secret ceremony on the Vineyard. But within hours — before Caroline could start packing in earnest — John phoned to say the wedding was off.

Caroline, like her mother, was relieved. Not that they didn't like Daryl; both Jackie and her daughter were very supportive when they learned of Hannah's stormy relationship with Jackson Browne. And Daryl more than met

Jackie's exacting financial standards; the star of such hit films as *Splash*, *Roxanne*, and *Steel Magnolias* was the stepdaughter of billionaire Chicago financier Jerry Wexler.

Yet Jackie did not feel that a sexy blond movie star would be the right match for Camelot's torchbearer. Nor was she convinced that the delightfully flighty actress was temperamentally suited to her son. "She felt Daryl was not," Jackie's friend Ed Klein observed, "the most stable person for John."

At first Caroline defended her brother's right to fall in love with and marry anyone of his choosing. But as their roller-coaster affair progressed — the couple's bitter rows on the streets of New York were grist for the city's tabloids — Caroline came to agree with Mom. When John asked "Old Married Lady" what she thought of his marrying Miss Hannah, she answered point-blank, "Kiddo, she's nice, but she's not the one." Caroline, who clung so desperately to every vestige of privacy, also worried that her brother would "never again know a moment's peace" if he married someone with Daryl's star power.

November 22, 1993. It was thirty years to the day that Caroline sat clutching her teddy bear in the passenger seat of a Secret Service car, rushing back to the White House on the news that her father had been murdered. This was a day for Jack's widow and their kids to hide from the spotlight, to avoid anything that would only serve to magnify the pang of loss that, all these decades later, were still keenly felt.

Caroline stuck close to home, immersing herself in such quotidian tasks as taking Jack to the park, helping Rose with her homework, exercising at a nearby gym (like Mom, she also kept fit running around the Central Park reservoir), and starting on her Christmas list. "Caroline seemed to have come into her own in the last few years," said her friend Alexandra Styron, daughter of writers Rose and William Styron. "I'd never seen her happier than she was now. She looked beautiful. She was stick thin. Her skin was glowing. She and Ed were as much in love as any married people I had ever seen."

John, meantime, had a new woman in his life. Like Daryl, Carolyn Bessette was blond, stunning, and sleek — five feet eleven inches tall and 135 pounds. But where Daryl was fragile and quirky, Bessette, a personal shopper catering to celebrity clients at Calvin Klein, was poised, chic, and very much in control.

Caroline was soon pelting her brother mercilessly with questions about "this new girlfriend of yours." When she brought the kids by to play with Grand Jackie, the woman who might replace Daryl was Topic A.

Like her mother, Caroline always tended to

worry more about John's emotional well-being than about the physical dangers he courted on a regular basis. For as long as Caroline could remember, their mother had made a point of indulging, even encouraging John's instinctive adventurous streak. Whether he was rock climbing, scuba diving, skiing, Rollerblading, or just threading his bike through Manhattan traffic, Jackie took unalloyed pride in her son's fearless athleticism. She did not even object when he disappeared into the wilderness for days at a time.

Caroline was certainly more prudent than her brother, but she also shared her mother's laissez-faire attitude when it came to John's penchant for risk taking. Caroline had heard the stories about John kayaking in the wild for days or swimming out to the horizon and vanishing — only to magically reappear a few feet from shore. John's friends had that nickname for him — "Master of Disaster" — and while Caroline felt a recurring urge to caution her little brother, she also had faith in his ability to emerge from almost any dicey situation unscathed. He had, after all, done it so many times before.

For both Jackie and Caroline, flying was an entirely different matter. John had first secretly begun taking flying lessons on Martha's Vineyard in 1988. After he finally got up the nerve to tell his mother, she demanded that he stop. Jackie did not wish to alarm her son, but she confided in Maurice the primary reason for her concern: In the latter years of her life Jackie had a recurring premonition that John would be killed piloting his own plane. Caroline's reasons were more prosaic: Her brother was notoriously accident-prone and absentminded, so much so that he kept his apartment keys — which he lost numerous times — on a chain attached to his pants. Out of respect for their mother's feelings, John put aside his dreams of becoming a licensed pilot — at least for the time being.

On November 22, Caroline was at home with her children, busying herself with chores in the annual effort to keep her mind off her father's assassination when the call came from the hospital. Jackie had been spending the day doing what, next to playing with the grandkids, she most loved — jumping fences, at the Piedmont Hunt in Virginia — when she was thrown from her horse.

An ambulance was summoned, and Jackie, described by one onlooker as looking like a "broken doll," remained unconscious for a full thirty minutes before coming to. Sighed a relieved Middleburg Police Chief Dave Simpson, "She gave us quite a scare."

Just to be safe, Jackie was transported to Loudon Hospital Center, near Middleburg, where she remained under observation for the next twenty-four hours. When told of her mother's accident, Caroline was on the phone to the doctors with a barrage of questions. She remained calm, for two reasons: First, no one was more accustomed to dealing with crises of this sort than Caroline Kennedy. Then there was the simple fact that, however dramatic the fall may have appeared, it was just one of many spills both Caroline and her mother had taken over the years. If anyone knew how to take a fall from a horse, it was Jacqueline Bouvier Kennedy Onassis.

But Caroline, herself the victim of stalkings and threats that the general public knew nothing about, was shocked to learn that while her mother rested in the hospital on the thirtieth anniversary of JFK's assassination, an armed drifter was apprehended as he drove through New Jersey asking directions to Jackie's weekend retreat. "Caroline and Jackie both knew there were plenty of kooks out there," said a Doubleday colleague of Jackie's. "It came with the territory." Agreed Jamie Auchincloss: "My niece grew up with the knowledge that people — dangerous people — could strike at any time. But she's never been the kind of person who let that defeat her. She got that strength from Jackie."

Whatever stresses mother and daughter may have endured, Caroline — like everyone else — marveled at Jackie's ageless beauty. GRANDMA JACKIE — LOOKIN' GOOD, declared one front-page headline alongside a photo of the still-sleek former First Lady leaning into a stroller with Caroline at her side.

Caroline, in particular, took pride in her mother's youthful appearance — though she had been frustrated in her efforts to get Jackie to stop smoking. That Christmas, Caroline urged her mother to go ahead and cruise the Caribbean with Maurice aboard the *Relemar*. It would be a relaxing change for her, a chance to get away. But during the cruise, Jackie began to feel stabbing pains in her abdomen. Nor could she shake a persistent cough. Though she simply suspected she was suffering from the flu, they decided to cut the vacation short and rush back to New York Hospital–Cornell Medical Center.

It fell to Dr. Carloyn Agresti, a leading head and neck surgeon, to deliver the news. A biopsy of one of Jackie's lymph nodes revealed that she was suffering from a particularly aggressive form of cancer, non-Hodgkin's lymphoma. If there was any hope of beating the disease, she would have to start chemotherapy immediately.

Caroline was curious when she and John were summoned to 1040 Fifth Avenue; their mother had a flair for the dramatic and often kept things secret until the last possible moment. There was no way of knowing what news she might spring on them. But even with all they had already been through together, Caroline and John were not remotely prepared for the news they were about to receive. "I have cancer," she told them bluntly, and with that her children rushed to Jackie, hugged her, and began to weep.

Brushing away her own tears, Jackie quickly rebounded, reassuring Caroline and John that she intended to beat the odds. Incredibly, it was only now that she finally gave up the two-pack-a-day smoking habit she had so masterfully concealed from public view.

Whatever the outcome, the patient had no interest in lingering. Within days of receiving the diagnosis, Jackie had her lawyer draw up a living will that specified no heroic measures would be taken to keep her alive once death was a foregone conclusion.

Now that she was locked in her own struggle for survival, Jackie conspired with her children and Maurice to keep her illness a secret. The only member of the extended Kennedy clan they deigned to tell was Uncle Teddy.

While Jackie had always hidden behind dark glasses and a look of benign disinterest, Caroline had become expert at concealing her emotions behind a toothsome Kennedy grin. At home, she tried to keep up a brave front for the children. On several occasions, Marta Sgubin dropped in on the Schlossbergs to find Caroline sitting alone in the living room, eyes red from weeping.

"Caroline is a very brave person," Sgubin said, "but of course it was very hard. The thought of losing her mother . . ."

As Jackie underwent chemotherapy, it became increasingly obvious that she would not keep her secret for long. The unpleasant side effects — primarily bloating and hair loss — could not be concealed indefinitely beneath wigs, turbans, and slouchy sweaters. But even as speculation concerning Jackie's condition raged, Caroline saw no reason to go public; Jackie's daughter was proving herself to be the most resolutely private Kennedy of all. "Caroline wanted her mother to continue to stonewall," a family friend said. "When it came to the family's medical history, she believed in a total right to privacy — that, to be frank, it was nobody's damn business."

But by early February 1994, Jackie decided it was time to make a statement — if only to quell tabloid rumors that she was already at death's door. On February 11, Jackie told Nancy Tuckerman to talk to Robert D. McFadden of the *New York Times*. Tuckerman confirmed that Jackie was being treated for non-Hodgkin's lymphoma, and added that "the doctors are very, very optimistic."

Not surprisingly, the news made front-page headlines around the world. And once again Caroline found herself in the unenviable position of having to bear her private pain before the rest of humanity. "Most people think having the world share in your grief lessens your burden," Jackie had told Teddy White years before. "It magnifies it."

Since Jackie herself remained resolutely upbeat ("Even if I have only five years, so what? I've had a great run!"), Caroline tried not to let her mother see the slightest flicker of doubt. That March, as snowstorms bore down on the Northeast, Grand Jackie still delighted in leading Caroline's brood on "fantasy adventures" around her apartment. Caroline brought Rose, Tatiana, and Jack by 1040 Fifth every afternoon and stayed for hours. One arctic weekend, Jackie ventured into Central Park with Caroline and all the Schlossbergs and took part in a spirited snowball fight. At one point, Jackie grabbed a sled rope and pulled Rose and Tatiana across the snow.

"Caroline had an awful lot on her plate," said a former Metropolitan Museum colleague who remained a friend. "She was understandably very worried about her mother, but she also had her own family to think about." She was certainly not prepared for John's announcement to the family that he intended to launch an offbeat magazine that would blend politics and celebrity journalism.

"Why do you want to join the other team?" Caroline asked her brother half jokingly. "Traitor!" Caroline and her mother acknowledged that there was a family connection to the publishing world — from Jack's Pulitzer Prize to Jackie's employment history as a photojournalist and book editor to Caroline's own status as a published author. But they also saw a difference between those things and what John now had in mind — essentially a *People* magazine of politics.

Then there was the simple fact that, as Maurice Tempelsman noted, the chances of success for a new magazine were slim to almost nonexistent. Realizing full well that John wouldn't listen to them but would listen to Tempelsman, Jackie and Caroline urged Maurice to talk him out of it.

By mid-March, Caroline was encouraged by reports she was getting from Jackie's doctors. Although her mother looked terrible and felt worse, the experts insisted that it appeared as though her cancer was in remission as a result of the aggressive chemotherapy treatments. But one afternoon Jackie suffered a sudden and alarming spell of disorientation; she was not quite sure who or where she was. An MRI revealed that while the cancer had indeed vanished from her abdomen, neck, and chest, it had now spread to her brain and spinal cord.

Caroline was devastated. Now her mother would have to endure radiation therapy on top of chemotherapy, which would be delivered by shunt directly to the brain through a hole drilled in her skull. John and Caroline wept on each other's shoulders — but only when Jackie was out of earshot. "Got to keep strong for Mom" became their mantra.

That Easter, Grand Jackie joined Caroline and the Schlossberg children at the Bernardsville house, where they all sat in the kitchen dyeing eggs — a family ritual Caroline could trace back to her childhood in the White House. Caroline then watched as her mother, wearing one of her brightly colored turbans to conceal the effects of chemotherapy, clapped and laughed as Rose and Tatiana raced across the lawn with Jack toddling behind.

One of the friends who saw Jackie during this period was Peter Duchin, who described her as behaving "the way you would have expected her to behave — as if she intended to beat this thing." Caroline marveled that her mother seemed so cheerful, so upbeat, when it was all she could do to keep from "bawling like a baby."

That April, friends, relatives, and acquaintances from around the world called to express concern. Some, like Duchin and Carly Simon, made a point of seeing Jackie whenever they could; others simply asked Caroline to tell her mother she was in their prayers. Yet Jackie's only sister was, for the most part, nowhere to be seen.

Caroline was well aware of the rift between

her mother and Lee Radziwill. The mounting tension between the two had long troubled Caroline, who was not only Aunt Lee's namesake but a close friend to both of Lee's children, Tony and Tina. Given the dire circumstances, she expected Aunt Lee to make more of an effort to spend time with her only sister. Over lunch at Carly Simon's, a guest asked Jackie if she saw her sister often. "We've only seen each other once this whole year," Jackie answered. "I never could understand why Lee is so full of animosity."

The next day, Marta Sgubin called Caroline with the news that Jackie had collapsed in her apartment. She was rushed to New York Hospital, where doctors operated on a perforated ulcer — a side effect of chemotherapy. Visiting her mother at the hospital, Caroline was struck by the irony that Richard Nixon was down the hall, having suffered from a stroke. Nixon died eight days after Jackie was admitted, on April 22, 1994.

Once she was back home from the hospital, Jackie broke out her trademark pale blue stationery, sat down, and began writing notes to her children — letters that were to be opened only after her death. She needed to write them now, she told Maurice, while her mind was still sharp.

To John, she wrote, "I understand the pressures you'll forever have to endure as a Kennedy, even though we brought you into this

433

world as an innocent. You, especially, have a place in history.

"No matter what course in life you choose," she wrote, "all I can do is ask that you and Caroline continue to make me, the Kennedy family, and yourself proud."

Despite the fact that Caroline had excelled academically, become a lawyer, written a book, and skillfully run several charities, Jackie still viewed her essentially as a wife and mother. "The children have been a wonderful gift to me," Grand Jackie wrote, "and I'm thankful to have once again seen our world through their eyes. They restore my faith in the family's future. You and Ed have been so wonderful to share them with me so unselfishly."

Caroline watched helplessly as her mother's condition deteriorated with alarming speed. She still saw the grandchildren whenever she felt strong enough — at least several times a week — but now the treasure hunts and fantasy adventures were replaced with quiet talks or games led by Caroline and Marta as Jackie watched from the living-room sofa.

When she felt the occasional (and unexplained) surge of energy, Jackie grabbed Maurice's arm and they returned to Central Park. "Oh, isn't it something?" she whispered as they strolled down Fifth Avenue in early May. "One of the most glorious springs I can

434

remember — and after such a terrible winter!"

As the days progressed and her mother's pain grew more excruciating, Caroline was overcome with despair and helplessness. According to John's friend Steven Styles, Jackie phoned her son and sobbed, "I don't think I can take it anymore." She had said much the same thing to Caroline.

On Sunday, May 15, 1994, Jackie took Maurice's arm and went for a walk through her beloved Central Park. She knew it was going to be her last. Caroline, dressed in jeans, a blue-and-white-striped T-shirt, and sneakers, walked a few feet ahead, carrying Jack in one arm and pushing a blue stroller with the other hand. She turned to see that her mother was grimacing with pain; Jackie could only manage a few halting steps before having to turn back.

The next day, Jackie, feeling weak and disoriented, returned yet again to New York Hospital. Caroline was told that her mother was now suffering from pneumonia and that she was being put on antibiotics. She was also told that the cancer had spread to Jackie's liver, and there was nothing more that could be done to arrest its spread. In the short run, Jackie's doctors recommended that she remain in the hospital so that her pneumonia could be brought under control.

Caroline was not surprised that her mother

refused to stay. With no interest in prolonging the inevitable, Jackie instructed the doctors to stop treating her pneumonia and on Monday discharged herself from the hospital.

On May 18, Carly Simon received the dreaded phone call from Marta Sgubin. "Caroline," Sgubin said, "wants you to come over now." Jackie's stepbrother, Yusha Auchincloss, got the call in Newport and drove at breakneck speed, praying that he'd make it to New York in time.

Simon and Auchincloss were among those few close friends and family members summoned to Jackie's bedside for a final farewell. When they got there, they encountered hundreds of New Yorkers — reporters, camera crews, well-wishers, and the merely curious — who pressed against the blue police barricades that had been set up on the sidewalk outside 1040 Fifth Avenue.

John agreed to welcome those who had been summoned in the foyer of his mother's apartment; Caroline, undone by what was transpiring, simply sat on a bench in the hallway and gently wept. Sitting next to her was Ed Schlossberg, who put a comforting arm around his wife.

For the next twenty-four hours, Caroline, John, and Maurice took turns at Jackie's bedside. "As you can imagine," Nancy Tuckerman said, "it was a very emotional time for everyone." Caroline and her brother spelled each other, reading to Jackie from her favorite works of literature — passages from Isak Dinesen and Colette as well as poems by Robert Frost, Emily Dickinson, and Edna St. Vincent Millay.

Aunt Lee arrived that evening, followed closely by Uncle Teddy and his second wife, Victoria Reggie. Hours later, Lee emerged from her sister's bedroom in tears. "Caroline," said another friend who had been summoned to say good-bye, "was clearly not impressed."

At one point, Jackie came to long enough to see that John and Caroline were exhausted. "It's late," she whispered. "Go home and get some sleep. . . ." Uncle Teddy convinced Caroline and John to leave, but they returned in a matter of hours.

It was shortly after noon on Thursday, May 19, when Monsignor Georges Bardes of St. Thomas More Church came to the apartment to administer last rites. When Caroline's Uncle Bobby lay dying in Los Angeles, visitors were permitted to visit him only two at a time. Now they filed in two by two — Aunt Ethel and Aunt Pat, Aunt Eunice and Uncle Sargent, Carly Simon and Bunny Mellon — to sit by the bed, hold her hand, share memories, or even tell some funny stories.

At 9:15 p.m., Jackie slipped into a final

coma. Caroline and John, who had been comforting each other in the next room, joined Maurice at their mother's bedside. An hour later, Jackie's heart stopped. Caroline was inconsolable; her sobs were clearly audible to family members who had gathered in the living room. Within moments everyone was crying. "She just," a stunned Nancy Tuckerman said of her best friend, "sort of slipped away. . . ."

Outside, the world waited for news — any news — concerning Jackie's condition. Uncle Ted suggested that perhaps a statement should be issued or that Tuckerman might, as she had so often before, speak for the family. Caroline, ever mindful of how zealously Jackie had guarded her privacy, saw no reason to make a formal announcement of any sort. At this moment, she harbored only resentment toward the press for maintaining a ghoulish deathwatch outside her mother's building. "We don't owe them anything," she told her brother.

But the media would learn the sad truth soon enough. The best way to break the news, John argued, was for a family member to speak directly to the press and conclude by asking to be left alone to grieve. The next morning, he stepped before a sea of microphones outside 1040 Fifth Avenue. "Last night, at around ten-fifteen, my mother passed on," John said. "She was surrounded by her friends and family and her books and the people and things that she loved. And she did it in her own way, and we all feel lucky for that, and now she's in God's hands.

"There's been a generous outpouring of good wishes from everyone in both New York and beyond," he added. "And I speak for all our family when we say we're extremely grateful. And I hope now that you know, we can just have these next couple of days in relative peace."

Not likely. As Caroline predicted, the press and public were more relentless and intrusive than ever. Uncle Teddy argued for a large public funeral, instead of the private affair Caroline insisted upon. In fact, Jackie had specified only that she wanted the service to be held at New York's St. Ignatius Loyola — the Upper East Side church where she had been baptized and confirmed — and that she be interred next to JFK at Arlington. Beyond that, she left it up to her children to sort out the details.

Caroline stood firm. She did, however, agree to have speakers set up outside the church so that ordinary people gathered on the streets could hear the service. Too distraught to compile the guest list or make the arrangements, Caroline turned those tasks over to John.

Caroline made one more concession to her Uncle Teddy. True to Kennedy form, there

439

would be a wake, and it would be held at Jackie's apartment. The crowd outside 1040 Fifth kept a respectful distance as more than a hundred mourners, including numerous celebrities, arrived in a steady stream of limousines. But when John and Caroline appeared, there was pandemonium. Hiding her tears behind dark glasses, Caroline clung to her brother as he put a protective arm around her and tried to usher her into the building. At one point, a woman in the crowd grabbed Caroline's arm and would not let go until a nearby policeman pried her loose.

The next morning, eight pallbearers — seven of Jackie's nephews and John Walsh, the Secret Service agent who had become a father figure to Caroline — carried Jackie's heavy mahogany coffin up the church steps. Among the hundreds of artists, writers, business leaders, social lions, entertainment figures, and politicians were two other first ladies: Lady Bird Johnson and Hillary Rodham Clinton.

In planning the service, John explained, "three things came to mind over and over again and ultimately dictated our selections. They were her love of words, the bonds of home and family, and her spirit of adventure." All this, he said, was by way of trying to "capture my mother's essence."

On one thing they could all agree: Lee Radziwill would not be speaking at her sister's funeral. Caroline in particular was in no mood to forgive her aunt for not spending more time with her dying sister. Lee's daughter, Tina, was asked to give a reading, however. And Tony, another favorite of Aunt Jackie's, was named an honorary pallbearer.

Caroline's part in her mother's service would reflect their mutual love of poetry, and of one poet in particular. After the celebrated soprano Jessye Norman sang "Ave Maria," Caroline stood to read from the collected works of Edna St. Vincent Millay. The slim volume had been presented to Jackie the day she graduated from Miss Porter's School — her prize for winning Miss Porter's literary award. Jackie loved Millay, and Caroline picked out a favorite passage from "Memory of Cape Cod":

Let me listen to the wind in the ash . . .
it sounds like surf on the shore.

Yet again, Ted delivered the eulogy. "Jackie's love for Caroline and John was deep and unqualified," he said. "She reveled in their accomplishments, she hurt with their sorrows, and she felt sheer joy and delight in spending time with them. At the mere mention of their names, Jackie's eyes would shine and her smile would grow bigger."

Caroline and John escorted their mother's casket to La Guardia Airport and watched as it was loaded onto a chartered 737. When they arrived at National Airport in Washington, President Clinton was on the tarmac to meet them. Their motorcade proceeded to Arlington, where Caroline and John clung to each other as their mother's casket, covered with ferns and a cross of white lilies, was placed next to Jack's. On either side lay Caroline's stillborn sister and her brother Patrick, whose birth she had so eagerly anticipated as a little girl.

Caroline, who could recall watching her mother light the Eternal Flame thirty-one years before, listened as President Clinton praised Jackie's "dignity and grace and uncommon common sense. In the end, she cared most about being a good mother to her children, and the lives of Caroline and John leave no doubt that she was that, and more."

The children — first Caroline, then John — gave brief readings. Then sixty-four bells — one for each year of their mother's phenomenal life — rang out from Washington's National Cathedral, and Caroline and John knelt down to kiss their mother's coffin just as Caroline had kissed her father's coffin when she was a girl of six. His sister stepped back, but John walked the few steps over to the spot where JFK lay and touched his gravestone. Caroline's grief had been etched on her face for days, and she marveled at how John had somehow managed to keep it all together in public. Now she watched as her brother stood, gazed down at his parents' graves, and brushed a tear from his eye. As he turned back toward her, Caroline reached out and pulled John toward her.

That night, the family flew back to New York, and Caroline's limousine wended its way through the streets of the city toward her Park Avenue apartment. She was staring vacantly out the window when her car stopped at a red light. There, standing on the corner, was a man reading the New York *Daily News*, its photo of Caroline's mom and banner headline clearly visible:

MISSING HER

She is like a rock.
She knows John would want her
to pick up and move on with her life.

— *Caroline's cousin,*
Joe Gargan

She has a strong sense
of personal responsibility.
She knows she has serious work to do.
And in that sense,
I've always felt
she's very much a Kennedy.

— *David McCullough,*
historian and friend

She is her mother's daughter.

— *Letitia Baldrige*

He and Caroline were best friends.
There was a genuine love between
them.

— *Richard Wiese,*
John's friend

8

"My mommy cries all the time. My mommy cries all the time." It had been thirty years since Caroline pleaded with Sister Joanne Frey to do something — *anything* — to ease her mother's grief. Through her quiet grace and natural sense of dignity, the public Jackie had somehow managed to hold herself — and the nation — together in one of her darkest hours. But it was too much to expect Jackie to conceal her sorrow from her daughter. This was more than just a sad memory for Caroline; it was a heavy psychological burden she would have to shoulder her entire life.

Caroline would never blame her mother for sinking into a deep depression following JFK's death, or for failing to shield her little girl from the pain. Yet now that she faced a similar situation with her own children, Caroline was determined that they not be scarred emotionally as she had been scarred.

There had scarcely been enough time to prepare herself, much less her children, for the possibility of their grandmother's death. When it happened, Caroline sat down with five-year-old Rose and four-year-old Tatiana (Jack was only sixteen months old at the time) and tried to explain to them that their Grand Jackie had gone to heaven. Still, for months afterward, Tatiana would periodically ask when their grandmother would lead them on another adventure through her apartment.

Uncle John had always been there for Caroline's children; next to their own very hands-on father, John was easily the most important male figure in their lives. Now that Jackie was gone, he was spending more time with them than ever — steering Jack's stroller down East Seventy-eighth Street, pushing Tatiana on the swings in Central Park, buying cotton candy for Rose from a street vendor.

Caroline had more than just the children to worry about. Maurice Tempelsman, whom she had come to regard as a stepfather (and surrogate grandfather to her children), was crushed by the death of the woman he had loved for nearly twenty years. He had suffered a major heart attack in 1988, and now Caroline was concerned about the impact her mother's death would have on his health. "Caroline and John called him every day to cheer him up," said a friend of Tempelsman's.

"They told him that he would always be a part of their family. That's what their mother would have wanted."

An even more pressing concern for Caroline was John. Now that Mom was no longer around, responsibility for looking after the Prince of Camelot — protecting him from himself, essentially — fell to his big sister. "Gee, kiddo," Caroline joked with her brother, "it's a rotten job, but somebody's got to do it." Certainly no one was better equipped for the assignment than Caroline. Even as a small child, recalled Nanny Maud Shaw, "Caroline had the knack for bossing John without getting his back up."

There was ample cause for concern. To begin with, John was seeing Carolyn Bessette but still seemed very much involved with Daryl Hannah. Less than two weeks after their mother's funeral, Caroline watched as Daryl cavorted with John and the Kennedy cousins on the lawn at Hyannis Port.

By all accounts, Daryl was ready for marriage. But Caroline reminded her brother that there were more pressing matters to attend to. Under Maurice's guidance, their mother had amassed a $150 million fortune. Jackie had named Maurice and her lawyer, Alexander Folger, as executors, but ultimately it was up to her children to make certain that her final wishes were carried out.

It was no surprise that the bulk of the estate was divided up between Caroline and John. To Nancy Tuckerman, she left $250,000. Tina and Tony Radziwill each received $500,000 in trust (in a final snub, Jackie made no provision for her envious sister, Lee, "because I have already done so during my lifetime"). To Provi Paredes, her longtime maid, Jackie bequeathed $50,000, while another niece, Janet Auchincloss Rutherford's daughter Alexandra, received $100,000.

Jackie's will contained more than a simple list of bequests. Attached to the document was a chilling assessment of outstanding security risks to Caroline and John prepared by Jackie's chief bodyguard, former Secret Service Agent John Viggiano. In addition to stalker Kevin King, Viggiano identified three other men who posed a threat to Caroline. According to Viggiano, a Brooklyn man was convinced that he, not Ed Schlossberg, should be married to Caroline — and had made several calls to Schlossberg at his office to tell him so. Another man, identified by Viggiano as someone who abused his own two children, believed he was actually married to Jackie. In the months before Jackie's death, he had made several menacing calls to Caroline and John, insisting they were both his children. Perhaps most frightening was the double murderer who appeared at the front door of Jackie's apartment building to proclaim that he was in love with her and the children. "The mental instability of many of the individuals involved," Viggiano concluded, "and the harassing nature of their communications, represent a significant threat to the personal security of Mrs. Onassis' descendants."

Aside from her ongoing efforts to keep her precise address out of the newspapers, Caroline believed there was not much she could do about the threats. John, meanwhile, paid little heed to the warnings. He was too preoccupied with ongoing plans to launch his new political magazine. A still-dubious Caroline asked what they intended to call it. "*George*," he proudly replied.

"What?"

"*George* — as in Washington," he said, studying Caroline's befuddled look. "You know, the father of our country?"

John's publishing ambitions aside, Caroline breathed a sigh of relief two months later when Daryl headed back to Los Angeles — and the arms of off-again, on-again lover Jackson Browne. The focus now shifted to the mystery woman John had been seen with occasionally since the fall of 1993 — Carolyn Bessette.

Meantime, the world was still trying to find ways to say good-bye to Jackie. The end had come with such stunning swiftness — the public was made aware of her illness just four months before her death — that, for many, the full reality had yet to sink in. Caroline was particularly touched when, the first summer following Jackie's death, the City of New York paid tribute to its most famous citizen by naming the Central Park reservoir after her. "She was as much a part of this park," said one park worker who had watched her take one of her runs along the 1.57-mile jogging path, "as this body of water." Plans had already been set in motion to rename the former High School of Performing Arts on Forty-sixth Street — inspiration for the hit 1980 movie *Fame* and the subsequent TV series of the same name — as Jacqueline Kennedy Onassis High School.

Neither of Jackie's children wanted to live in Jackie's Fifth Avenue apartment; it was simply filled with too many memories. Besides, Maurice was warning Caroline that the taxes on Jackie's estate were going to be hefty — it would be wise to unload any real estate they had no intention of using. So in January 1995, oil tycoon David Koch paid $9.5 million for Jackie's apartment. Caroline could not bring herself to watch movers empty the apartment of her mother's belongings. John, on the other hand, plopped down on the curb opposite the building's entrance and observed the transition in silence. "That's the kind of thing you'd expect John to do," John Perry Barlow said of his friend, who by this time had already moved into a penthouse at 20 North Moore Street in New York's trendy Tribeca district. "John was a very sentimental guy."

On January 22, 1995, Rose Kennedy died at the age of 104. Caroline felt the loss, coming eight months after her mother's death, more keenly than John. With reason. Rose's longtime secretary, Barbara Gibson, claimed that Jackie "kept John, in particular, away from Rose. . . . Jackie didn't want the children to be 'too Kennedy.' I noticed that she felt most strongly about John not being too close to his grandmother. She seemed to want to keep him really close to her. In the end, it worked, because although Caroline and Rose were close — writing to each other regularly — Rose hardly had much to do with John at all."

Perhaps, but he clearly had the family knack for politics — or at least that's what party leaders devoutly believed. Ever since he'd graduated from Brown, John had been besieged with offers to run for office in New York and Massachusetts. Caroline had had her share of offers as well, though she was far too private a person ever to subject herself — or her family — to the scrutiny a campaign would entail. She counseled her brother to think twice before running for office "just because somebody wants to run a Kennedy."

Nor was Caroline entirely sold on *George*, reminding her brother of Maurice's cautionary words about the magazine business. In March 1995, Hachette-Filipacchi, publishers of twenty-two magazines, from *Road and Track* to *Elle*, agreed to bankroll *George* to the tune of $20 million over a five-year period. But Caroline cautioned John to beware of anyone seeking merely to trade on his star power as a Kennedy. "My sister is a smart woman, a very smart woman," he told a friend. "I respect her opinion more than anyone's."

There was no doubt, of course, that investors in *George* were banking heavily on John to lure not only advertisers and subscribers but interview subjects as well. "He has access," said Hachette's U.S. chief, David Pecker, "to almost everyone." *George*'s backers would not be disappointed in that respect; John put the full force of his celebrity behind the magazine.

As the September launch of *George* approached, however, Caroline noticed that her brother was looking drawn and fatigued. For no apparent reason, he had also lost fifteen pounds in three weeks. In view of their own father's history of Addison's disease — a potentially fatal autoimmune disorder — and Jackie's battle against lymphoma, Caroline urged her brother to see a doctor. John checked into New York Hospital for tests and later phoned his sister with the news. Caroline was relieved when noted New York endocrinologist James Hurley told John he was merely suffering from a hyperactive thyroid.

Exactly one week before announcing the birth of his new magazine venture to the world, John slipped a small emerald-and-diamond ring on Bessette's finger and asked her to marry him. Her reply: "I'll think about it."

John was mystified and, he told his sister, more than a little hurt. Carolyn had typically played hard to get — that, frankly, was a large part of her appeal to someone so accustomed to being pursued by women. Caroline had always been there to provide moral support for her little brother, but she did not blindly endorse his choices. For the past two years, Caroline had stood on the sidelines and watched as Bessette used her former boyfriend, Calvin Klein underwear model Michael Bergin, to make John jealous. They had had furious rows over Bergin, who was a full decade younger than John and for a time loomed over Times Square on a billboard, clad only in his Calvin Klein briefs.

Bessette also had a reputation as a denizen of New York's nightclub scene. A regular at such fashionable spots as the Buddha Bar, the Merc Bar, and MK, Bessette, like many other young "fashionistas," had developed a taste for cocaine. Even though Bessette friends would insist that her recreational drug use never developed into anything approaching addiction, Caroline worried about her brother's exposure to the downtown drug culture.

John, as it turned out, did have what his friend John Perry Barlow called a "Bohemian streak" that included the occasional joint. "John was certainly not a pothead," Barlow said, "but he wanted to lead the life he wanted to lead. This was one of the reasons he held off on starting a political career. He knew everything he did would be scrutinized, and he didn't want to put himself or his family's reputation in peril."

John did promise his sister that, if Bessette did decide to accept his marriage proposal, he would have Maurice Tempelsman review the terms of their prenuptial agreement. Caroline did not have to remind John of their mother's parting words concerning Maurice: "You will do well to seek his advice."

Medical scares and romantic disappointments notwithstanding, John appeared fit and confident when he stepped before more than 160 reporters on September 8, 1995, to announce the birth of *George*. Caroline, watching her brother's presentation on the evening news, laughed as he segued from quip to quip. "I don't think I've seen as many of you in one place since they announced the results of my first bar exam," he announced. After declaring that he hoped to end up as president — "of a very successful publishing venture" — John volunteered answers to a barrage of personal questions before anyone could bother to ask them: "Yes. No. We're merely good friends. None of your business. Honest, she's my cousin from Rhode Island. I've worn both. Maybe someday, but not in New Jersey." Caroline, more in awe than ever of her brother's winning charm and seemingly effortless wit, called to congratulate him. However, like Maurice, she was still not entirely convinced that *George* was going to make it.

With John as its formidable front man, *George* at first appeared to be a stupendous success — but at a personal cost. All the time John was spending away from Bessette — not to mention the fact she could no longer venture out in public without being hounded by the paparazzi — was stressing their relationship to the limit. Caroline understood what Bessette was going through and urged John to be patient. "You can't expect her to adjust to this life overnight," she told her brother. "Be fair — you've grown up with all this craziness and it can *still* get to you."

John did not always take his sister's advice, though Caroline's opinion clearly mattered more to him than anyone else's. And vice versa. "One rarely made a decision," said a board member of Harvard's Kennedy School, "without checking with the other."

"They may have disagreed about things and argued now and then the way brothers and sisters do," noted one of the few friends Caroline and John shared. "But there was never a rift or any time of prolonged bitterness. John and Caroline were just utterly, totally devoted to each other — and they loved being around each other, which you can't always say about families."

Since the death of their mother, Caroline had, in the words of one friend, become her brother's principal "sounding board and confessor." They were still speaking to each other on the phone every day and often met for lunch at favorite out-of-the-way hangouts. One of their more high-profile haunts was San Domenico on Central Park South, where they usually picked a secluded spot toward the rear of the restaurant. "They would spend hours at the table and laugh a lot," San Domenico's manager, Marisa May, said. "He would always kiss her when he said good-bye."

Just as frequently, they might be spotted at Coco Pazzo, a bustling Italian eatery just five blocks from the Schlossbergs' apartment. "Caroline could always make John laugh," John Perry Barlow said. "She is a very sophisticated person and has this very dark sense of humor. She sees the foibles in people and has a very trenchant way of commenting on them. Caroline isn't mean-spirited by any means, but you don't want to be the butt of her jokes if you can help it. She is very surgical, very precise." Agreed longtime friend George Plimpton, "In the company of her friends and her family, Caroline can be — and often is — absolutely hilarious."

Barlow felt that Caroline's quick wit was "a defense mechanism against all the bullshit she had to go through." Caroline was, like her mother, also a skilled mimic who delivered startlingly accurate impersonations of politicians, show-business figures, and social lions alike. Uncle Teddy was a favorite target, as was Jackie. "Caroline would assume her mother's regal posture, then do the slow, breathless voice," said a friend of John's. "It wasn't disrespectful at all. Imitation is the sincerest form of flattery, and Jackie knew that better than anyone. Back in the White House, she used to do everyone from Lyndon Johnson to Nehru! Frankly, Jackie thought Caroline's impersonation of her was hysterical."

While John tried to sort out his public and private lives, Caroline became increasingly determined to carry on their parents' legacy. She became president of the Kennedy Library Association and — by way of paying tribute to her mother's love of ballet and urban preservation — served on the boards of the American Ballet Theatre and the Citizens Committee for New York City. Caroline attacked each job with the ferocity for which her family was famous. "She can be funny and disarmingly . . . well, normal," said a senior staff member at the Kennedy Library. "But most of the time she is all business — calm and self-assured, always, and very focused. Her eyes really bore in when she's talking to you, and there is none of that Jackie breathlessness to her voice. You get the impression of someone who is on a mission, whereas with John everything is much more laid-back."

Caroline also drew on a wealth of personal experience to write *The Right to Privacy*, her second with Ellen Alderman. Once again, Caroline and her law-school pal hit the road to interview average people who felt that their right to privacy had been violated. Among them: a young couple in Iowa who discovered a two-way mirror in their hotel room, a high-school senior whose boyfriend secretly videotaped them having sex — then showed the tape to his buddies — people whose photos had been used without their permission, and those whose identities were stolen via information gleaned over the Internet. Caroline flew to Beverly Hills to in-

460

terview publisher Larry Flynt, whose *Hustler* magazine had soared to success on the strength of nude Jackie photos published in 1973. Flynt had lost a 1982 suit brought by an animal trainer who was appalled when Flynt published a photo of her with her diving pig in *Chic*. "You wouldn't mistake his office for someone else's," said Caroline, who did the interview surrounded by statues of copulating nudes. As for the pig owner's case, "Somebody's picture gets used without their consent?" Kennedy asked with a shrug. "That doesn't seem as terrible to me as it might to somebody else."

The topic seemed perfectly suited to Caroline, whose entire life had been lived in the proverbial fishbowl. She had been so intent on leading a normal existence — Caroline and John both managed to ride the subway without being harassed — that the press seemed surprised she would venture forth as an author yet again. "Kennedy must emerge, blinking, into the light," wrote *Time*'s Elizabeth Gleick, "to promote the book."

"It's something I've dealt with my whole life," Caroline conceded. But, she also hastened to add, "most of the time I can just go about my business. You know, from time to time a camera will click or someone will approach . . . but not all the time, not at all. I know people don't always believe this, but

461

my life is much more private than most people think."

The most troubling case Caroline and Alderman encountered had nothing to do with celebrity at all, but with women who were strip-searched by Chicago police after failing to pay their parking tickets. In that instance, Caroline allowed, being famous would be a help, not a hindrance. "So maybe I wouldn't get strip-searched," she said. "That's the upside." With the name Caroline Kennedy (sans Schlossberg) on the cover, *The Right to Privacy* leaped onto the *New York Times* bestseller list.

Caroline was still doing book signings and interviews when, in late February 1996, John and his girlfriend were videotaped screaming and shoving each other while walking their dog in New York's Washington Square Park. When she saw the "Brawl in the Park," Caroline, like the rest of the viewing public, was reminded of John's many public battles with Daryl Hannah.

John was, said John Perry Barlow, "profoundly embarrassed by the whole thing. It was very undignified — and so unlike John." Caroline was less than forthcoming when asked to give the Kennedy family's reaction to John's widely reported donnybrook with Bessette. "It's private," she said with a sniff. "I don't want to talk about it. John's doing fine."

In truth, John was anguished about the unseemly spectacle he had caused, and apologized repeatedly to Caroline for holding the whole family up to ridicule. Mom, they both agreed, would have been furious. Caroline was thoroughly familiar with her brother's temper — in college, he had put his fist through a wall after one especially frustrating quarrel with Jackie. But Caroline was far more concerned about her brother's state of mind and the effect the mercurial Ms. Bessette was having on him. "Caroline doesn't like to see John yanked around by a woman," said one of John's Brown buddies. "In that respect, she's a lot like their mother."

Caroline and John were learning that if you were a Kennedy, you were never out of the spotlight for long — even in death. In April 1996, Jackie took center stage again when 1,195 lots from her estate were auctioned off by Sotheby's in New York. The historic auction, approved by Jackie prior to her death, poured another $34,461,495 into Caroline and John's coffers.

In the months before the cataloging of Jacqueline Kennedy Onassis's possessions began, Caroline had sorted through everything — separating what she and John might want to keep for sentimental reasons from what the Kennedy Library could use for its archives and displays. Caroline would ultimately oversee the donation of more than forty-five hundred photographs, thirty-eight thousand pages of documents, and two hundred works of art and artifacts — including the wedding dress her mother wore when she married John Fitzgerald Kennedy.

There were those, however, who viewed the sale of JFK's golf clubs, rocking chair, and humidor — not to mention John's high chair and Jackie's clothes and jewelry — as nothing less than sacrilege. Caroline shrugged off the criticism. Without putting her mother's belongings on the auction block, Maurice reminded her, Jackie's estate would be decimated by estate taxes. "It's what," Caroline replied to the critics, "my mother wanted." No one doubted that Jackie would have been pleased with the outcome. Said her friend Dina Merrill, "Are you kidding? I'm sure Jackie would have been *thrilled*."

She would not have been thrilled about the direction in which John was taking *George*. When Drew Barrymore appeared on the September 1996 cover reenacting Marilyn Monroe's famous rendition of "Happy Birthday, Mr. *Pres-i-dent*" song to JFK, eyebrows soared along with sales. "If I don't find it tasteless," John responded to critics, "I don't know why anyone would. It's part of the iconography of American politics — an enduring image." Caroline said nothing publicly, but, according to one friend, she was "hurt and

464

upset that he would do something so obvious and so crass. What would their mother have thought? Caroline let John know how she felt, and he sort of stuck to his guns. But I think he knew he'd made a serious mistake."

Caroline could not stay mad at John for long. Even before the Drew Barrymore debacle subsided, Caroline was trying on the dress she was to wear at her brother's top secret wedding. She had kidded with her brother that it would be an impossible stunt to pull off, but on September 21, 1996, John Kennedy and Carolyn Bessette were wed in a private ceremony that caught the press and public completely off guard.

The triumph was especially sweet for the acutely privacy-conscious Caroline, who with John planned and stage-managed the entire affair. Over the course of four days, the forty guests who could be counted on to keep a secret began arriving by private plane and boat at Cumberland Island off the coast of Georgia. Guests stayed at the island's only hotel, the Greyfield Inn, where, according to caterer Jodee Sadowsky, everyone "was forced to really rough it. The inn only has bathtubs. There's only one shower, and it's outdoors. So every morning everyone stood on line. Maria Shriver was right behind me in her fuzzy slippers."

Caroline set up headquarters in the inn's large kitchen and began issuing orders. "I was told she takes charge wherever she goes," Sadowsky said. "She certainly did there." While Ed Schlossberg looked after the kids and stayed out of his wife's way, Caroline conspired with Uncle Ted to make everything run as smoothly as possible. "It was always Ted and Caroline," Sadowsky said, "whispering to each other, eating together, plotting something."

The ceremony, held inside the tiny Brack Chapel of the First African Baptist Church, was a family affair. Tony Radziwill was best man. Caroline was matron of honor, and her daughters, Rose and Tatiana, were flower girls. Three-year-old Jack Kennedy Schlossberg was the ring bearer. When Carolyn made her entrance in a $40,000 floor-length silk crepe gown, little Jack shouted, "Why is Carolyn dressed like *that?*" Caroline rolled her eyes and laughed.

"Carolyn came in the church looking like some beautiful ghost," said John Perry Barlow, one of the few non–family members present. Her hair was pulled back, held in place by a comb that had belonged to Jackie, a gift from Caroline.

At the wedding dinner that night, Uncle Teddy once again reduced everyone present to tears with a heart-tugging toast. "I know that Jack and Jackie would be very proud of them," he said, "and full of love for them as they begin their future together."

Incredibly, it would be two days before the press reported the story. At one point, an enterprising photographer for the *National Enquirer* had flown over the chapel in a small plane. Members of the wedding stood on the lawn and, in unison, pointed an obscene gesture in the plane's direction. "Of course," Sadowsky said, "you didn't see that in the pictures."

Caroline was "overjoyed," Marta Sgubin said, "at seeing John so happy. We all were." But Caroline worried that the press, which had already anointed her the "New Queen of Camelot," might make life unbearable for the high-strung Mrs. Bessette-Kennedy, as she now preferred to be known.

Only days after John and Carolyn returned from their honeymoon — three days in Turkey followed by a ten-day Aegean cruise aboard the schooner *Althea* — Caroline threw a postwedding party for her new sister-in-law at the Schlossbergs' apartment. When she arrived, the guest of honor was mobbed by photographers. "Please!" Carolyn pleaded as she shielded her eyes from the blinding flash of the cameras. "I can't see."

Carolyn confided to John's sister that she was totally unprepared for the onslaught, and that much of the time the paparazzi made her feel like "a hunted animal." According to friends of Bessette-Kennedy, Caroline offered words of sympathy and encouragement. As time went on, she told Carolyn, the pressure would ease up and she would become more adept at handling it. "John and I have had to deal with reporters and photographers our whole lives," she said, "but you're still new at this. It will get easier."

But it never did. "Carolyn said some of the photographers made her life hell — that no one understood what it was like to not be able to walk out your front door without somebody shoving a camera in your face," said John's friend Lloyd Howard. "Carolyn admired John for the way he handled it, and she said she was learning from him. But it was hard."

"Carolyn was a tempestuous, passionate human being," John Perry Barlow said. "She could feel everything." Now she was crumbling under the strain, said another friend, "and taking John right along with her." At one point, he became so enraged at a photographer in a parked car that he climbed onto the hood, pressed his face to the windshield, and began shouting, "I know who you are, and I'm going to get you! Leave us the hell *alone!*" When the stunned photographer rolled down her window, he reached inside and grabbed her by the collar.

Caroline had gently prodded her brother about starting a family, but it quickly became apparent that Carolyn was not about to subject a child to what she was going through —

at least not yet. "They wanted," Barlow said, "things to kind of settle down first." They had, however, already picked out the name for a son: Flynn.

It hardly mattered that John and his young wife had made the conscious decision not to have children right away. There was ceaseless speculation that Carolyn had had several miscarriages, that the couple was battling infertility, and that Carolyn and John were no longer sleeping together. Caroline watched helplessly as these and other unfounded rumors sent John's wife into an emotional tailspin.

At first overlooking the fact that his wife was beginning to show the signs of severe depression, John decided to make his first foray into politics. In January 1997, when incumbent New York Senator Daniel Patrick Moynihan made it known he would not be seeking reelection in 2000, John approached New York State Democratic Chair Judith Hope and told her he was interested in running for Moynihan's seat. Caroline urged her brother to think it through. If he was determined to run, then of course she would back him. But was he ready to make the sacrifices a life in office entailed? Was Carolyn ready? In the end, John decided she was far too fragile at the moment to be able to withstand a campaign. He was putting off his political ambitions — for now. (Hillary Clinton would ultimately be elected to fill Moynihan's seat.)

As much as she worried about the health of John's marriage, Caroline was even more concerned about John's renewed fascination with flight. Since their mother was no longer there to put her foot down, John was determined to earn his pilot's license. As a big step in that direction, he had bought his first ultralight — a Buckeye powered parachute — in August 1996. The powered parachute did not require a pilot's license, so, after just two hours of instruction, John took to the skies. Still, over the next two years, neither Caroline nor John's wife made an issue of the Buckeye powered parachute. The two women viewed it not so much as an aircraft as a grown-up's toy. After all, as John repeatedly pointed out, one was not even required to have a license to operate it.

Caroline understood better than most why her brother felt compelled to pilot his own flying machine — any flying machine. When he was a little boy, Caroline had disabused John of the notion that Air Force One was actually his private plane. And as an adult, one of the few places he could find real freedom from the cameras and the microphones and the prying eyes of the public was at the controls of his own plane.

The idea of taking off into the sunset may well have appealed to several of their Kennedy cousins as the family reeled from two scandals that summer of 1997. Congressman Joe Kennedy was in the middle of a run for Massachusetts governor when he came under heavy fire for arranging an annulment of his twelve-year marriage to Sheila Rauch. Joe's younger brother Michael's story was far more tawdry: He was accused of sleeping with his family's underage baby-sitter.

Just as he had with the Drew Barrymore–Marilyn Monroe cover, John decided to create a little controversy to boost flagging magazine sales. Breaking ranks with his Kennedy cousins, John used his editor's letter in the September 1997 issue to brand Joe and Michael "poster boys for bad behavior." He wrote that "one left behind a bitter wife. Another, in what looked to be a hedge against mortality, fell in love with youth and surrendered his judgment in the process." To spice things up, John struck a nude pose — in shadow — for the photo that accompanied the letter. Under the heading "Don't Sit Under the Apple Tree," John was shown sitting on the ground, his gaze directed upward at the forbidden fruit.

Michael was deeply wounded by the sneak attack but said he still viewed John as "not just my cousin but my friend." Joe was not quite so charitable. "I guess my first reaction was 'Ask not what you can do for your cousin, but what you can do for his maga-

471

zine.' " Shortly after, he pulled out of the race for governor.

Caroline was stunned by her brother's unprovoked attack on his own family. As much as their mother had disapproved of the Hickory Hill gang, she'd always believed in presenting a united front to the world. Caroline harbored her own serious misgivings about the clan, but she nevertheless shared Jackie's view. The notion that John would turn on his own family to sell a few magazines was, said a friend, "repugnant to her. She asked John why he would do such a thing. It struck her the way it struck a lot of people, as being just a dumb thing to do."

George, as expected, flew off newsstands that week, and John celebrated by taking an eight-day kayaking trip to Iceland with three friends. As soon as John returned, he and Carolyn hopped a commuter flight to Martha's Vineyard. There they joined Caroline and Ed for a dinner party honoring Bill and Hillary Clinton on August 20 — exactly one week after the President had privately confessed to his wife that he'd indeed had a sexual relationship with Monica Lewinsky.

Prior to the August 20 dinner, Caroline, who felt a strong personal connection to the Clintons, had been sailing with the President and First Lady aboard Ted Kennedy's sailboat, the *Maya*. About to turn forty, Caroline was as svelte as her mother was in her prime — and proved it by taking to the beach in a black two-piece identical to one her mother had worn in the 1980s. There was even conjecture among Jackie's friends that it was, in fact, the very same suit.

The sailing trip was not altogether carefree. For the first time, Caroline found herself torn between John and Uncle Teddy, who was still fuming over the editorial broadside John had leveled at his cousins. Caroline stood by her brother, but she also promised to have a talk with him.

Of equal concern was Carolyn Bessette-Kennedy's rocky mental state. With John devoting so much time to his magazine and the paparazzi still pursuing her through the streets of New York, Carolyn felt abandoned. Over the next several weeks, Caroline sat by helplessly as her brother and his wife engaged in pitched battles on the street, aboard crowded airplanes — and behind closed doors.

"It was clear there was resentment on Carolyn's part," said photographer David McGough, who observed the couple frequently during this period. "She certainly didn't try to hide it." When John mysteriously severed a nerve in his hand and had to be rushed to the hospital for emergency surgery, the official explanation — that it was a simple "kitchen accident" — proved unconvincing. "They were both volatile, highly physical," said a friend of the couple's. "Caroline knew that, and she worried that things were going to get out of hand."

If his marriage was falling to pieces, John was not about to let on to anyone — including Caroline. His hand and forearm bandaged and in a brace as a result of his so-called kitchen accident, John flew off just days later for a historic first meeting with Cuban dictator Fidel Castro. John regaled his sister with a detailed account of his five-hour dinner with Castro and told her that Fidel claimed to be a great admirer of their dad. He even apologized to John and to Caroline for refusing Lee Harvey Oswald an entry visa into Cuba in October 1963, which in all likelihood would have resulted in Oswald's not being in Dallas the following month.

As the holidays approached, there were more heated confrontations with the press. At one point, John turned a videotape on his pursuers and promised it would be used as Exhibit A in a lawsuit against them. Later, Carolyn would chase after a female photographer and spit in her face.

Caroline understood John's need to get away. That did not, however, prevent her from letting him know how frightened she was when she learned he was again secretly taking flying lessons — this time at the Flight Safety Academy in Vero Beach, Florida.

Just five days later, Caroline sat staring at

her television, numb with disbelief. Michael Kennedy, the networks were reporting, had been killed in Aspen after colliding with a fir tree during a typically reckless Kennedy game of night football on skis. Michael's sister Rory cradled his bleeding head and tried to revive him as his children knelt in the snow and sobbed. Michael was thirty-nine.

Caroline knew how hard this tragedy would hit her hypersensitive brother, who only five months before had skewered Michael in the pages of *George*. At the funeral in Centerville, Massachusetts, John was more openly emotional than he had been at any of the previous funerals he'd attended — and there had been many. Tears rolled down his cheeks as he tightly embraced Michael's brother Douglas, but clearly all was not forgiven. Oldest brother Joe — the other "poster boy for bad behavior" — turned a cold shoulder to John.

"Caroline felt badly for her brother," another mourner recalled. "She was devastated by the senselessness of Michael's death, but she also knew John was feeling badly about what he'd done. She was pretty teary, too, but I think it also had a lot to do with the guilt she knew John was carrying around."

Both Caroline and Carolyn saw Michael's death as just one more indication of the impulsive streak that ran through the Kennedy males. Now Caroline and Uncle Teddy joined

Carolyn in pressuring John to quit his flying lessons — if for no other reason than to reduce the strain on his beleaguered bride. Caroline also nudged her little brother to remember their mother's wishes. John grudgingly agreed, informing his flight instructors that "personal and family conflicts" were forcing him to quit.

A few weeks later, after a highly publicized visit to the White House and a string of galas, balls, and black-tie dinners, all seemed to be well with the Kennedy-Bessette marriage. John told Caroline that his wife was happier now and finally learning to live in the unremitting klieg-light glare. They had achieved, he told his sister, a certain "equilibrium" in their lives. Carolyn was now so comfortable, in fact, that he was able to talk her into letting him resume his flying lessons.

"Caroline knew they had problems, and of course she sympathized with her brother," a friend said. "John tried not to be too critical of his wife to Caroline, but of course she knew all about their fights. So when it looked like Carolyn had finally come to terms with being in the spotlight, Caroline was thrilled."

Caroline was not overjoyed, however, when John told her that he had earned his pilot's license that April. She loved her brother and thought of him as being, as she once said, "very intelligent and highly capable." But there was also no denying that John was profoundly absentminded. It was an opinion shared by virtually everyone who knew him, including his flight instructors. He had a problem with concentration and with "multitasking" — an aptitude required of any pilot who wished to become instrument-certified.

No one, not even close friends and family, would agree to go up with John at the controls. Caroline declined. So did Uncle Teddy. Even Willie Smith, his closest Kennedy relative, refused.

And Caroline's brother faced plenty of added distractions in the fall of 1998 — not the least of which were the plummeting sales of *George*. Caroline knew that John was working until late at night, coming into the office on weekends and taking business trips abroad without Carolyn. She, in turn, was spending more and more time with her fashion-industry pals and her sister, Lauren, who, after a year in Hong Kong, had settled into her own penthouse apartment two blocks from 20 North Moore Street.

Caroline was all too aware of the gossip swirling around her brother and his mercurial wife. There were rumors of infidelity (hers and his), of drug abuse on her part (cocaine and antidepressants), and of sexual estrangement. At one point, he confessed to Caroline that his wife had moved into the spare bedroom. Still, they appeared very much in love when they accompanied Caroline and Ed to the gala reopening of the newly restored Grand Central Station. Showing up hand in hand at a benefit at New York's Tavern on the Green that December, they gave no hint of the trouble that was simmering beneath the surface. Within three months, they would be seeing a marriage counselor.

As the situation deteriorated, Caroline became less and less tolerant of her sister-in-law's behavior. Specifically, she disapproved of those denizens of the fashion world Carolyn seemed to be spending increasing amounts of time with. "Carolyn was causing her brother a lot of unnecessary pain," said a colleague from John's days in the district attorney's office, "and, frankly, that pissed Caroline off."

The state of John's marriage was not the only topic on the agenda during Caroline's daily phone chat with John. In late 1998, they found themselves locked in a bizarre legal battle with Sheldon Streisand, older brother of longtime Kennedy supporter (and heavyweight Democratic Party fund-raiser) Barbra Streisand. Twenty years earlier, Jackie had entered into a real-estate investment partnership with Sheldon Streisand through a trust set up for Caroline and John. The trust invested $780,000 in Western Properties Associates, in return for 99 percent of the profits. For a minimal investment, Streisand, who managed the partnership, received the remaining 1 percent. Western Properties invested in shopping malls in California, Utah, and the state of Washington.

Caroline and John filed a lawsuit against Streisand, claiming that he gave a half interest in the partnership to his wife without their permission. Charging that Streisand had engaged in the "rankest form" of double-dealing, Caroline and her brother went on to describe his actions as "blatant and deceitful" — a "sordid saga of partnership pilfering." Streisand, not surprisingly, denied all claims of wrongdoing.

Perhaps not so coincidentally, John took a potshot at Sheldon Streisand's famous sister in *George*. In its "Editor's Picks" column, the magazine said Barbra "went too far" when, based on her "blind faith in Clinton," she urged everyone to vote for the Democrat running for Congress in his or her particular district.

An enraged Streisand fired back. "The next time you write something," she said in a letter to John, "it would be good to check your facts, not to mention the Constitution. Who could have imagined that in this day and age, journalists would question a person's right to express his or her views? So much for freedom of speech. What will be next: Do I dare say freedom of the press?"

At the time, Streisand's "blind faith" in the

President was being put to the test as the sordid Monica Lewinsky affair snowballed into a full-scale impeachment trial. The Lewinsky scandal and all that followed was nothing short of a godsend for *George*, which would post record advertising of $1 million for the April 1999 issue.

Caroline, however, was more acutely aware of the immense strain on her friends the Clintons — especially the psychic pain that had been inflicted on Chelsea over the course of the year. The emotional connection Caroline felt with Chelsea was strong — not only were they both the only daughters of young liberal Democratic presidents, but they were the daughters of young liberal Democratic presidents whose reputations had been tarnished by scandal and sexual innuendo. "It's very different, say, from what Tricia and Julie Nixon went through," said the daughter of a U.S. senator and friend of the Kennedys'. "The Nixon girls never believed their father betrayed their mother, the way Caroline and Chelsea constantly have their dads' infidelities thrown in their face. Caroline identified with Chelsea in many ways, and that was one of them. That's why she thought she could help Chelsea get through that very tough time in her life."

Toward that end, Caroline spent hours talking to Chelsea on Martha's Vineyard and followed up over the fall and winter months with phone calls and letters. When her brother gloated over the impact the scandal was having on magazine sales, Caroline told him to remember the human cost involved and "how you feel when they talk about Dad."

Or, for that matter, when they talked about *him*. Each week, the tabloids were still filled with stories speculating on the health of the Kennedy-Bessette marriage. But by May 1999, when she sat on John's lap and they nuzzled at the White House Correspondents' Dinner, it appeared that they were back on track. Locals had never seen John and Carolyn happier than when they arrived to spend Memorial Day weekend on Martha's Vineyard.

They were also more than a little alarmed one blustery day to see John aloft in his Buckeye ultralight powered parachute — "a flying lawn mower," one neighbor called it — careening past high-tension power lines toward earth. John managed a crash landing, breaking his left ankle in the process.

Caroline could not resist teasing her accident-prone little brother, who now had his leg in a cast and was forced to hobble around on crutches. But she also insisted that he stop flying the "flimsy contraption."

There was still, of course, the question of whether he should be flying at all. The ultralight crash gave Caroline yet another opportunity to raise the issue with John. He had also told her he was trading up from his single-engine Cessna to a faster Piper Saratoga. Was he sure he could handle it?

As usual, John blithely dismissed his sister's concerns. He reminded Caroline that he had been trained at one of the best flight schools in the country and insisted — "for the hundredth time" — that he was not about to take any chances in the air. Inevitably, talk turned to more mundane matters. Caroline was finalizing plans for the long-anticipated Schlossberg-family rafting trip in Idaho. About their cousin Rory's wedding at Hyannis Port . . . "Yes, yes, Carolyn and I are going," John assured his sister. "I promised I would."

He was the Kennedy who loved us all,
but especially cherished his sister,
Caroline.

— *Ted Kennedy*

Her mother gone.
Her father murdered. . . .
She's alone now.

— *Jack Valenti*

You just keep going along.
You just keep going along,
or you're left behind.

— *Caroline*

9

July 21, 1999
4:30 p.m.

Caroline did not have to ask her uncle; he promised he would be there to identify the bodies when this terrible moment came. The ashen-faced senator stood on the deck of the navy salvage vessel USS *Grasp*, anchored seven and a half miles southwest of Martha's Vineyard. After four days of searching, a remote-operated underwater camera had spotted the wreckage of John's Piper Saratoga lying upside down at a depth of 116 feet. A ten-foot section of the cabin remained intact. Inside, John was still strapped into his cockpit seat; on the murky, rocky ocean floor, the bodies of Carolyn and Lauren Bessette were found several yards away.

Now Ted, flanked by his sons Ted Jr. and Rhode Island Congressman Patrick Kennedy, drew a deep breath as the *Grasp*'s large grappling arm pulled the first of the bodies up to the water's glistening surface. Uncle Teddy, expressionless behind dark glasses, watched as the remains of John and the Bessette sisters were placed in three metal caskets. Several crew members, including those with the grim duty of handling the bodies in their respective caskets, fought back tears.

After the *Grasp* docked at Woods Hole, the bodies were loaded into a van. Around 7:10 p.m., the bodies were wheeled into the morgue of Barnstable County Hospital. Caroline knew that, under Massachusetts law, an autopsy would have to be performed on the body of the pilot. But she and Ted had both been outraged when JFK's autopsy photos were made public in the early 1980s. Now there was the distinct possibility that someone might obtain copies of these autopsy pictures and sell them to the tabloids — or post them on the Internet.

Ted and his niece agreed that the best way to keep this from happening was not to take any photos at all. But local authorities insisted; autopsy photos were mandated by state law. Ultimately, a compromise was reached: The customary photographs were taken during the four-hour procedure, but it was agreed that the film would be developed only if there were some future legal need. No autopsies were performed on the bodies of the Bessette sisters.

Caroline and the relatives of the Bessette women could take some solace in the fact that the victims did not suffer. All three died instantly when the plane hit the water at more than sixty miles an hour. After consulting by phone with Caroline and the Bessettes' mother, Ann Marie Bessette Freeman (Carolyn's parents had divorced when she was six), Uncle Ted moved to have the bodies cremated as quickly as possible.

Much had already been made in the media about the likelihood of a wrongful-death suit. John took off not only with a severely injured foot that may have made it difficult to operate the brakes and the rudder, but under questionable conditions at night and without being instrument-certified. Then there was the irrefutable fact that John's family had a reputation for recklessness.

Caroline was acutely sensitive to the situation. She had lost her adored John, but Ann Freeman now grieved for two daughters killed in a plane piloted by Caroline's brother. After Caroline conferred with Ann Freeman and with Uncle Ted, the bodies were rushed to the crematory in nearby Duxbury. The ashes of John, Carolyn, and Lauren were then turned over to Ted.

Even before the bodies were located off Martha's Vineyard, Caroline had begun planning the funeral — sadly, a task that was by now second nature. She and Ted were never closer than at times like these, but still they clashed over the details. Five years before, she had fought bitterly against Ted's attempts to stage a large public funeral for Jackie at St. Patrick's Cathedral.

Now Ted, pointing to the fact that the entire nation had held its breath during the search for John, again argued for a spectacular funeral mass at St. Patrick's. Several Kennedy relatives, including Aunt Eunice, sided with Uncle Ted. But Caroline, now known in family circles for her steel will, held her ground. She did not want her brother's funeral to devolve into a tacky media circus. "Caroline has vivid memories of Bobby's funeral there," a friend said. "It was very traumatizing and overwhelming for a ten-year-old girl, and she just didn't want to dredge all that up. That's why she didn't want her mother's funeral at St. Patrick's, and that's why she didn't want John's there either."

Caroline did want a comparatively small family service, and she wanted it to be held at the church that had meant so much to their little family of three — St. Thomas More, the modest, neo-Gothic stone church on East Eighty-ninth Street where Jackie took her children to mass every Sunday, and where Caroline now worshipped with *her* children. Wherever the memorial service was held, there was really no way to stave off the inevitable media onslaught — especially since the President and First Lady Hillary Clinton would be heading up a long list of dignitaries in attendance.

Caroline, meanwhile, shook her head in disbelief as the unfolding drama took an unexpected turn in Washington. In a hastily called press conference, President Clinton was forced to defend himself against criticism that the search-and-rescue effort — the most extensive ever for a private plane — had cost taxpayers millions of dollars. Citing the "role of the Kennedy family in our national life" and the number of losses the family had suffered over the years, Clinton was unapologetic. It was, he said, "the right thing to do."

Clinton had also cleared the way for John to be interred at Arlington alongside his parents and his two siblings. But when it became clear that Carolyn would not be permitted to join him, Ann Freeman objected. A second option — interring John and his wife at the Brookline cemetery where Rose, Joe, and a number of other Kennedys were buried — was also rejected by Freeman. Her girls, she pointed out, were really not connected to Massachusetts. Caroline also had her doubts; she had spent time at Graceland around the time of Elvis's death and did not want her brother's final resting place turned into a shrine.

John had once mentioned to Caroline in passing that he wanted to be buried at sea. Whether he was serious or merely musing at the time, it seemed now to be the only viable solution for both families.

On Thursday morning, July 22, 1999, Caroline and sixteen other relatives of the deceased boarded the navy destroyer *Briscoe*. She slumped in a wooden folding chair, eyes concealed behind dark glasses, as the ship headed out to sea. Tony Radziwill, now losing his decade-long battle with cancer, had been pushed on board in a wheelchair. John, perhaps to show his faith in his favorite cousin's recovery, had made Tony executor of his estate. "John is my brother," Tony said. "I love him and will miss him forever."

When the *Briscoe* stopped not far from where John's plane had gone down, Caroline and the others moved to the stern. Charles O'Byrne, the priest who married John and Carolyn, conducted the fifteen-minute ceremony with the help of two navy chaplains. Then Caroline and the others climbed down a ladder to a platform not far above the waterline. Three officers stood by, each holding a silver urn. As a brass quintet from the Newport Navy Band played the Navy Hymn, Caroline scattered her brother's ashes over the waves.

While the *Briscoe* turned and headed for shore, Caroline embraced Uncle Ted, kissed Tony on the cheek, and spoke with members of the Bessette family. As they shared words of comfort through their tears, thousands of flower petals — the blossoms that were to have decorated the tables at Rory Kennedy's now-canceled wedding reception — fluttered off the *Briscoe*'s fantail.

The many sad ironies of this moment did not escape Caroline, not the least of which was the fact that John's ashes were being scattered within sight of their mother's house — and on what would have been Rose Kennedy's 109th birthday. Hundreds of miles to the south, off the coast of Virginia, five thousand crew members aboard an aircraft carrier observed a moment of silence. Their ship was the *John F. Kennedy*, so christened by nine-year-old Caroline Kennedy in 1967.

Incredibly, no detail escaped Caroline's notice. She even had time to monitor the press, so she would know what was being said about her brother and who was saying it. Printed invitations for the New York memorial service, the design of which Caroline had personally approved, went out to invited guests. Far more than John, who had long ago learned to court favor with reporters, Caroline had a rule about dealing with the press that was more ironclad than ever: No one spoke with the press without express permission from her. Anyone who did was cut off, and instantly. It was a lesson learned by a few of John's closest friends, who, after uttering only words of praise for him, received a phone call saying their invitation to the memorial service was being rescinded.

In an effort not to disrupt her own children's lives any further, Caroline tried to remain as upbeat in their presence as humanly possible. "She wanted to make sure the kids didn't see her cry," said Betina Lovell, a longtime friend of Carolyn's and an acquaintance of the Kennedys'. Although Marta Sgubin did nearly all of the cooking for the Schlossbergs, Caroline took it upon herself to prepare breakfast for the kids every morning — a task she insisted on performing even on the day of her brother's memorial service. "Her heart must have been breaking," Lovell said.

An hour after cooking breakfast for her children, Caroline combed Tatiana's hair, straightened Jack's tie, and headed out the door of their apartment building. Blue police barricades had been set up on the street, and paparazzi and fanny-pack-wearing tourists alike pressed against them to snap photos of Caroline and her family. Holding tight to Jack's hand, her head held high and eyes straight ahead, Caroline stepped to the waiting limousine that would take the Schlossbergs to St. Thomas More Church.

When she got there five minutes later, most of the 315 invited guests had already filed inside. Chelsea Clinton and her parents were among them, along with John's childhood hero Muhammad Ali, old college buddies, a few *George* staffers, and famous faces from his dad's era like Arthur Schlesinger Jr. and Robert McNamara. Uncle Ted Kennedy stepped to the podium and performed the onerous task for which he was now far too well prepared.

"He had amazing grace," Ted told the mourners. "He accepted who he was, but he cared more about what he could and should become." Ted pointed out that John flew his own plane because "that was how he wanted it. He was the king of his domain."

Ted spoke of John's accomplishments — the founding of *George* and his work for the philanthropic Robin Hood Foundation — but his voice quavered when he began to talk about the special feelings John had for his sister. John "celebrated her brilliance," he said, "and took strength and joy from their lifelong mutual-admiration society. . . . John was one of Jackie's two miracles."

Ted promised that John's life "will live forever in our beguiled and broken hearts. We dared to think . . . this John Kennedy would live to comb gray hair, with his beloved Carolyn by his side. But, like his father, he had every gift but length of years."

Sobs inside the dimly lit church were audible; nearly everyone was either crying or about to. Everyone but Caroline, who had never broken down in public and was not about to now. As her uncle left the pulpit, Caroline rose to embrace him.

It was impossible to ignore the presence of the First Family or the indisputable eloquence of Ted Kennedy's eulogy. But Caroline was the emotional focal point of the service; all eyes were on her, as they had been for days.

With a dignity of purpose worthy of her mother, Caroline recalled that Jackie had instilled a love of literature in both her children. She then recited a few lines from one of the plays John had performed in at Brown, *The Tempest*. " 'We are such stuff as dreams are made on,' " she said, " 'and our little life is rounded with a sleep.' " Rose, Tatiana, and Jack then lit candles while Wyclef Jean sang a favorite reggae tune of John's.

After the service, Caroline greeted mourners warmly, thanked them for coming, and sometimes put a comforting arm around a less stoic friend or relative. At one point, she turned to Stephen Styles, another of John's college pals, and mused, "It's as if the natural order of things has been somehow shifted, ruined even. . . ."

Leaving the church, eleven-year-old Rose stuck her tongue out at photographers gathered across the street. Her mother, however, managed a wan smile, and even rolled down her window to wave at the thousands of spectators who lined the streets.

Caroline, who felt it was important Carolyn and Lauren not be eclipsed by her brother

("John wouldn't have wanted that"), took special care to spend time with Carolyn's family. The following evening, she and Uncle Teddy led a group of twenty-five Kennedys to the memorial for Lauren Bessette at the Episcopal Christ Church in Greenwich, Connecticut.

There would be more heartache just three weeks later, when Tony Radziwill lost his battle with cancer. At the funeral of her brother's cousin and best friend, Caroline's face was etched with grief — though once again she managed to otherwise appear cool and in control.

"Tony's death had been expected for some time," said a friend of the Radziwills', "but Caroline never expected to be attending his funeral without John. They were like brothers. Her kids liked Tony and were at his funeral, too. All she could tell them was that these two guys who loved each other so much were now in heaven together."

However overwhelmed she may have felt, Caroline was forced to face some hard legal realities. While the National Transportation Safety Board moved ahead with its investigation, aviation experts took to the airwaves in a media stampede to assign blame for the crash.

Since investigators had determined that mechanical failure did not cause the crash, attention naturally focused on the pilot. As consensus built that the NTSB would likely find that pilot error was to blame, Ann Freeman moved to have herself named administrator of the Bessette sisters' estates — a legal maneuver that would enable her to file wrongful-death lawsuits against "unknown parties" in the future.

Caroline might have anticipated that, when John's will was read on September 24, 1999, it would only exacerbate tensions between the Kennedy and Bessette-Freeman clans. John bequeathed the vast majority of his $100 million–plus estate to a trust set up in 1983. The primary beneficiaries: Caroline and her children. (In addition to leaving Rose, Tatiana, and Jack his half of Red Gate Farm — now valued at well over $8 million — John bequeathed to Jack "a scrimshaw set previously owned by my father.")

Had Carolyn survived her husband, she would have received only John's belongings and their apartment at 20 North Moore, then valued at more than $2 million. The Bessette-Freeman family's reaction was predictable. "They were shocked and very, very upset," said a friend of Ann Freeman's. "It had nothing to do with money and everything to do with fairness."

Uncle Teddy, no stranger to such matters, urged Caroline to deal directly with Ann Freeman in an effort to forestall a messy lawsuit. She did not have to be persuaded;

Caroline had no interest in having the horrifying details of her brother's death rehashed in court or seeing him depicted as reckless and incompetent. Moreover, Caroline was genuinely sympathetic to the feelings of Carolyn's parents.

By way of circumventing the anticipated lawsuit, Caroline met over the course of five months with Ann and her surviving daughter, Lisa Bessette, to work things out. Reaching an accord would not be so easy, however. The two families had never been close prior to the accident, and they would discover that, besides their shared grief, they had little in common. Caroline and the Bessette family would not finalize a deal until July 2001 — just ten days before the end of the two-year deadline for Ann Freeman to file a wrongful-death suit. In return for not bringing action, Caroline agreed to pay her sister-in-law's family an estimated $10 million — though it was unclear how much of that figure was paid by the insurers of John's plane. "Don't assume," said New York aviation attorney Jim Kreindler, "that the Kennedy estate is paying a nickel."

In those first months following the crash, Caroline picked up the pieces of her brother's life — literally and figuratively. The wreckage of the Piper Saratoga was crated by the NTSB and turned over to Caroline. Anxious that fragments might find their way into the hands of souvenir hunters, she kept the plane's twisted remains in a warehouse for several months before having them destroyed.

Caroline also had someone recover her brother's white convertible from the Essex County Airport in New Jersey. In all the confusion, it had been left unclaimed in the airport parking lot for eleven days. She personally saw to it that the apartment was emptied of John's personal belongings and sold ("All of this was just so painful," said a family friend). Additionally, Caroline arranged the sale of John's 50 percent interest in *George* magazine to Hachette-Filipacchi (the magazine folded soon thereafter).

One of the more touching casualties of the crash was John's dog, Friday, who had not been aboard the plane but nonetheless grieved for his owner. At first Friday was taken, along with Carolyn's cat Ruby, to live with Jackie's longtime butler, Ephigenio Pinheiro, on Martha's Vineyard. Later, Friday went to live with the Schlossbergs on Park Avenue.

She would allow no one outside the family to witness her grief, but behind the serene facade so reminiscent of her mother's, Caroline was teetering on the edge of a nervous breakdown. "Caroline was so close to John, and she was crushed by his death — shattered," Marta Sgubin said. "She was weeping constantly. Many times after the funeral, I saw Ted, without a word, put his arms around her and hold her as she wept onto his shoulders."

Still sticking to their usual schedule — "She didn't want to disrupt the children's lives," Sgubin said — Caroline packed up the family for Martha's Vineyard that August. It was on the Vineyard that Caroline had helped Chelsea Clinton get through the dark days of the Lewinsky scandal and her father's impeachment. They had forged a strong bond over the years, and now Chelsea was back sailing with the Schlossbergs, doing whatever she could to bolster her friend's spirits.

Returning to Red Gate Farm had not been easy. No sooner did Caroline open the door than memories came flooding back. Wherever she looked — on fireplace mantels, on tabletops and bookshelves — were framed photographs of her mother and brother. Overcome, Caroline went to her bedroom, closed the door, and cried. Once she pulled herself together, Caroline asked Rose and Tatiana to help her pack some of the photos away. Looking around at the bare surfaces, she changed her mind and told the kids to help her put the pictures back where they were.

Inevitably, there would be a flurry of reports that Caroline intended to sell her mother's Martha's Vineyard estate because of all the memories it held. Not far from the estate, on the beach where debris from the crash first washed up, local residents had put up a rustic wooden cross entwined with grapevines. The names of Carolyn and John were printed on the cross, and prayers and wishes were scrawled on stones piled at its base. Caroline had to pass this makeshift shrine whenever she strolled this far down the beach.

Nevertheless, Caroline had no intention of selling Red Gate Farm. Instead she gave the nod to Ed to remodel the main house so that it would be more suitable for her young family. In no time, Ed began peeling back the roof and tearing down walls. The notoriously frugal Caroline kept close tabs on expenditures — so close that local contractors began referring to Red Gate Farm as "Home Depot."

In the meantime, Caroline's in-laws and a few select Kennedy relatives tried to persuade her to focus more on her own feelings and less on how they might affect the children. "They talked to her about sharing her grief with her husband and kids," Stephen Styles said, "about opening up to them in a way her mother — whom she really takes after — seldom did."

Caroline turned to her closest Kennedy cousin for help in coming to terms with the latest tragedy in her life. Coincidentally,

Maria Shriver had just published *What's Heaven?*, a bestselling book about grief and loss inspired in part by the devastating consequences of the Kennedys' stiff-upper-lip approach to tragedy. "When I was growing up, there was a lot of loss around," said Shriver, who would prove instrumental in getting Caroline to be more open with her children. "I also grew up at a time when you didn't talk about it. I'd think, I know somebody just died, but nobody's talking about it, so I better not talk about it either. Even though I knew the whole world was talking about it. . . ."

On October 3, Caroline made her first public appearance since John's death, hosting a dinner to celebrate the Kennedy Library's twentieth anniversary. "There are a few people I would like to salute," she said, staring out over a sea of faces from her father's New Frontier. "The first is my brother, John, who brought his own sense of purpose and idealism to the public service which I wish we can all continue." When her brief remarks were over, she rushed backstage and broke down sobbing.

There would never be even the slightest crack in the mask Caroline showed to the public. But now, thanks in large part to Maria Shriver, she understood that trying to pretend nothing had happened could have negative consequences for her children.

"Sometimes I cry in front of the kids," Caroline told a friend. "I don't think it's healthy bottling things up inside, and I think it's important they understand that."

Caroline suffered a setback in late November 1999, as she approached her forty-second birthday — and what would have been John's thirty-ninth. Memories of their joint birthday celebration — including the one just days after their father's murder — came flooding back. For the sake of the children, she agreed to have a small birthday party on November 26 — halfway between John's on November 25 and Caroline's on November 27. There was a cake with a single candle, which everyone blew out.

Three days later, however, Caroline nearly broke down at a political fund-raiser for her uncle. "Without Teddy," she said, "I don't think I could have gotten through the past few months." The pain was far from over. "Caroline is still very sad," Sgubin said nearly a year later, "but at least with Ted there, she is never alone."

Just as he had always done, Ted stepped into the void for the children, too. "Dear Uncle Teddy," Jack Schlossberg wrote on lined school paper after the crash that took the life of his godfather, "Will you be my godfather now? Love, Jack."

Indeed, Caroline would never take her uncle for granted. "I have an appreciation," she said, "for how lucky I am to be in our family."

Now it fell on Caroline to take on not only the causes that John championed but the remainder of all the charities their mother had supported as well. On December 7, 1999, she showed up at a Robin Hood Foundation reception to present one of four John F. Kennedy Jr. Hero Awards. Caroline told the crowd she was there to "support what John — to continue what he cared about." When one of the honorees, Marc Washington, broke down recounting his brother's death, Caroline gave him a hug and told him to "stay strong."

For her part, Caroline found solace in simple daily routine. Every morning, she put Jack on the crosstown bus to Collegiate, the West Side school Uncle John had attended as a boy. Then she often walked Rose and Tatiana the ten blocks to her alma mater, Brearley. While Caroline served on Brearley's Board of Trustees (and in 2003 would help pick a new headmistress), Ed pitched in to design the school's computer lab.

From Christmas pageants to assemblies to school sporting events, either Ed or Caroline — or, more frequently, both — was sure to be in attendance. Usually it was Ed who manned the camcorder. "It's hard to imagine," another Collegiate mom said, "but there they are just like any proud parent videotaping every moment of their child's fourth-grade graduation."

For Caroline, however, some of the simplest tasks were becoming increasingly difficult — and sometimes painful — to perform. Her hands were often red and the joints of her fingers swollen. To further complicate matters, Caroline had lost a startling amount of weight — nearly twenty pounds — in the months following John's death. Like John, who had gone through a similar drop in weight caused by an overactive thyroid, Caroline wondered if she might be suffering symptoms of the autoimmune disorder that her father had battled for years — Addison's disease.

The speculation ended one morning she woke up with searing pain, barely able to move her fingers. Doctors reportedly diagnosed her as suffering from rheumatoid arthritis, another autoimmune disorder that essentially causes the body to attack its own joints. The stress of John's death, they believed, had aggravated an already existing condition — and caused the sudden weight loss.

That Caroline might suffer from arthritis should not have been altogether surprising, since both the Bouviers and Kennedys had a family history of the disease. Both of Caroline's parents had suffered from it, though they managed to conceal the fact from the public.

In the months following John's death, Caroline's symptoms appeared to subside, and she took the children on a number of trips — adventures designed to take everyone's mind off the tragic loss of Uncle John. They visited the Virginia horse country where Jackie used to ride with Caroline, Civil War battlefield sites like Antietam, and Ireland, where they stayed at a modest bed-and-breakfast in Kenmare and reconnected with their Fitzgerald-Kennedy roots.

"That's always been a Kennedy-family message," Joe Gargan observed, "to pick up and carry on." In spite of it all, Gargan insisted, Caroline remained "full of life, full of laughter." She jumped back into the New York social whirl on May 13, when she donned a sequined Carolina Herrera gown for the gala season opening of the American Ballet Theatre at New York City's Metropolitan Opera House. Caroline, who had chaired the event ever since Jackie's death, seemed relaxed, even jovial. Later, over dinner, she turned to Aileen Mehle and asked, "Next to mine, which is the most beautiful dress in the room?"

Still, there was no way of escaping the fact that John had left a giant hole in Caroline's life. For ten years running, brother and sister had presented the foundation's Profile in

Courage Awards together. Now, in May 2000, Caroline stepped up to present each award — a $25,000 stipend and a silver lantern designed by Ed Schlossberg — alone. While a videotaped 1999 interview with John loomed above them on a giant screen, Caroline sat waiting in the dark to present the awards. "I felt John's absence," Kennedy Library Foundation Chairman Paul Kirk Jr. said, "but I felt his presence more." Agreed Caroline, "No matter how much we miss John today, he was . . . *is* smiling on these awards." It had been, said Kirk, "an emotional morning."

No one played a larger role than Ed Schlossberg in helping his wife through this difficult period. "Ed does for Caroline what Maurice did for Jackie," said a New York gallery owner who has been a longtime friend of the Schlossbergs. "He's a safe harbor for her. He has no interest at all in the limelight, but he's not thrown by it either. He can cope with the media in a way Carolyn Bessette couldn't. What words would I use to describe his attitude toward Caroline? 'Fiercely protective.' " As for Caroline's opinion of Ed: "She fell in love with him as an artist — she is as proud of him and his accomplishments as he is of her. They argue sometimes about the small stuff, sure — with three kids, how could you not? But they are rock solid as a couple."

On one issue in particular, Ed and Caroline were in complete agreement: Rose, Tatiana, and Jack would be taken to as few public events as possible, thereby shielding them from the paparazzi who had dogged Caroline's every move as a child and as a teenager. An exception was made in April 2001 for the opening of Dad's thirty-year retrospective at New York's National Arts Club. The children waited in a back room until Caroline felt that the crowd had thinned out enough for them to be brought into the main gallery area.

Caroline and Ed also made a point of taking the kids to Ellis Island, the site of one of their father's most ambitious undertakings — the American Family Immigration History Center. Ed had spent five years working on the interactive-media display consisting of a Web site and forty-one computers. Tapping into a database of more than 17 million people who passed through Ellis Island from 1892 to 1924, the Web site made it possible for people to determine once and for all if their ancestors entered the country via the famous immigration center. As it turned out, everyone on the Schlossberg side of the family was descended from Ellis Island immigrants.

For all the distractions in their lives, getting through the first anniversary of John's death was especially hard for Caroline. The milestone was marked with countless newspaper and magazine articles, television specials and documentaries, and a number one *New York Times* bestselling book.

Caroline handled it the way she had every other anniversary of a family death — by trying hard to ignore it. The Schlossbergs did nothing to mark the day, and in fact tried to keep the children from reading about it or watching coverage on television. Instead they spent the day as they did most days in July — relaxing at their summer house in Sagaponack, Long Island.

That summer, Caroline was thinking as much about her father's legacy as she was about the senseless accident that took her brother's life. Uncle Teddy had approached her to make a speech, prefacing his request with, "I've got something fun for you to do." Caroline had turned down the chance to chair the 1992 Democratic National Convention, but now, eight years later, Ted was asking his niece to address the convention in Los Angeles — the same city where JFK was nominated forty years earlier. In what was touted as "Kennedy Night" at the convention, Caroline and four other family members — Uncle Teddy, Maryland Lieutenant Governor Kathleen Kennedy Townsend, Patrick Kennedy, and Robert F. Kennedy Jr. — paid tribute to the glory days of Camelot.

"I know that my father's spirit lives on," Caroline told the convention and a prime-time television audience of millions. "Now it is our turn to prove that the New Frontier was not a place in time but a timeless call." As she appealed to voters to back the party's choice for president, Al Gore, she evoked the name of her brother. "I thank all Americans for making me and John, and all our family, a part of your families — for reaching out and sustaining us through the good times and the difficult ones, and for helping us to dream my father's dream." Caroline then claimed to have "a special sense of kinship" with Gore, whose parents were among several matchmakers who had helped bring Jack Kennedy and Jacqueline Bouvier together. "I wouldn't be here," Caroline quipped, "if it weren't for the Gore family."

Increasingly, Caroline was stepping out of the shadows and into the spotlight that was for so long occupied by Jackie and John. "I get a sense that it was her brother's death," said family friend John Siegenthaler, "that has made Caroline feel an obligation to become more involved in public life."

In April 2001, Caroline presided over the celebrity-packed gala opening of "Jacqueline Kennedy: The White House Years," a lavish exhibition of Jackie's trendsetting Camelot-era fashions at the Metropolitan Museum of Art in New York. Unaware that Laura Bush had long idolized her mother, Caroline virtually ignored the new First Lady when she arrived, perfunctorily thanking Mrs. Bush "for coming tonight." But Jackie's daughter went out of her way to praise the newly elected senator from New York, Hillary Clinton, who deigned to make her appearance only after Laura had departed, as the woman who "interpreted the role of First Lady for our times."

Just a few days later, Caroline dazzled balletomanes at the American Ballet Theatre's annual fund-raising dinner. When a reporter noted that she was more visible than she had been in decades, Caroline grinned and said, "Yes, and I'm having a very good time!" In May, she was back on the television talk-show circuit to announce the winners of the 2001 Profiles in Courage Awards.

That summer, between visits to Sagaponack and Martha's Vineyard, Caroline was confronted with a ticklish legal dilemma stemming from John's death. For years, Marta Sgubin had lived in a seventh-floor, two-bedroom apartment just a few blocks from the Schlossbergs, at 929 Park Avenue. The apartment was actually owned by John, who had left her $1 million in his will for the express purpose of purchasing it. But Ed reportedly believed that the apartment should remain in the family, and that while Marta was welcome to continue living there, it should not be sold to her.

By July, Sgubin was threatened with eviction by the building's co-op board. "When Caroline goes away for a weekend, she has this woman, who is totally devoted, take care of her children," the building's board chairman, Susan Thomases, explained. "That makes the apartment the equivalent of a servant's quarters, and it's a precedent that we cannot allow. We do not want this woman kicked out. We do not wish to embarrass her. We want her to have it. Clearly, this is some control issue on the part of Caroline, [who] will neither sell it nor give it to her." Regardless of who wound up actually owning the apartment, Sgubin would continue to reside there.

When she wasn't attending openings and dinners and award ceremonies — or trying to keep her beloved former governess from being evicted — Caroline was quietly working on her third book. "There are parts of my heritage," she told journalist Elizabeth Kastor, "I think people would really respond to. I will always have my personal and private memories, but I think there are aspects of that which are not only interesting but also helpful. It's good to be able to share it, and not have it be such an isolated thing."

The way she chose to share those memories was through *The Best-Loved Poems of Jacqueline Kennedy Onassis,* an anthology that also included recollections by Caroline as well as poems Jackie herself wrote. To compile the book, Caroline culled through volumes of her mother's poetry collections — works by the likes of Emily Dickinson, Robert Louis Stevenson, e.e. cummings, Robert Frost, Shakespeare, W. B. Yeats, and Homer. But she also used as her guide the scrapbook started when Caroline and John were small. When she opened the book, crammed with poems and drawings scrawled in crayon on construction paper as well as programs and term papers from Radcliffe and Brown, a valentine to her mother fell out. Attached to it was a baby tooth — from either Caroline or John, she couldn't remember. "I need," Caroline said, examining the tooth, "to do a little conservation work here."

Caroline made a point of showing the scrapbook to her own children. "Look at this!" she said. "How hard we had to work for my mother! We really had to do something good. You guys have had it too easy till now." From then on, the Schlossberg kids were required to contribute poems of their own.

Of all the selections in *The Best-Loved Poems of Jacqueline Kennedy Onassis*, Elizabeth Bishop's "One Art" was the one that most reminded Caroline of John. The poem, which deals with loss, begins with trivial everyday losses — an hour misspent, lost door keys ("John was constantly misplacing things," Caroline recalled) — then moves on to more significant things, ending with the loss of a loved one.

"Occasionally, a poem comes to us almost like a message in a bottle," Caroline wrote in the introduction to one chapter. "When it is passed from one person to another it deepens in meaning in an almost mystical way. There are poems . . . that meant something to my father, my mother, and my brother."

Yet Caroline still grew impatient whenever she was asked about what it was like to grow up Kennedy. "For me, it is my life," she said. "It's my family, it's the people that I'm with every day. I think that I'm really lucky because our family is so strong, and the people in it really care about each other. In that way, whatever is going on outside, or in other people's minds, is less important than the relationships we have with each other."

Once again, Caroline took to the airwaves with her newest title — willingly talking about her parents' love of literature and what it meant to her and her brother, but essentially nothing more. Not surprisingly, she proved a huge draw at book signings around the country, sometimes selling thousands of copies at a single sitting. The book, far and away Caroline's biggest success yet, would sell well over a half million hardcover copies.

One of the reasons, her publisher theorized, was an upsurge in interest in poetry following the terrorist attacks of September 11, 2001. "People were becoming more spiritual, more introspective," one bookseller suggested, "and I think they found comfort in this slim volume, which was also a young American woman's heartfelt tribute to her mother."

Caroline was already finishing up another anthology by the time *The Best-Loved Poems* hit the bookstores, this one an updated version of the book that catapulted her father to national prominence. *Profiles in Courage for Our Time* was a collection of essays by various writers honoring fourteen winners of the Profile in Courage Award, including such "modern-day political heroes" as Georgia Congressman John Lewis, Wisconsin Senator Russell Feingold, Arizona Senator John McCain, and former President Gerald Ford.

If Caroline seemed even more tense than usual doing interviews to promote *Profiles in Courage for Our Time*, she had ample reason. That spring the sensational murder trial of Ethel Kennedy's nephew Michael Skakel, accused of bludgeoning fifteen-year-old Martha Moxley to death in 1975, was in full swing. Unlike her cousin Robert F. Kennedy Jr., who went so far as to proclaim Skakel's innocence in a lengthy *Atlantic Monthly* article, Caroline refused to take part in the clan's all-too-familiar habit of covering for its own.

At the conclusion of the two-month-long trial, Skakel was convicted of murder and given close to the maximum sentence: twenty years to life.

Caroline may well have been in no mood to sympathize with men accused of violent attacks on women. On May 5, 2002, a man showed up at the Schlossbergs' building and told the doorman he had an appointment with Caroline. When the stranger gave his name — Sidney Waite — the police were called immediately. Waite, a thirty-nine-year-old Canadian psychiatric patient with delusions of being Caroline's long-lost brother, had been sending the Schlossbergs unwanted letters and packages — more than forty over a two-year period. In several of the letters, he asked for money.

Waite pleaded guilty to aggravated harassment and was ordered to leave the country. Manhattan Criminal Court Judge William Harrington warned Waite that, if he did not stay away from Caroline and her family for at least three years, he would be sentenced to a one-year jail term.

For all the public pressures Caroline faced, few were aware of the near-constant threat from stalkers. "There are so many crazies out there," she told an old friend of her mother's who voiced concern. "You just can't let it get to you."

But by the summer of 2002, Caroline was

being stalked again — by her old nemesis, rheumatoid arthritis. Her hands were once again noticeably swollen, and the pain in her knees reportedly began to make even walking difficult. At one point there was widespread speculation that Caroline, who at times appeared to have difficulty getting up out of her chair, might be forced to undergo joint-replacement surgery on her hands and knees.

"It's sad," Jackie's cousin John David said. "Caroline has always been such an athletic, active person. She loves cycling, swimming, riding, and was a great outdoorswoman. Now she has to curtail her activity quite a bit because of the pain."

Smaller tasks requiring manual dexterity also presented special challenges. Caroline now used a silver stylus to punch out numbers at the ATM machine, as well as on her cell phone. Of particular concern was the impact the disease might have on her ability to continue writing — a process that she had now come to love. So that she would not have to struggle with a pen or typing words on a keyboard, Ed set up a voice-activated software program that enabled Caroline simply to dictate her copy directly into her computer. While prescription drugs were available to keep the disease's symptoms at bay for long stretches of time, Caroline would continue to suffer from crippling and excruciatingly painful flare-ups.

Undaunted, Caroline took on one of her biggest challenges yet in October 2002, signing on as chief fund-raiser for the beleaguered $12 billion New York City public-school system. The idea was first broached by Nicole Seligman, Caroline's old Harvard buddy and a bridesmaid at her wedding. Seligman happened to be married to New York City Schools Chancellor Joel Klein.

With Caroline's new position came a desk of her own at Tweed Courthouse, the school system's headquarters, and an annual salary of one dollar. "She brings visibility and smarts and pizzazz, and that can't but help," observed Beth Lief, founding president of the nonprofit New Visions for Public Schools.

Jackie's daughter also brought her A-list connections to the job — though even that was not enough to silence the inevitable skeptics. Caroline handled her critics with a deft touch reminiscent of her dad. In an otherwise tame and uncharacteristically civilized interview, radio talk-show host Don Imus could not resist alluding to the fact that Caroline sent all three of her children to private schools. So what public school do your kids go to? he wanted to know.

Probably the same one yours do, she volleyed back. Imus, whose principal residence was a waterfront estate in pricey Westport, Connecticut, quickly changed the subject.

It was not long before even these few

517

critics fell silent. In her first nine months as the school system's head rainmaker, Caroline managed to raise more than $45 million.

Not that the children themselves were all that impressed. When Caroline visited one New York City school, the adults were bubbling over with excitement. The pupils, however, stared blankly when the "special visitor" they had been told to expect walked into their classroom.

"Do you have any idea who this is?" their teacher asked.

The staring continued, until one girl finally raised her hand. "Britney Spears?" she volunteered.

Caroline was delighted. "I was very flattered, actually," said the forty-five-year-old mother of three. "I thought it was great."

By the spring of 2003, Caroline carried a crushing load of charitable responsibilities — from her new duties as chief New York City public-school fund-raiser (she still served on the board of Brearley) to the Kennedy Library to the litany of nonprofit organizations she inherited from Jackie and John. Yet, incredibly, she made time to embark on yet another book tour in support of her latest literary effort.

Released on Memorial Day, 2003, *A Patriot's Handbook: Songs, Poems, Stories and Speeches Celebrating the Land We Love* paid homage to everything from Woody Guthrie's

"This Land Is Your Land" to Ronald Reagan's 1989 farewell speech to her own father's inaugural address. Caroline described *A Patriot's Handbook* as "my collage of America." Hitting stores as the war in Iraq was winding down, the book rode a tsunami of patriotism onto the *New York Times* bestseller list.

Yet Caroline was in no mood to celebrate. Her publicity tour had scarcely gotten under way when Boston University historian Robert Dallek claimed in his new book *An Unfinished Life* that JFK had conducted a secret affair with a nineteen-year-old White House intern named Mimi. Marion "Mimi" Beardsley Fahnstock, now sixty and living not far from Caroline on New York's Upper East Side, stepped forward to confirm that she had indeed had an affair with President Kennedy that lasted from June 1962 until his death.

Had it not been for Bill Clinton's sexual encounters with White House intern Monica Lewinsky, this revelation might otherwise have gone unnoticed. JFK's numerous liaisons were, after all, well documented. But the parallels between Clinton and Kennedy — and Mimi Fahnstock's startling admission nearly forty years after the fact — proved irresistible to headline writers.

The day the story hit the papers, Caroline

showed up for a scheduled 8:00 a.m. meeting with Kathryn S. Wylde, president of the philanthropic Partnership for New York City. "I brought it up," Wylde said of the screaming headlines, "because it was the elephant in the room. I said, 'This must be very hard for you.' She rolled her eyes and said, 'What are you going to do?'" Then she laughed.

Family and friends, however, worried that this latest attack on the integrity of her father — the one person she most revered and whose legacy she now carried forward alone — hit Caroline hard. "These have been a tough few years for Caroline, with the deaths of her mother and brother," Marta Sgubin said. "It's so sad that tales like this about her father are still coming out."

"I'd hope that by now Caroline is immune to all these revelations about her father's infidelities," mused her uncle Jamie Auchincloss. "But I'm sure it's still tough for her to hear these things."

At store signings for *A Patriot's Handbook*, a seemingly unflappable Caroline blithely dismissed any questions about the latest scandal. "I don't," she would say with a casual smile, "want to talk about that."

"I see Caroline every day," Sgubin went on, "and as good as she looks, you don't know what she's going through privately. I know this is hurtful, especially without her brother around to help her through this."

John Perry Barlow agreed. "If you're in the position Caroline is in and you don't have a sense of humor about it, you'll go crazy," he said. "Caroline and John could always roll their eyes at one another. Now she has no one to roll her eyes with.

"Caroline knows she's not responsible for what her father might have done," Barlow added, "but of course it still hurts — how could it not? When you're in Caroline's position, you have to just let the waves crash over you — cover your head as best you can and go on."

Perhaps even more hurtful was the persistent gossip revolving around the state of her brother's turbulent marriage to Carolyn Bessette. In its August 2003 issue, *Vanity Fair* ran a book excerpt contending, among other things, that Bessette had a serious cocaine habit, that John was tortured by fears that his wife was cheating on him, and that their marriage had completely unraveled by the time of their deaths. The cover story also claimed that Caroline and Carolyn had feuded bitterly ever since the Kennedy-Bessette wedding, when John's sister supposedly criticized the bride for showing up late.

Caroline had been aware that the story was in the works. But its timing — *Vanity Fair* ran its piece to coincide with the fourth anniversary of her brother's plane crash — took Caroline by surprise. The allegations were, said one of John's closest friends, "for the most part grotesquely misdirected and out of context. Carolyn was intensely passionate, and the relationship was tumultuous, but were they split? No. Were they headed for divorce? No. Frankly, I don't think either one of them was capable of living without the other."

As for Carolyn's alleged drug use: "She was a thoroughbred, she was high-strung, but she was no lunatic. Carolyn was still upset by the media-zoo atmosphere that had persisted since their wedding, but she did not have a cocaine problem."

Nor did Barlow, who had also known Caroline since she was twenty, see any indication of a feud between John's wife and his sister. "Caroline and Carolyn were very different stylistically," he said, "but they appreciated those differences in each other. Caroline knew this was the love of John's life." Barlow, one of the few non–family members invited to John's wedding, remembered that Carolyn was indeed late — and that "nobody gave a damn. We were all just sort of wandering around, talking, having a good time. When she appeared, we all just gasped. She took your breath away. Caroline and Carolyn got along great that day, and no one — not John, not Carolyn, not Caroline — ever once mentioned to me that there was tension between John's sister and his wife. There were times when Caroline was unhappy with the fact that John was having trouble in his marriage, sure. But the idea that Caroline and Carolyn were feuding is nonsense."

Still, when heading into another media storm, Caroline "knows how to deal," Barlow said. "Caroline can maintain a level of public equanimity even when she's heartbroken. There's a difference between being stoic, which implies some degree of denial, and being dignified. Jackie suffered, and so does Caroline, but she doesn't burden you with that. Caroline is dignified."

What made the sordid headlines more difficult to ignore was the fact that now all three children — Rose, fourteen, Tatiana, thirteen, and ten-year-old Jack — were old enough to understand what was being said about their revered grandfather and their beloved uncle. What's more, they faced the prospect of being teased about it by schoolmates, or at the very least knowing that other kids were snickering behind their backs. Where once it was just Jackie, Caroline, and John against the world — and later just Caroline and John — three new Kennedys would now have to learn what it meant to "circle the wagons," as Caroline liked to say.

On any given weekday, she could be seen striding purposefully down Park Avenue in jeans, white shirt, dark glasses, and sandals.

In a gesture so reminiscent of her mother, she would reach up and run her hand through long, blonded hair. Even on near-perfect days like these, she would say, the reality of all that had happened would creep back into her consciousness. "You don't think about it all the time," she once said. "Sometimes you're just walking down the street and it just hits you, you know. It just hits you. . . ."

She was, from the day her father set foot in the White House, Camelot's princess — the beguiling little girl with the huge blue eyes, a sprinkling of freckles, a pony named Macaroni, and a mischievous baby brother. No one then could have imagined — or would have wanted to — that the adored only daughter of Jack and Jackie Kennedy would be fatherless at five and, not so far in the future, the sole survivor of her immediate family.

Perhaps more than any other American's, Caroline's personal life paralleled that of the country. Her private tragedies were our national ones — from the assassinations of her father, Jack, and her Uncle Bobby to the untimely deaths of her mother and her brother. John would be remembered for delivering history's most famous salute at their father's state funeral, but it was Caroline who would remember it all, and become a repository of her family's — and the nation's — grief.

While her glamorous mother became the most celebrated American woman of the twentieth century and her charismatic brother reigned as the "Sexiest Man Alive," Caroline never veered from her assigned role as dutiful eldest child. She excelled at everything she chose to do — as student, author, philanthropist, wife, and mother — yet shunned the spotlight. It would take John's senseless death to coax the intensely private Caroline out of the shadows and compel her to assume the full burden of her family's formidable legacy.

Over the course of her life, Jack Kennedy's cherished "Buttons" would endure one hammer blow after another, then be forced to confront her grief in public. And, like the other three people who rounded out their little family, she did it without complaint. As the public got to know the grown-up Caroline better, it became increasingly clear that, like Jackie, she displayed what Arthur Schlesinger called "a certain gallantry." She could not escape her destiny any more than her father, mother, and brother could escape theirs. From the beginning, Caroline was — and remains — America's Daughter.

ACKNOWLEDGMENTS

Daughter. Sister. Wife. Mother. *Survivor.* In the course of writing three books on the Kennedy family — *Jack and Jackie, Jackie After Jack,* and *The Day John Died* — I was always fascinated by the fact that, in the end, the story of her remarkable family always seemed to come back to Caroline. Though strong, determined, and intelligent like her parents and her brother, Caroline was also less flamboyant and more centered — qualities that, in the end, looked as if they might save her from a fate similar to that suffered by so many Kennedys. In a sense, the little girl who charmed the world would grow up to be the most courageous Kennedy. She'd have to be, since Caroline alone would witness the extinction of her immediate family — and then be left to carry on in their names. Ultimately, in a family saga punctuated by tragedy, Caroline's story of love and loss may be the most heartbreaking of all.

A daunting amount of research is required for any comprehensive biography, and this was particularly true of *Sweet Caroline*. Fortunately, over the years I have interviewed hundreds of Kennedy sources — including family members, friends, colleagues, classmates, neighbors, and the journalists and photographers who have covered them. Given Caroline's penchant for privacy, in particular, a relative handful have asked to remain anonymous.

Once again I am privileged to be working with the wonderful people at William Morrow. I owe a special debt of gratitude to my editor, Maureen O'Brien, for her insight, her dedication, and her friendship. My thanks extend to the larger William Morrow/HarperCollins publishing family, notably Jane Friedman, Cathy Hemming, Michael Morrison, Laurie Rippon, Lisa Gallagher, Debbie Stier, Rome Quezada, James Fox, Beth Silfin, Chris Goff, Kyran Cassidy, Richard Aquan, Brad Foltz, Michelle Corallo, Kim Lewis, Betty Lew, Christine Tanigawa — as well as Goldberg-McDuffie Communications.

I have thanked my agent, Ellen Levine, so many times and in so many ways over the past twenty years that this time I thought I might as well do it in Japanese. *Domo arrigato*, Ellen, for your wisdom, your passion, and most of all, for being a true friend. My thanks as well to Ellen's longtime associates

Diana Finch and Louise Quayle, and to her new colleagues Melissa Flashman and Julia TerMatt.

My daughters, Kate and Kelly, are still a more or less constant source of amazement (and amusement). We are all indebted to their grandparents, Edward and Jeanette Andersen, for being a continuing source of knowledge and, more important, wisdom. My wife, Valerie, is, as she has been ever since we met as undergraduates at Berkeley in the late 1960s, not only my partner in life but my best friend.

Over the years, the memories and insights of hundreds of people — some, sadly, no longer with us — have gone into my four books about Jack, Jackie, John, and now Caroline. To these individuals and others, I owe my profound thanks. Among them: John Perry Barlow, George Plimpton, Hugh "Yusha" Auchincloss, Jamie Auchincloss, Arthur Schlesinger Jr., Marta Sgubin, Pierre Salinger, Theodore Sorensen, Letitia Baldrige, Kitty Carlisle Hart, Sister Joanne Frey, Charles Spalding, Jacques Lowe, John Kenneth Galbraith, George Smathers, Dr. Bob Arnot, Julie Baker, Michael Cherkasky, Priscilla McMillan, Godfrey McHugh, John Sargent, Evelyn Lincoln, John Husted, Michael Berman, Larry Newman, Cleveland Amory, Roy Cohn, Angie Coqueran, Roswell Gilpatric, Oleg Cassini, Clare Boothe Luce,

Alfred Eisenstaedt, Helen Thomas, James O'Neill, Carolina Herrera, Andrew Nurnberg, Aileen Mehle, Nancy Dickerson Whitehead, Betty Beale, Megan Desnoyers, Tom Freeman, Molly Fosburgh, Perri Peltz, Gloria Swanson, June Payne, Dorothy Oliger, Patricia Lawford Stewart, Dudley Freeman, Hazel Southam, Brad Darrach, Angier Biddle Duke, Terry L. Birdwhistell, Sandy Richardson, David McGough, Theodore H. White, Charles Bartlett, Charles Furneaux, David Halberstam, Dr. Janet Travell, Jack Anderson, Jeanette Walls, Farris L. Rookstool III, Tobias Markowitz, Kyle Bailey, Bia Ayiotis, Lloyd Howard, Michael Gross, Earl Blackwell, James Price, Doris Lilly, Vincent Russo, John Marion, Lois Cappelen, Keith Stein, Billy Baldwin, Michelle Lapautre, Ralph Diaz, Bill Moyers, Jack Tabibian, Ham Brown, Jeanette Peterson, Lawrence Leamer, Janet Lizop, Malcolm Forbes, Robert Drew, Roy Cohn, Larry Lorenzo, Cranston Jones, Lawrence R. Mulligan, Kenneth P. Norwick, Wendy Leigh, Jonathan Soroff, Barry Schenck, Norman Currie, Wikham Boyle, David Plotkin, Yvette Reyes, Alex Gotfryd, the Countess of Romanones, Rosemary McClure, Betsy Loth, Ricardo Richards, Charles Collingwood, Dorothy Schoenbrun, Anne Vanderhoop, Drew Middleton, Paula Dranov, Ray Whelan Jr., Arthur Marx, Michael Gross, Donna Smerlas, Dale Stier,

Diana Brooks, Valerie Wimmer, Michael Shulman, Arlette Santos, Jean Chapin, and Gary Gunderson.

My thanks as well to the staff of the John F. Kennedy Library and Museum, the New York Public Library, the Gunn Memorial Library, the Columbia University Oral History Project, the Butler Library, the United States Secret Service, the Bancroft Library at the University of California at Berkeley, the Federal Bureau of Investigation, Scotland Yard, Concord Academy, the Metropolitan Museum of Art, the Radcliffe Archives, Harvard University, Sotheby's, the New Milford Public Library, the Silas Bronson Library, the Edgartown Library, the Robin Hood Foundation, the Brookfield Library, the Southbury Library, the Archdiocese of New York, St. Thomas More Church, the Barnstable Public Library, Redwood Library and Atheneum of Newport, Martha's Vineyard Airport, Globe Photos, Corbis, Corbis Sygma, Sipa Press, the Associated Press, AP–Wide World Photos, Reuters, Graphictype, and Design to Printing.

SOURCE AND CHAPTER NOTES

The following notes have been compiled to give a general view of the sources drawn upon in preparing *Sweet Caroline*, but they are by no means all-inclusive. I have respected the wishes of those interview subjects who asked to remain anonymous and accordingly have not listed them either here or elsewhere in the text. The archives and oral history collections of many institutions — including the John Fitzgerald Kennedy Library, the Lyndon Baines Johnson Library, the libraries of Harvard, Stanford, Columbia, Yale, Brown, and Princeton Universities — yielded a wealth of information. Millions of words have been written about Caroline's family over the decades, appearing in such publications as the *New York Times*, the *Washington Post*, the *Wall Street Journal*, the *Boston Globe*, the *Los Angeles Times*, *Time*, *Newsweek*, *Life*, *Vanity Fair*, *The New Yorker*, *The Times* of London, and *Paris-Match* — not to mention carried on the Reuters, Associated Press, Gannett, Knight-Ridder, and United Press International wires.

CHAPTER 1

Interview subjects included Kyle Bailey, John Perry Barlow, Julie Baker, Marta Sgubin, Dr. Bob Arnot, Keith Stein, Jack Tabibian, Lloyd Howard, Anne Vanderhoop, Lois Cappelen, Larry Lorenzo, George Plimpton.

Published sources included "Tragic Echoes," *Newsweek*, July 26, 1999; Angie Cannon and Peter Cary, "The Final Hours," *U.S. News & World Report*, August 2, 1999; "He Was America's Prince," *Time*, July 26, 1999; "Charmed Life, Tragic Death," *People*, August 2, 1999; "Sister, 'Close Confidant,' Awaits News," *USA Today*, July 19, 1999; Dr. Bob Arnot, "FAA False Visibility Reports: Lost in the Darkness and the Haze," *2000 Eve's* magazine, March 2000; "Aircraft's Reputation Called Good," Associated Press, July 18, 1999; "More Tears: JFK Jr., Wife and Her Sister Presumed Dead in Plane Crash," *New York Post*, July 18, 1999; "Sad Vigil," New York *Daily News*, July 19, 1999; Maggie Haberman and Alex Devine, "Caroline Keeps Private Vigil on L.I.," *New York Post*, July 19, 1999; "Goodbye," *New York Newsday*, July 23, 1999; Katy Kelly, "Caroline Loses Brother She Could Lean On," *USA Today*,

July 23, 1999; "Farewell, John," *Time*, August 2, 1999.

CHAPTERS 2 AND 3

These chapters were based in part on conversations with George Plimpton, John Kenneth Galbraith, Sister Joanne Frey, Jamie Auchincloss, Yusha Auchincloss, Arthur Schlesinger Jr., Letitia Baldrige, Pierre Salinger, Jacques Lowe, Theodore Sorensen, John Husted, Patricia Lawford Stewart, Chuck Spalding, Ham Brown, Priscilla McMillan, Evelyn Lincoln, Angier Biddle Duke, George Smathers, the Countess of Romanones, Roswell Gilpatric, Oleg Cassini, Charles Furneaux, Willard K. Rice, Mollie Fosburgh, Dr. Janet Travell, Theodore White.

For these and subsequent chapters, the author drew on Secret Service and FBI files, as well as White House staff files and numerous oral histories — most notably those oral histories given by Jacqueline Kennedy Onassis, Rose Fitzgerald Kennedy, Robert F. Kennedy, Maud Shaw, Nancy Tuckerman, Richard Cardinal Cushing, Robert McNamara, J. B. West, Leonard Bernstein, Walter Lippmann, Thomas "Tip" O'Neill, Torbert MacDonald, Paul "Red" Fay, Dave Powers, Peter Lisagor, Hale Boggs, Hugh Sidey, William Walton, Arthur Krock, Eunice Kennedy Shriver, Pamela Turnure, Douglas Dillon, Dean Rusk,

Stanley Tretick, Leverett Saltonstall, John W. McCormack, Kaye Halle, Dinah Bridge, John F. Dempsey, Claiborne Pell, Sargent Shriver, Mark Shaw, Dean Acheson, Katharine Graham, Father John C. Cavanaugh, Peter Lawford, John Sherman Cooper, Aaron Shikler, and Janet Lee Bouvier Auchincloss.

Additional published sources included Maud Shaw, *White House Nannie: My Years with Caroline and John Kennedy, Jr.* (New York: New American Library, 1965); Mary Van Rensselaer Thayer, "First Years of the First Lady," *Ladies' Home Journal*, February 1961, and Mary Van Rensselaer Thayer, *Jacqueline Bouvier Kennedy* (Garden City, N.Y.: Doubleday, 1961); "How to Be a Presidential Candidate," *The New York Times Magazine*, July 13, 1958; "Behind the Scenes," *Time*, May 5, 1958; "This Is John Fitzgerald Kennedy," *Newsweek*, June 23, 1958; Fletcher Knebel, "What You Don't Know About Kennedy," *Look*, January 7, 1961; Luella R. Hennessey, "Bringing Up the Kennedys," *Good Housekeeping*, August 1961; "Queen of America," *Time*, March 23, 1962; "JFK: The Man, the President," *Boston Globe*, October 20, 1979; Mary Barelli Gallagher, *My Life with Jacqueline Kennedy* (New York: David McKay, 1969); J. B. West, *Upstairs at the White House* (New York: Coward, McCann & Geoghegan, 1973); "One of Their Own," *Time*, August 31,

1962; John Davis, *The Kennedys: Dynasty and Disaster* (New York: McGraw-Hill, 1984); Hugh Sidey, "The First Lady Brings History and Beauty to the White House," *Life*, September 1, 1961; Lawrence K. Altman and Todd S. Purdum, "In J.F.K. File, Hidden Illness, Pain and Pills," *New York Times*, November 17, 2002.

CHAPTERS 4 AND 5

Author interviews included George Plimpton, Yusha Auchincloss, Jamie Auchincloss, Letitia Baldrige, Peter Duchin, Sister Joanne Frey, Chuck Spalding, Pierre Salinger, Charles Bartlett, Larry Newman, Theodore White, Halston, Robert Drew, Alfred Eisenstaedt, Nancy Dickerson Whitehead, Charles Collingwood, Betty Beale, Clare Boothe Luce, Godfrey McHugh, Billy Baldwin. Oral histories included Lorraine Cooper, Helen Thomas, Albert Gore, Liz Carpenter, Lucius Clay, Jacob Javits, Nicholas Katzenbach, Rafer Johnson, Admiral George Burkeley, Laura Knebel, Averell Harriman, and Hubert H. Humphrey. Correspondence between Lyndon Johnson and Jacqueline, Caroline, and John Kennedy Jr. courtesy of the LBJ Library.

Published materials included: William Manchester, *The Death of a President* (New York: Harper & Row, 1967); Jacqueline Kennedy,

"How He Really Was," *Life*, May 29, 1964; Kenneth P. O'Donnell and David F. Powers with Joe McCarthy, *Johnny, We Hardly Knew Ye* (Boston: Little, Brown, 1970); Jim Bishop, *The Day Kennedy Was Shot* (New York: Funk & Wagnalls, 1968); Theodore Sorensen, Kennedy (New York: Harper & Row, 1965); "The Assassination of President Kennedy," *Life*, November 29, 1963; *The Warren Commission Report* (Washington, D.C.: U.S. Government Printing Office); Lady Bird Johnson, *A White House Diary* (New York: Holt, Rinehart & Winston, 1970); Ben Bradlee, *Conversations with Kennedy* (New York: W. W. Norton & Co., 1975) and *A Good Life* (New York: Simon & Schuster, 1975); Shana Alexander, " 'Congratulations,' Whispered Jackie, 'And Thanks for My Birthday Letter,' " *Life*, September 4, 1964; "Mini Trend Setter," *Time*, August 11, 1967; Jack Anderson, *Washington Exposé* (Washington, D.C.: Public Affairs Press, 1967); Arthur Schlesinger Jr., *Robert Kennedy and His Times* (Boston: Houghton Mifflin, 1978).

CHAPTERS 6 AND 7

These chapters were based in part on author interviews and conversations with Arthur Schlesinger Jr., John Perry Barlow, Peter Duchin, Kitty Carlisle Hart, Pierre Salinger, Jack Anderson, David Halberstam, George

Plimpton, Aileen Mehle, Bobby Zarem, Yusha Auchincloss, Malcolm Forbes, James Young, Jamie Auchincloss, John Marion, Larry Newman, John Sargent, Earl Blackwell, Charles Damore, Doris Lilly, Roy Cohn, David McGough, Brad Darrach.

Other published sources for this period included: B. Drummond Ayres Jr., "Carrier Kennedy Is Handed Over to Navy by Caroline," *New York Times*, September 8, 1968; "And There Were Jackie, John and Caroline," *New York Times*, September 20, 1969; "The Happy Jackie, the Sad Jackie, the Bad Jackie, the Good Jackie," The *New York Times Magazine*, May 31, 1970; "Caroline Kennedy Has Given Up the Convent," *Women's Wear Daily*, September 23, 1970; Jurate Kazickas, "Almost a Teen-Ager, Caroline Kennedy Talks About Her Life," *New York Times*, October 18, 1970; "John-John, Caroline Revisit White House," United Press International, February 5, 1971; "The Question Is Academic: Caroline Kennedy Will Go to Concord," Associated Press, May 11, 1972; "Caroline Is 16 and It's No Secret," United Press International, November 27, 1973; Andy Warhol, *The Warhol Diaries* (New York: Warner Books, 1989); Peter Collier and David Horowitz, *The Kennedys: An American Drama* (New York: Summit, 1984); Miguel Acoca, "A Caper for Caroline," *Washington Post*, August 16, 1972; " 'Widow Kennedy' Wasn't for Jackie," Associated Press, May 27, 1995; "Here Comes Caroline," *Women's Wear Daily*, July 18, 1975; Bernard Weinraub, "Bomb Kills a Doctor Near a London Home of Caroline Kennedy," *New York Times*, October 24, 1975; "Caroline Barely Escapes London Bomb," Associated Press, October 24, 1975; Jane Perlez, "The Object of Caroline's Affections," *New York Post*, November 5, 1975; Kitty Kelley, *Jackie Oh!* (Secaucus, N.J.: Lyle Stuart, 1979); "Art News: Caroline Has Beau," United Press International, October 31, 1975; "She's the Queen of the Hop: Caroline's All-Knight Parties," Associated Press, November 6, 1975; Kiki Levathes, "Portrait of Caroline as a Photographer," New York *Sunday News*, November 23, 1975; Lester David, "She's Rebel Caroline Oh! At 21," New York *Daily News*, November 26, 1978; "Caroline Shifts to Pop Paper," *New York Post*, August 23, 1977; Alex Drehsler, "Warrant Withdrawn for Caroline Kennedy," *Newsday*, January 14, 1978; "Caroline Kennedy in Love," *Fair Lady*, May 21, 1980; C. David Heymann, *A Woman Named Jackie* (New York: Lyle Stuart/ Carol Communications, 1989); John J. Miller, "Agony of Romance Gone Sour for Caroline Kennedy," *New York Post*, October 31, 1980; "Caroline Kennedy," *Washington Post*, March 1, 1981; Mike Pearl and George Carpozi Jr., "Caroline's Pursuer Is Bloody but Unbowed: Guilty but He Still Wants Her," *New York*

Post, October 17, 1981; Thomas Hanrahan, "Caroline Pursuer Sent to Hospital," New York *Daily News*, October 31, 1981; Sam Rosensohn, "Caroline, Will You Marry Me?" *New York Post*, October 22, 1981; "Psychiatric Exam Ordered for Miss Kennedy's Suitor," Associated Press, November 1, 1981; Harrison Rainie and John Quinn, "Caroline Kennedy's Secret Fantasy," *Boston Herald*, April 29, 1984; "Caroline Denies David 'Coverup,' " Reuters, October 18, 1984; Joe Sciacca, "Feds Nab Caroline Kennedy Stalker," *Boston Herald*, December 8, 1984; Mei-Mei Chan and Kitty Bean Yancey, "Publicity-Shy Caroline Is Engaged," *USA Today*, March 3, 1986; Desson Howe, "Caroline Kennedy Engaged to N.Y. Designer," *Washington Post*, March 3, 1986; James A. Revson, "Caroline's Intended," *Newsday*, March 4, 1986; Stephanie Mansfield, "Camelot II: The Wedding in Hyannis," *Washington Post*, July 19, 1986; Alton Slagle, "Echoes of Camelot: Once Again, Caroline Wins America's Hearts," July 20, 1986; Lester David, "A Girl for Caroline," *McCall's*, September 1988; James Dindall, "Caroline Kennedy Is Open About Her Book, Closed About Her Life," *Newsday*, February 21, 1991; Alan Mirabella, "Following in Her Father's Footsteps," *Ladies' Home Journal*, May 1991; John McDonald, "Caroline Kennedy a Target in Bomb Scare?" *Newsday*, September 9, 1991; Susan Linfield,

"Who's Guarding Our Rights? An Exclusive Interview with Caroline Kennedy," *McCall's*, November 1991.

CHAPTERS 8 AND 9

Information for these chapters was based in part on conversations with John Perry Barlow, Marta Sgubin, Keith Stein, Jerry Wiener, David McGough, Michael Berman, Angie Coqueran, Bia Ayiotis, Howie Montaug, Wikham Boyle, Frank Ratcliff, Pierre Salinger, Michael Cherkasky, Jonathan Soroff, Michael Gross, Jack Tabibian, Anthony Comenale, Jeanette Walls, Joe Duran, Arthur Marx.

Published sources included: Larry Sutton, "Caroline's Turn," New York *Daily News*, May 21, 1994; Jonathan Alter, "Her Cocoon of Values," *Newsweek*, May 30, 1994; Marylou Tousignant and Malcolm Gladwell, "In Somber Ceremony Jacqueline Kennedy Onassis Is Laid to Rest," *Washington Post*, May 24, 1994; Ellen O'Hara, "Love and Loss," *Ladies' Home Journal*, August 1994; Wendy Leigh, "Caroline's Precious Legacy," *McCall's*, September 1994; Elizabeth Gleick, "Those Prying Eyes," *Time*, November 6, 1995; Mark Marvel, "Life & Liberty: An Interview with Ellen Alderman and Caroline Kennedy," *Interview*, December 1995; Patricia Morrisroe, "Caroline Rising," *Vogue*, November 1995; Martha Sherrill, "Private People, Public Lives," *Harper's Bazaar,* November 1995; Tina Brown, "A Woman in Earnest," *The New Yorker,* September 15, 1997; Senator Edward Kennedy, "Caroline Kennedy: The New Frontier woman," *Mirabella,* October 1998; Salvatore Arena, "Kennedys vs. Kin of Barbra in Mall Deal," New York *Daily News,* November 17, 1998; Jeannie Williams, "Caroline Spends Anniversary in Private Grief," *USA Today,* July 20, 1999; "Caroline Inherits Legacy," Knight-Ridder, July 18, 1999; Susan Schindehette, "Two Shattered Families," *People,* August 9, 1999; Michelle Green, "Life Without John," *Good Housekeeping,* October 1999; Daniel Jeffreys, "Now Caroline Is Going It Alone," *New York Post,* July 28, 1999; Robert Gearty and Leo Standora, "And Then There Was One — Caroline," New York *Daily News,* July 20, 1999; "Kennedy Family Wanted Dignified Burial at Sea," *Cape Cod Times,* July 26, 1999; "And Then There Was One," *Time,* July 26, 1999; Anthony Wilson-Smith, "The Curse of the Kennedys," *Maclean's,* July 26, 1999; Barbara Kantrowitz, "The Last Child of Camelot," *Newsweek,* August 2, 1999; "Prince of the City," *New York,* August 2, 1999; "A Sad Goodbye," *Newsweek,* August 2, 1999; Talk of the Town, *The New Yorker,* August 2, 1999; David Michaelis, "Great Expectations," *Vanity Fair,* September 1999;

Jane Farrell, "An Unbreakable Bond," *McCall's*, October 1999; "John Kennedy: A Tribute," *George*, October 1999; Jill Smolowe, "Caroline Kennedy: Profile in Courage," *People*, May 29, 2000; Deborah Orin, "Camelot Revived for One Night in L.A.," *New York Post*, August 16, 2000; Elizabeth Kastor, " 'You Just Keep Going,' " *Good Housekeeping*, October 2001; CNN/Larry King interview with Caroline Kennedy transcript, May 7, 2002; Abby Goodnough, "Caroline Kennedy Takes Post as Fund-Raiser for Schools," *New York Times*, October 2, 2002; Laurence Michie, "At the Kennedy Compound," *Vineyard Gazette*, June 20, 2003; Barbara Kantrowitz, "Juggling Kids, Career and History," *Newsweek*, May 12, 2003; Abby Goodnough and David M. Herszenhorn, "Kennedy Finding Her Footing as Schools' Rainmaker," *New York Times*, June 4, 2003.

SELECTED BIBLIOGRAPHY

Acheson, Dean. *Power and Diplomacy.* Cambridge, Mass.: Harvard University Press, 1958.

Adams, Cindy, and Susan Crimp. *Iron Rose: The Story of Rose Fitzgerald Kennedy and Her Dynasty.* Beverly Hills, Calif.: Dove Books, 1995.

Amory, Cleveland. *The Proper Bostonians.* New York: E. P. Dutton & Company, Inc., 1947.

Andersen, Christopher. *Jack and Jackie: Portrait of an American Marriage.* New York: William Morrow and Company, Inc., 1996.

———. *Madonna Unauthorized.* New York: Simon & Schuster, 1991.

Anson, Robert Sam. *"They've Killed the President!": The Search for the Murderers of John F. Kennedy.* New York: Bantam, 1975.

Anthony, Carl Sferrazza. *As We Remember Her.* New York: HarperCollins, 1997.

Baldwin, Billy. *Billy Baldwin Remembers.*

New York: Harcourt Brace Jovanovich, 1974.

Baldrige, Letitia. *Of Diamonds and Diplomats.* Boston: Houghton Mifflin, 1968.

Beard, Peter. *Longing for Darkness: Kamante's Tales from "Out of Africa."* San Francisco: Chronicle Books, 1990.

Beschloss, Michael R. *Kennedy and Roosevelt: The Uneasy Alliance.* New York: Norton, 1980.

——. *Taking Charge: The Johnson White House Tapes, 1963–1964.* New York: Simon & Schuster, 1997.

Birmingham, Stephen. *Jacqueline Bouvier Kennedy Onassis.* New York: Grosset & Dunlap, 1978.

——. *Real Lace: America's Irish Rich.* New York: Harper & Row, 1973.

Bishop, Jim. *The Day Kennedy Was Shot.* New York: Funk & Wagnalls, 1968.

Blair, Joan, and Clay Blair Jr. *The Search for JFK.* New York: Berkley, 1976.

Bouvier, Jacqueline, and Lee Bouvier. *One Special Summer.* New York: Delacorte Press, 1974.

Bouvier, Kathleen. *To Jack with Love, Black Jack Bouvier: A Remembrance.* New York: Kensington, 1979.

Braden, Joan. *Just Enough Rope.* New York: Villard, 1989.

Bradlee, Ben. *A Good Life.* New York: Simon & Schuster, 1995.

———. *Conversations with Kennedy*. New York: Norton, 1975.

Brady, Frank. *Onassis*. Englewood Cliffs, N.J.: Prentice-Hall, 1977.

Brando, Marlon, with Robert Lindsey. *Songs My Mother Taught Me*. New York: Random House, 1995.

Bryant, Traphes, and Frances Spatz Leighton. *Dog Days at the White House*. New York: Macmillan, 1975.

Buck, Pearl S. *The Kennedy Women: A Personal Appraisal*. New York: Harcourt, 1969.

Burke, Richard E. *My Ten Years with Ted Kennedy*. New York: St. Martin's Press, 1992.

Burns, James MacGregor. *Edward Kennedy and the Camelot Legacy*. New York: Norton, 1976.

———. *John Kennedy: A Political Profile*. New York: Harcourt, 1960.

Cameron, Gail. *Rose: A Biography of Rose Fitzgerald Kennedy*. New York: Putnam, 1971.

Cassini, Oleg. *A Thousand Days of Magic*. New York: Rizzoli, 1995.

———. *In My Own Fashion: An Autobiography*. New York: Simon & Schuster, 1987.

Cheshire, Maxine. *Maxine Cheshire, Reporter*. Boston: Houghton Mifflin, 1978.

Clarke, Gerald. *Capote*. New York: Simon & Schuster, 1988.

Cohn, Roy. *McCarthy*. New York: New

American Library, 1968.

Collier, Peter, and David Horowitz. *The Kennedys: An American Drama.* New York: Summit Books, 1984.

Dallek, Robert. *An Unfinished Life: John F. Kennedy, 1917–1963.* New York: Little, Brown, 2003.

Damore, Leo. *The Cape Cod Years of John Fitzgerald Kennedy.* Englewood Cliffs, N.J.: Prentice-Hall, 1967.

Davis, John. *The Bouviers: Portrait of an American Family.* New York: Farrar, Straus & Giroux, 1969.

———. *The Kennedys: Dynasty and Disaster.* New York: McGraw-Hill, 1984.

Dempster, Nigel. *Heiress: The Story of Christina Onassis.* London: Weidenfeld & Nicolson, 1989.

DuBois, Diana. *In Her Sister's Shadow: An Intimate Biography of Lee Radziwill.* Boston: Little, Brown, 1995.

Duchin, Peter. *Ghost of a Chance.* New York: Random House, 1996.

Evans, Peter. *Ari: The Life and Times of Aristotle Socrates Onassis.* New York: Summit Books, 1986.

Exner, Judith Campbell, as told to Ovid Demaris. *My Story.* New York: Grove, 1977.

Fay, Paul B., Jr. *The Pleasure of His Company.* New York: Harper & Row, 1966.

Fisher, Eddie. *Eddie: My Life, My Loves.* New

York: Harper & Row, 1981.

Fontaine, Joan. *No Bed of Roses: An Autobiography.* New York: William Morrow, 1978.

Frank, Gerold. *Zsa Zsa Gabor: My Story.* New York: World, 1960.

Fraser, Nicolas, Phillip Jacobson, Mark Ottaway, and Lewis Chester. *Aristotle Onassis.* Philadelphia: Lippincott, 1977.

Frischauer, Willi. *Jackie.* London: Michael Joseph, 1967.

———. *Onassis.* New York: Meredith Press, 1968.

Galbraith, John Kenneth. *Ambassador's Journal: A Personal Account of the Kennedy Years.* Boston: Houghton Mifflin, 1969.

Gallagher, Mary Barelli. *My Life with Jacqueline Kennedy.* New York: David McKay, 1969.

Giancana, Antoinette, and Thomas C. Renner. *Mafia Princess: Growing Up in Sam Giancana's Family.* New York: William Morrow, 1984.

Goodwin, Doris Kearns. *The Fitzgeralds and the Kennedys: An American Saga.* New York: Simon & Schuster, 1987.

Granger, Stewart. *Sparks Fly Upward.* New York: Putnam, 1981.

Halberstam, David. *The Best and the Brightest.* New York: Random House, 1969.

Hall, Gordon Langley, and Ann Pinchot. *Jacqueline Kennedy.* New York: Frederick Fell, 1964.

Hamilton, Nigel. *JFK: Reckless Youth.* New York: Random House, 1992.

Heymann, C. David. *A Woman Named Jackie: An Intimate Biography of Jacqueline Bouvier Kennedy Onassis.* New York: Lyle Stuart/ Carol Communications, 1989.

Kelley, Kitty. *His Way: The Unauthorized Biography of Frank Sinatra.* New York: Bantam, 1986.

——. *Jackie Oh!* Secaucus, N.J.: Lyle Stuart, 1979.

——. *Nancy Reagan: The Unauthorized Biography.* New York: Simon & Schuster, 1991.

Kennedy, Caroline. *The Best-Loved Poems of Jacqueline Kennedy Onassis.* New York: Hyperion, 2001.

——. *Profiles in Courage for Our Time.* New York: Hyperion, 2002.

——. *A Patriot's Handbook: Songs, Poems, Stories, and Speeches Celebrating the Land We Love.* New York: Hyperion, 2003.

Kennedy, Caroline, and Ellen Alderman. *In Our Defense: The Bill of Rights in Action.* New York: William Morrow, 1991.

——. *The Right to Privacy.* New York: Vintage, 1997.

Kennedy, John F. *Profiles in Courage.* New York: Harper & Row, 1965.

——. *Why England Slept.* New York: Wilfred Funk, 1940.

Kennedy, Rose Fitzgerald. *Times to Remember.*

New York: Doubleday, 1974.

Kessler, Ronald. *Inside the White House.* New York: Pocket Books, 1995.

Klein, Edward. *Just Jackie: Her Private Years.* New York: Ballantine Books, 1998.

Koskoff, David E. *Joseph P. Kennedy, A Life and Times.* Englewood Cliffs, N.J.: Prentice-Hall, 1974.

Krock, Arthur. *Memoirs: Sixty Years on the Firing Line.* New York: Funk & Wagnalls, 1968.

Kunhardt, Philip B., Jr., ed. *Life in Camelot.* Boston: Little, Brown, 1988.

Lash, Joseph P. *Eleanor and Franklin.* New York: W. W. Norton, 1971.

Latham, Caroline, with Jeannie Sakol. *The Kennedy Encyclopedia.* New York: New American Library, 1989.

Lawford, Patricia Seaton, with Ted Schwarz. *The Peter Lawford Story.* New York: Carroll & Graf, 1988.

Lawliss, Charles. *Jacqueline Kennedy Onassis.* New York: JG Press, 1994.

Leamer, Laurence. *The Kennedy Women: The Saga of an American Family.* New York: Villard, 1994.

Leigh, Wendy. *Prince Charming: The John F. Kennedy Jr. Story.* New York: Signet, 1994.

Lilly, Doris. *Those Fabulous Greeks: Onassis, Niarchos, and Livanos.* New York: Cowles, 1970.

Lowe, Jacques. *Jacqueline Kennedy Onassis: A*

Tribute. New York: Jacques Lowe Visual Arts, 1995.

——. *JFK Remembered*. New York: Random House, 1993.

Mailer, Norman. *Of Women and Their Elegance*. New York: Simon & Schuster, 1980.

——. *Marilyn*. New York: Grosset & Dunlap, 1973.

Manchester, William. *The Death of a President*. New York: Harper & Row, 1967.

——. *Portrait of a President: John F. Kennedy in Profile*. Boston: Little, Brown, 1962.

Martin, Ralph. *A Hero for Our Time*. New York: Ballantine, 1984.

Moutsatsos, Kiki Feroudi. *The Onassis Women*. New York: G. P. Putnam's Sons, 1998.

McCarthy, Joe. *The Remarkable Kennedys*. New York: Dial, 1960.

Montgomery, Ruth. *Hail to the Chiefs: My Life and Times with Six Presidents*. New York: Coward-McCann, 1970.

O'Connor, Edwin. *The Last Hurrah*. New York: Bantam, 1970.

O'Donnell, Kenneth P., and David F. Powers, with Joe McCarthy. *"Johnny We Hardly Knew Ye."* Boston: Little, Brown, 1970.

O'Neill, Tip, with William Novak. *Man of the House: The Life and Political Memoirs of Speaker Tip O'Neill*. New York: Random House, 1987.

Ogden, Christopher. *Life of the Party: The Bi-*

ography of Pamela Digby Churchill Hayward Harriman. New York: Warner, 1994.

Oppenheimer, Jerry. *The Other Mrs. Kennedy.* New York: St. Martin's, 1994.

Parmet, Herbert S. *J.F.K.: The Presidency of John F. Kennedy.* New York: Dial, 1983.

——. *Jack: The Struggles of John F. Kennedy.* New York: Dial, 1980.

Parker, Robert. *Capitol Hill in Black and White.* New York: Dodd, Mead, 1987.

Pepitone, Lena, and William Stadiem. *Marilyn Monroe Confidential.* New York: Pocket Books, 1979.

Reed, J. D., Kyle Smith, and Jill Smolowe. *John F. Kennedy Jr.: A Biography.* New York: People Profiles/Time, 1998.

Reeves, Richard. *President Kennedy: Profile of Power.* New York: Simon & Schuster, 1993.

Reeves, Thomas C. *A Question of Character: A Life of John F. Kennedy.* Rocklin, Calif.: Prima, 1992.

Salinger, Pierre. *P.S.: A Memoir.* New York: St. Martin's, 1995.

——. *With Kennedy.* Garden City, N.Y.: Doubleday, 1966.

Schlesinger, Arthur M., Jr. *A Thousand Days.* Boston: Houghton Mifflin, 1965.

Sgubin, Marta. *Cooking for Madam: Recipes and Reminiscences from the Home of Jacqueline Kennedy Onassis.* New York: A Lisa Drew Book/Scribner, 1998.

Shaw, Maud. *White House Nannie: My Years*

with Caroline and John Kennedy, Jr. New York: New American Library, 1965.

Shulman, Irving. *"Jackie"!: The Exploitation of a First Lady.* New York: Trident, 1970.

Sidey, Hugh. *John F. Kennedy, President.* New York: Atheneum, 1964.

Sorensen, Theodore C. *Kennedy.* New York: Harper & Row, 1965.

Spada, James. *John and Caroline: Their Lives in Pictures.* New York: St. Martin's, 2001.

———. *Peter Lawford: The Man Who Kept the Secrets.* New York: Bantam, 1991.

Spignesi, Stephen. *The J.F.K. Jr. Scrapbook.* Secaucus, N.J.: Carol, 1997.

Stack, Robert, with Mark Evans. *Straight Shooting.* New York: Macmillan, 1980.

Storm, Tempest, with Bill Boyd. *Tempest Storm: The Lady Is a Vamp.* Atlanta: Peachtree, 1987.

Summers, Anthony. *Goddess: The Secret Lives of Marilyn Monroe.* New York: Macmillan, 1985.

Swanson, Gloria. *Swanson on Swanson.* New York: Random House, 1980.

ter Horst, J. F., and Ralph Albertazzie. *The Flying White House.* New York: Coward, McCann & Geoghegan, 1979.

Thayer, Mary Van Rensselaer. *Jacqueline Bouvier Kennedy.* Garden City, N.Y.: Doubleday, 1961.

Thomas, Bob. *Golden Boy! The Untold Story*

of William Holden. New York: St. Martin's, 1983.

Thomas, Helen. *Dateline: White House.* New York: Macmillan, 1975.

Tierney, Gene, with Mickey Herskowitz. *Self-Portrait.* New York: Simon & Schuster, 1979.

Travell, Janet. *Office Hours: Day and Night.* New York: World, 1968.

Vidal, Gore. *Palimpsest: A Memoir.* New York: Random House, 1995.

Warhol, Andy. *The Andy Warhol Diaries.* Ed. Pat Hackett. New York: Warner, 1989.

The Warren Report. New York: Associated Press, 1964.

Watney, Hedda Lyons. *Jackie.* New York: Leisure, 1971.

West, J. B., with Mary Lynn Kotz. *Upstairs at the White House.* New York: Coward, McCann & Geoghegan, 1973.

White, Theodore H. *In Search of History.* New York: Warner, 1978.

——. *The Making of the President 1960.* New York: Atheneum, 1961.

Wills, Garry. *The Kennedy Imprisonment.* Boston: Atlantic/Little, Brown, 1981.

ABOUT THE AUTHOR

CHRISTOPHER ANDERSEN is the author of twenty-four books that have been translated into more than twenty languages. A former contributing editor of *Time* and senior editor of *People*, Andersen has also written hundreds of articles for a wide range of publications, including *Life* and the *New York Times*.

To receive notice of author events and new books by Christopher Andersen, sign up at www.authortracker.com.

The employees of Thorndike Press hope you have enjoyed this Large Print book. All our Thorndike and Wheeler Large Print titles are designed for easy reading, and all our books are made to last. Other Thorndike Press Large Print books are available at your library, through selected bookstores, or directly from us.

For information about titles, please call:

(800) 223-1244

or visit our Web site at:

www.gale.com/thorndike
www.gale.com/wheeler

To share your comments, please write:

Publisher
Thorndike Press
295 Kennedy Memorial Drive
Waterville, ME   04901